The Power of Greed

THE POWER OF GREED

Collective Action
in International
Development

Michael Rosberg

THE UNIVERSITY
OF ALBERTA PRESS

The University of Alberta Press
Ring House 2
Edmonton, Alberta, Canada T6G 2E1

Library and Archives Canada Cataloguing in Publication

Rosberg, Michael, 1943–

The power of greed : collective action in international development / Michael Rosberg. Includes bibliographical references and index.

ISBN 0-88864-429-9

1. Economic assistance – Developing countries.
2. Self interest – Developing countries. 3. Economic development projects – Social aspects – Developing countries. 1. Title.

HD82.R6825 2004   338.91′09172′4   C2004-906824-5

Copyediting by Peter Midgley.
Indexing by Judy Dunlop.
Maps by Wendy Johnson.
First edition, first printing, 2005.
All rights reserved.
Printed and bound in Canada by Houghton Boston Printers, Saskatoon, Saskatchewan.

The University of Alberta Press is committed to protecting our natural environment. As part of our efforts, this book is printed on New Leaf Paper: it contains 100% post-consumer recycled fibres and is acid- and chlorine-free.

The University of Alberta Press gratefully acknowledges the support received for its publishing program from The Canada Council for the Arts. The University of Alberta Press also gratefully acknowledges the financial support of the Government of Canada through the Book Publishing Industry Development Program (BPIDP) and from the Alberta Foundation for the Arts for its publishing activities.

Canada Council   Conseil des Arts
for the Arts   du Canada

For Arnie & Judy
For Ari & Amira, Jewel & Keino
For Nathan, Miriam & those I await
—My past, my present and my future

Contents

Figures

Acknowledgements

FOR YEARS I HAVE WAITED for somebody else to write this book. I was sure a more experienced development practitioner and scholar would eventually report that working with poor people in developing countries would be more effective than working against them, as I think we generally do. My wife kept insisting I had the ability to do it. My children endured my monologues and polemics on the topic and encouraged me too. My stepson dazzled me with his analysis of Belizean politics and poverty that related well to what I had been thinking, and in return, prompted me to share and develop more of my ideas out loud. But after years of waiting, when nobody made my observations the point of their book, I decided I had to do it myself. As it happened, many people helped me along the way:

My doctoral supervisor, Professor Arnold Strickon, Ph.D., Chair of the Department of Anthropology at the University of Wisconsin-Madison, challenged me as nobody had done before. Arnie was an original: funny but knowledgeable and demanding, critical but full of praise when I produced work of quality. Other intellectual stimulation was provided by Professors Marion Brown, Eugene Wilkening and Gene Havens, to name but a few.

Acknowledgements

Dr. Strickon's closest colleague and friend was Dr. Sidney Greenfield, now Professor Emeritus of the University of Wisconsin-Milwaukee. He, along with Dr. Strickon, created the concept of Populational Decision-Making which I have used throughout my career. I lean heavily on their ideas in this book. To my delight, Dr. Greenfield graciously agreed to write the introduction to this book which, I feel, adds greatly to it.

In San Andrés, Islas, Colombia, it was Randel (*Guata*) Watson, a school teacher and seminary graduate, who helped me make sense of the economic, political and anthropological complexities of that place. But I also gained from exposure to the unique intelligences possessed by Carlos Benjamin Corpus H., William Francis, Harrington McNish, William F. Myles B., Kent Francis J., Julio and Carlos Bush, Edburn Newball, Rojelio Robinson, Alberto Douglas H., Luis H. Soto, Remijio Barker, Juan Ramirez, Raphael Archbold, Manuel Pusey, Vanderbilt Bowie, Miss Mercedes Hooker, Miss Rilla Myles, and Miss Una and Miss Lucy Pomare. There is an additional list of students, fishermen, *lancheros*, colleagues and friends in San Andrés too long to be included here. But all of them educated me in ways necessary to write this book.

My writing efforts were intellectually and morally supported by Canadian friends and colleagues too including Dr. Sid Brownstein, Dr. Walter and Mrs. Teena Hendelman, and by my brother-in-law, Bert d'Antini. I also wish to thank Vivian Cummins, the knowledgeable, efficient and ever-cheerful librarian at the Norman Paterson School of International Affairs Reference Library at Carleton University. Special thanks are extended to my friend Oscar Brown S. from the Canadian Co-operative Association (CCA) with whom I worked closely on development projects for many years and from whom I learned tremendously. Special thanks are also extended to my good friend Raúl Eluchans, formerly the Director of Program Management with CCA, who read early drafts of the manuscript and who provided elegant and perceptive feedback and unflagging encouragement.

In Belize, I am grateful for the support and encouragement of my academic colleagues and friends Dr. Joseph-Ernest Aondofe (Joe) Iyo, and Dr. Thippichetti Thiagarajagan, both from the University of Belize. I am also grateful to the former Director of the Central Statistical Office, Sylvan Roberts, for guidance, and the Head Librarian of Belize, my sister-in-law, Joy Ysaguirre. I want to thank my friends and colleagues from consultancy assignments who taught me so much, especially Melva Johnson, Adele Catzim and Sandra Paredez. Mr. Lloyd Pandy and his wife, Dr. Carla Barnett, have been especially supportive and greatly appreciated too. As in San Andrés, I have a list of friends to thank in Belize City and Gale's Point Manatee Village too long to include here specifically but of great value to me nonetheless.

Neither could this publication have taken such beautiful and accurate form without the unflagging assistance and support of the staff at The University of Alberta Press (UAP) including the Director, Linda Cameron, my constant guide and Editor, Michael Luski, the Copy Editor, Peter Midgley, the Marketing Co-ordinator, Cathie Crooks, and freelance designer, Robert Tombs.

However, I want to end where I began, by acknowledging my greatest debt of gratitude for support and encouragement to my wife, Jewel, and to my beloved children Ari, Amira, and Keino, my stepson.

Abbreviations

CACM — Central American Common Market
CARICOM — Caribbean Common Market
CAT$ — Ca$h For Any Thug With $pirit
CCA — Canadian Co-operative Association
CIDA — Canadian International Development Agency
EGS — Employment Guarantee Scheme
FS — Financial Services
GOB — Government of Belize
GRO — Grass Roots Organization
IDB — Inter-American Development Bank
IMF — International Monetary Fund
LDM — Leader-disciplining Mechanism
MSES — Micro- and Small Enterprises
MVP — Most Valuable Player
NDDP — National Dairy Development Board
NGO — Non-Governmental Organization
ODA — Overseas Development Assistance
OPEC — Organization of Petroleum Exporting Countries

Abbreviations

PLA Participatory Learning and Action
S&RH Sexual and Reproductive Health
SAP Structural Adjustment Program
TA Technical Assistance
UB University of Belize
UN United Nations
UNIA United Negro Improvement Association
USAID United States Agency for International Development
WOCCU World Council of Credit Unions
WTO World Trade Organization

Introduction

Sidney M. Greenfield

MICHAEL ROSBERG ACKNOWLEDGES that after half a century of concerted effort by many well-trained and dedicated people, development has not worked, nor have the lives of the poor throughout the world been significantly improved by the multitude of undertakings and the expenditure of billions of dollars. In the engrossing and stimulating pages of *The Power of Greed: Collective Action in International Development*, he seeks to understand the reasons for this. In rethinking the assumptions on which development programs are based, he employs a theoretical framework the late Arnold Strickon and I developed in the 1970s and early 1980s. Writing this introduction provides me with an opportunity to comment on the subject of this provocative book, its use of our populational decision-making model and its potential value for revising the thinking about development.

The Historical Context of Development

In July of 1944, as the fighting in Europe was coming to an end, representatives of the victorious allied nations met at Bretton Woods, New Hampshire, to plan the rebuilding of a continent that had been devastated by warfare. Based on their understanding as to what had caused the war, and to prevent a repetition of a depression of the magnitude of the one that had immediately preceded it, the International Monetary Fund (IMF) and the World Bank were created; subsequently, the World Trade Organization (WTO) came into being. All three became the centerpieces of what was intended to be a new world order.

The difficult task of ensuring global economic stability was assigned to the IMF. Those who participated in this UN Monetary and Financial Conference had been greatly influenced by the Great Depression of the 1930s in which widespread unemployment[1] had presented capitalism with its most severe crisis to date. The British economist John Maynard Keynes, who, as Stiglitz reminds us

> would later be a key participant at Bretton Woods, had put forward a simple explanation, and a correspondingly simple set of prescriptions: lack of sufficient aggregate demand explained the economic downturns; government policies could help stimulate aggregate demand. In cases where monetary policy is ineffective, governments could rely on fiscal policies, either by increasing expenditures or cutting taxes.[2]

The new World Bank, now working with the IMF, was to provide governments with loans that would enable them to stimulate demand, thereby preventing any future crises that would threaten the capitalist system.

These economic institutions, with these lofty goals, were predicated on a set of assumptions about how society was organized and operated that appeared so evident that neither the framers of the new system, nor those who were to implement it, had reason to make them explicit. They just took for granted that periodically some members of society would assemble the capital required to mobilize the factors that would result in the production of new goods and/or services. Moreover, the activity would be organized on a corporate model according to which other individuals would be brought together in an hierarchically ordered system to perform specialized tasks that, when done in concert, would result in the creation of commodities. The goods and services would be placed on the market for sale, with the profits belonging to those who owned the businesses. Individuals would be recruited to perform tasks in the producing units by offering them wages in the form of money that would differ in amount depending on the requirements of assigned activities and the supply of trained persons available to implement them.

It was further presumed that society's labour force would take their earnings home where they would be used to purchase in the market—from what had been supplied by the producing groups—what was needed for the sustenance of their dependents, who were mostly women related to them by marriage and their children. The possibility of the members of society being organized in extended families, large kinship, ethnic, or other groups, and hence potential wage earners having responsibilities to non-nuclear family members, was not even considered. Consumer purchases, plus those by producers in need of materials, constituted the demand Keynes and economists referred to. As demand grew, individuals, called entrepreneurs, would organize the production of additional commodities for which they would need more workers, leading to what in economic terms was called "growth." The male owners of the productive organizations would obtain the funds with which to purchase commodities for themselves and their dependents from the profits of their companies.

The founders of the new world order further presumed that money, earned as wages or as profits, was accepted as the measure of personal success and the overall symbol of individual prestige. Moreover, that the population had been (or were being) enculturated to think of themselves as independent individuals who made decisions and choices that would lead to their acquiring specialized skills for which there would be demand by employers. Specifically, they would seek jobs that in addition to providing income would define them socially and serve as their identities. Wages would enable them to purchase goods and services sufficient to attain a lifestyle defined as successful, or to mobilize capital with which to establish the production of new commodities. Agriculture, which occupied a progressively diminishing percentage of the labour force, was assumed to be organized in units worked by nuclear (farm) families that sold the harvests they produced and used the earnings (or profits) to purchase manufactured and other goods and services in the market. Ownership and its management on one side, and those who worked for them (actually their labour organizations) on the other, formed a major cleavage in society, with each group striving to increase its (relative) share of total earnings. This, in greatly simplified form, was the model of society implicitly assumed by the economists, politicians and planners who set out to rebuild Europe and to assist the rest of the world.

Those present at Bretton Woods made the further presumption that they were rebuilding societies organized as nation-states. Economists were familiar with making policy recommendations to governments for the stimulation of their respective growth. Now they were proposing a broader system to co-ordinate the market economies of the nations of the world. Governments, preferably elected by their citizens, were expected to serve as mediators preventing neither those who owned the productive units nor the workers from gaining sufficient control so as to destabilize the system, while also ensuring that there was enough aggregate demand for continued growth. Needless to say, in Europe and North America the oversimplified model of societal organization outlined approximated empirical reality in that it reflected the way most of the population lived and behaved. When Japan was defeated and occupied, the model for rebuilding was applied to this third member of the axis alliance. At great cost and with considerable investment capital and organizational input, Japanese society was reorganized under an American occupational authority along the lines of the Western social model with entrepreneurs, corporations and workers using their wages to support their dependents in a market system. The socio-economic transformation was so successful that in time the Japanese economy grew to become one of the largest in the world.[3]

The Soviet Union, like the United States, emerged from the war as a world power, but unlike capitalist America, it was committed to an alternative model for the production and distribution of goods and services and the two systems were unable to co-exist. Each saw the other as an actual or potential threat that was to have a considerable impact on the rest of the world and its development.

The proper name of the World Bank, The International Bank for Reconstruction and Development, reflects its original mission. Development was added to the name almost as an afterthought. At the time of its founding, most of the peoples of the world outside of Europe, with the significant exception of Latin America, were still colonies, and "what meager economic development efforts could or would be undertaken were considered the responsibility of their European masters."[4] But for our purposes, while the implicit sociological model on which the economic institutions for rebuilding Europe were based adequately reflected life and social reality there, and Japan and later South Korea were reorganized and transformed under American military occupation to reproduce them, for the most part they did not exist in the rest of the world. Production and distribution of goods and service, with the exception of what had been created with force by the colonial powers—that affected only a small part of the populations of Africa, South Asia and the Pacific—were not organized by entrepreneurs who employed their fellows for wages that their dependents used to purchase commodities in a growing system of markets.

When at the end of the war the colonial populations reacted to shed their former masters, they seemed to have no alternative models of political organization to follow. They responded to independence by adopting the nation-state organizational system, but unlike their colonial authorities, they were not organized internally according to the market model. Instead, the territories to become independent nations contained within them many diverse local populations each with its own language, belief system, culture, view of the world, traditions and systems for the production and distribution of goods and services. Unfortunately these specifics were little known to a new generation of elites who were educated in London, Paris, or other former colonial capitals. When they returned home to assume political leadership, instead of facing up to their domestic realities and undertaking nation building—if that was to be the choice—they found themselves wooed by both the Soviets and the Western bloc. They were presented with the choice of affiliating with the West, and adopting its capitalist political and economic model, or with the Soviets and their communist system. Unprepared for the daunting task, most leaders of new nations squandered the opportunity, appropriating for their personal use much of the resources advanced by their respective Cold War backer. While the threat of choosing sides presented considerable leeway, in either case they were expected to undertake economic development without having resources and organizational inputs sufficient to transform their highly diverse and internally competitive societies.

This was the broad setting for the beginnings of far too many development programs. Assuming that their target populations lived, thought and were organized in terms of market principles, and reinforced in this belief by government officials who often were more familiar with the culture of the development workers than of the peoples who lived outside their capital cities or in its urban peripheries, project after project was introduced that was not carried out as expected by those for whom they were intended. Although warned by an occasional anthropologist or others familiar with social life in the parts of the world where they introduced programs, the economists of the IMF and World Bank continued to proceed under the assumption that everyone lived in terms of the market system. When development did not happen, modernization theory came to the rescue.

The most influential theory in the social sciences during the second half of the twentieth century predicted that eventually all peoples and societies, no matter how isolated and distant they seemed to be, inevitably would become like us. All it would take was time. As those in the development field anxiously anticipated that the countless millions of the world's poor they were trying to help would modernize and behave in terms of market principles, new forces appeared on the scene that transformed the IMF and the World Bank.

In the 1980s, as part of the "Washington Consensus" between the IMF, the World Bank and the US Treasury about the "right" policies for developing countries, free market principles replaced the Keynesian orientation of the Fund.[5] Critics complained that given the end of colonialism and the fall of communism, the new approach, formulated in large part in reaction to events in Latin America, has given the international financial institutions [6]

> the opportunity to expand greatly their original mandates. Today these institutions have become dominant players in the world economy. Not only countries [governments] seeking their help but also those seeking their "seal of approval" so that they can better access international capital markets must follow their economic prescriptions, prescriptions which reflect their free market ideologies and theories.
>
> The result for many people has been poverty and for many countries social and political chaos. [7]

Rosberg has rightly chosen not to deal with these changes in the policies of the lending institutions, but like their predecessors, they too base their programs and policies on the assumptions that the peoples of the developing nations already have modernized, or soon will, and behave in terms of the market principles outlined above. But modernization theory was wrong. There are still far too many peoples in the interiors and urban peripheries of the nations of Asia, Africa and Latin America who, though they may watch Western television and Hollywood's movies, do not live their daily lives or base their survival strategies and decisions in terms of the goals, values and assumptions of the market. To illustrate this, let us examine how the people of Latin America may differ in their assumptions and make choices other than those taken as self-evident by the economists and development workers who have been so unsuccessful in trying to help them.

An Earlier World Order With Patronage and Clientage
as its System of Distribution

The second half of the twentieth century was not the first time Europeans imposed themselves and their cultural and organizational patterns on unwitting people in the name of helping them. In the sixteenth century, led by the Iberian kingdoms, Europeans began what their history books refer to as "the discoveries and conquests." Over the next several centuries they defeated and subjugated native peoples all over the world, reducing them to subservient status to be exploited economically when possible, replaced with their own excess numbers, or by slaves from Africa. The ideological justification for these actions ostensibly was religious. They were bringing God and His goodness and justice to the heathens and pagans. In so doing, they also imposed their forms of producing and distributing goods and service. And while capitalist markets for elite goods, participated in by royalty and a new class of long distance merchants, already existed, neither the majority of their own populations nor those they conquered lived their daily lives according to market principles. Europe, at the time, as Weber among others noted, was very much a "natural economy." What was produced came from the land that belonged to those who held legal—that is, political—title to it. In return for its use, the landowners appropriated the lion's share for themselves and (re)distributed the remainder in kind. The Iberian variant of the European natural economy was modified before it was brought to the Americas so that elite trade goods brought cash to the merchants involved in obtaining and selling them and to the nobles who both taxed and purchased them. After a series of organized Crusades against their Moslem foe who had taken the Holy Land in the eastern Mediterranean from them, items ranging from precious stones and metals to exotic foods such as sugar and spices became available in Europe and were distributed differently from locally produced items. The economy brought to the Americas combined the separate models of subsistence production and its distribution with the buying, selling and taxation of elite goods, in other words the natural economy and the capitalist market system. An idealized model of its operation was outlined in a little-read and greatly under-appreciated book written in the early fifteenth century by Pedro, Prince of Portugal. With respect to its impact on the non-European peoples effected by the Iberians, *O Livro da Virtuosa Bemfeitoria* (1946) may be thought of as a fifteenth-century precursor of Bretton Woods' attempt to create a world order, this one based on a different socio-economic model for the distribution of goods and services.

Some scholars acknowledge that the European expansion actually began with the landmark attack ordered by João I, King of Portugal, founder of the House of Avis, on the Moslem city of Ceuta across the straits of Gibraltar in 1415. Undertaken ostensibly to give his sons the opportunity to "win their spurs" in battle against the (Moslem) infidel, its success projected Portugal into a position of prominence in a turbulent Europe still torn by the Hundred Years War and the Great Schism.[8]

João's second son, Pedro, returned from the venture and undertook a translation of Seneca's treatise, On Benefits (De Beneficiis) that he completed in 1418. Later that year he promised to write a guide for the training of kings and great lords,[9] but a war with Castile delayed the endeavour, as did a period of official travel.

Second in line to the throne behind a sickly older brother, Pedro represented his father and his country on trips to the courts and councils of the continent between 1425 and 1428 and it was there that he learned of the threat posed by the Ottoman Turks. While traveling through Europe and the Holy Land, he collected maps and information that would be useful later for exploration and commercial expansion.

The guide, O Livro da Virtuosa Bemfeitoria, was completed in time to be dedicated to his older brother Duarte when he ascended to the throne in 1433.

Pedro's thinking reflects the culture and theology of his place and period. As was to be the case five centuries later at Bretton Woods, the nobles he was advising, like the presidents and legislators of the later period, were assumed to be the heads of national societies. Unlike the democratic and egalitarian leaders of the modern era with its secular and egalitarian beliefs, Pedro took the hierarchy of his era to be the natural order of the universe. Following St. Augustine, he maintained that humans were sinful by nature. For their own sakes, and to achieve the just and moral life God had intended for them, they needed constraints and direction that were provided by the beliefs of the church and the laws of the state, enforced by its rulers.

At the apex of the social order was the king who owed his allegiance, according to the prince, not to his subjects, but to God. His obligation was to implement the creator's divine plan. Below him, in descending order, were the organic parts or corporations of society such as the nobility, the church and the artisans, each with its own function. At the bottom were the poor.

Squalor, depravation and human misery, which were found in all societies, constituted the central problem Pedro addressed in his guide for rulers. Since humankind had been created by God, in His image, the prince reasoned, He could not have intended that any of His special creation suffer in a world whose perfection He was unfolding. Why was there poverty? Pedro's answer was that the rulers were failing in their duties, and to correct the problem he looked to Seneca's concept of the gift, or benefit. But unlike the Latin author who saw gift giving as an individual attribute, Pedro transformed it into the moral responsibility of those who occupied the highest stations in society. Kings and nobles who governed in God's name, he argued, should give from the abundance they had to those directly below them in the social order, and furthermore, inspired by the love and generosity of God and their social betters, each should bestow benefits to their immediate social inferiors. In this way the prince proposed a descending flow of resources through the hierarchical order of the society. When completed, the chain, or *cadea de bemfeitorias*, would help even the most humble and destitute, eliminating poverty and want, making society consistent with God's intent.

The benefits were to be given voluntarily, without expectation of return. Where immediate reciprocity between equals was made, Pedro maintained the transaction was not a gift; but a payment (*pagamento*), a reward or service.[10] The recipients of benefits were expected to show gratitude for and to reciprocate the gifts they received, first to God through acts of devotion such as prayer and the giving of alms, then as piety to parents, to the state as respect for the authority of is rulers, and finally as gratitude to their immediate benefactor which implied indebtedness and a sense of obligation. This was expressed as affection when the benefactor was a status equal or as submission, with loyalty implied, when he was a superior. Moreover, the recipient of a benefit was to praise, honour and give glory to his benefactor.

Looked at from the bottom up, in return for the benefits received that would abate their misery and need, the poor were expected to display the loyalty and deference characteristic of a medieval vassal to the state since they were to be indebted not just to their parents and to God, but also the nation and its rulers.

Pedro distinguishes four types of benefits: necessary—needed for physical and spiritual survival; profitable—intended to provide some comfort to those whose survival already is assured; honour-related benefits—to enhance the reputation and public image of the recipient; and agreeable, or pleasant—intended for those at the upper reaches of the social hierarchy.[11] Book III is devoted to petitions: how God, the saints and humans with access and control of greater resources may be asked for gifts and benefits.

In the early fifteenth century, though the kings and nobles of Portugal and the rest of Europe had considerably more than others in their kingdoms, especially the peasantry at the lower echelons of society who suffered great material want, they did not have the wherewithal to fuel the chain of benefits Pedro was proposing as the way to eliminate poverty. How were they to obtain the means that would enable them to implement this version of the patrimonial state in which they would behave responsibly and morally and implement God's intended design? The answer was not to be found in the pages of *O Livro da Virtuosa Bemfeitoria*, but in the life and deeds of the Portuguese Prince.

After the successful conclusion of the Ceuta affair, two schools of thought emerged as to the future direction to be taken by the nation. One, advocated by Pedro, proposed moving down the coast of Africa in search of discoveries and commercial expansion. The other supported further attacks on Moslem towns and villages. Amidst continuing conflict between the competing factions that was to last until the end of the century, in which first one side and then the other took control of the government and its "foreign policy," Pedro became regent shortly after his young nephew ascended to the throne as Afonso V in 1439. In the eight years he ruled there were no crusades and 198 leagues of the coast of West Africa were explored.

Under his direction the crown gave, as benefits, monopolies for trade in specific commodities and in newly discovered regions. Merchants were to pay the royal fifth and profess the loyalty and deference that was to become characteristic of the emerging patrimonial state. The crown further collected twenty per cent of the earnings from the landed properties in such places as Madeira where sugar cane had been planted and which by the end of the century were to earn profits that made both its settlers and the crown among the richest people in Europe. Other lands taken in conquest were given as benefits to nobles who also were to pay a fifth of all that was found, extracted or otherwise obtained. The recipients of these gifts in newly discovered parts of the world then gave rights and privileges (as benefits) to others below them who established settlements. In brief, the expansion, discoveries and conquests were to provide the resources that when distributed were to make possible the chain of patronage and clientage that was to eliminate hunger, misery and poverty.

Patronage in the model was the mechanism for distributing goods and services that moved down the hierarchically ordered socio-economic system that was to bring about God's intent for humanity, while clientage provided the reciprocity that maintained loyalty to and dependence on the expanding colonial order. Unlike the capitalist market system of a later period that was to emphasize providing opportunities, the patrimonial state with its patron-client system of distribution offered security, especially to those at the bottom who could petition for needed help with the legitimate expectation of receiving it. But greed was to prove to be a stronger motivator than the Christian morality proposed by the Portuguese Prince. European royalty came to assume it was divinely entitled to levels of conspicuous consumption that greatly diminished the obligation to provide benefits down the hierarchical chain.

In the New World the descendants of the recipients of royal benefits born and raised there, often in opulence and splendour that compared with that of royalty back home, in time came to challenge the legitimacy of the colonial authority while finding ways to evade paying the taxes that were intended to fuel the distributive chain. Those at the top enjoyed the gifts, but only grudgingly passed a fair share down the line. Consequently, the system gradually ground to a halt. Poverty grew worse as new peoples were brought into a (world) system that was intended only for those from Europe. Significantly, in the almost five centuries the system has been operational, the poor in the New World learned that no matter how bad things got for them, as long as they accepted the hierarchy and their place of dependence at the bottom, while giving loyalty and deference to those above them, at worst they would be able to petition and reasonably expect to obtain help they so desperately needed. Although the system did not provide them with opportunities to improve their lot, they could be secure in expecting to obtain what minimum was needed for their ultimate survival since the same still vital set of religious beliefs on which it was originally based still prevailed.

With the end of colonial authority and the establishment of independent nations throughout the Americas in the nineteenth century, the apex of the patrimonial order was relocated from the royal houses of Europe to the (now elected) governments in the capitals of the newly created nations. Instead of inheritance legitimizing sovereign authority, success in electoral contests now determined who was to control the resources of the new states and dispense benefits. Political elites and their voting networks replaced the crown and corporations of the old order. The patron-client system of distribution was adapted to the electoral process with loyalty transferred from the royal head of the empire to political groups that mobilized the votes needed to gain office. Politicians controlled benefits that they distributed, no longer to maintain a social order defined as moral, but rather to followers who brought home the vote. For those at the lower echelons this meant the need to find a patron who in return for electoral (and other) loyalty would provide needed resources given as benefits such as housing, jobs, or access to health care.

Unlike the more egalitarian system of Europe and North America, where in the last half a century women have moved in steadily growing numbers into the labour force and attained greater independence, in the patrimonial areas of Latin America women continue to be *casada*, a word in both Spanish and Portuguese than means married and housed.[12] A division of labour based on gender still prevails in which women tend to be confined to a domestic domain in which they are responsible for the care of children and the home while being protected by the men to whom they are related by blood or marriage, who function in the dangerous and threatening public arena (believed to be filled with rogues, thieves and scoundrels) that, again in contrast with Europe and North America, is political rather than commercial. Qualities such as manliness, dignity, generosity, and grandeur are stereotypic in this world that emphasizes the word as opposed to the deed. It is characterized more by the sociability of alliances and dependence (in a system of hierarchically ordered interdependence) in which an individual, especially one who is poor, seeks a good *patrón* (Spanish) or *patrão* (Portuguese),[13] than the individualistic independence of the North American and European public world of the market.[14]

A government contract in the new "democracies" remained a benefit whose function, in terms of the logic of the system, was to provide resources not just for the "profit" of the recipient, but also for him to distribute down the social order in the form of jobs and other benefits. Whatever the stated reason for it, be it to build a school, a hospital or a park, construction and completion is often secondary if not altogether unimportant. What is significant is whether or not the resources are used to provide benefits to those below in the hierarchy, and that all in the chain will provide the loyalty—i.e. votes—that will keep in office those who will continue the flow of goods and services to the members of the network. If it is, those at the bottom, the poor now affiliated with the winners, or those who promise support in the future, will be helped, even if only when they petition in times of dire need. In return, all in the network will reciprocate with loyalty, thereby maintaining the still hierarchical social order. This leads to understanding why many in Latin America, for example, may make choices they believe will provide them with security, often over, or along with, the opportunities offered them by those who see their behaviour exclusively in market terms.[15]

The Populational Decision-Making Model

Arnold Strickon and I proposed the populational decision-making framework as a way to model social processes as part of an attempt to re-conceptualize the study of social change. While working on a project on entre-preneurship,[16] we realized that the understanding of both entrepreneurship and development by economists, sociologists and students of business was based on the metaphor of organic growth that Robert Nisbet had shown to have dom-inated Western thinking about social change since the Greek era.[17]

When Joseph Schumpeter and other economists first turned their attention from the institutional processes that produced and maintained equilibrium states to entrepreneurship and the study of economic growth,[18] they focused on the movement of an economy (and a society) from a known state to an unknown one in the future. After World War II, the conceptualization was reversed. The imagery of organic growth implicitly accepted led to envisioning an inevitable movement from non- (or pre) industrialized, often non-market-oriented, "backward" states of the other economies in the world to that of the modern, Western one:

> In classic nineteenth-century tradition the traits and attributes of the contem-porary West were defined as characteristic of the typological construct called modernity, the direction in which mankind as a whole not only would move but should move. Its logical opposite, then, was used to establish a second cat-egory or type, traditional or underdeveloped. To these were added a third, defined as somewhat midway between underdeveloped and developed, called developing. In a page almost right out of the nineteenth century, students in the mid-twentieth century set out three stages of economic development for all of humanity. Not only the typology was composed of three stages that went from simple to complex, but to its proponents it represented the inevitable growth and development of human institutions.[19]

Given the inevitability of modernization implied by the model, it was not nec-essary to study other economic systems in their own right. The issue for the planners at the IMF, World Bank, representatives of helping governments and aca-demics was: how best was the transition—i.e., development—to be brought about?

Finding an answer was complicated by the implications of attempting to understand social reality in terms of metaphor. Thinking metaphorically may be helpful, even necessary, in beginning to comprehend complex issues. However, as Turbayne noted,[20] a consequence of this could lead to mistaking the model for the thing being modeled, to believing that what one likened reality to was reality. Strickon and I concluded that this was what had happened in the study of entrepreneurship and development. Likening economy, society and other institutions to the parts of a growing organism implied an understanding of the processes that brought about the growth. Since this was more than economic, other social scientists and historians were asked to explain how it worked. How do societies, cultures and institutions grow so that underdeveloped nations could move to more "advanced" stages? No one was able to provide answers and we found no examples showing the process by means of which a society, or set of institutions, was transformed by entrepreneurs.

Schumpeter suggested that entrepreneurs, as individuals, made decisions, and their resulting actions brought about change. Glade called for situational analysis at the micro level in terms of changing opportunity structures. If individuals perceived the opportunities and made the choices that took advantage of them, he maintained, change (meaning development) would take place. This may be so, but it still did not tell us how those behaviours affect the institutions that are assumed (by the metaphor and those in the social science community who accept it) to be the societal analogue of the organs of the growing organism.

Strickon and I had previously concluded that it was reliance by social theory on the metaphor of society as a growing organism that had prevented the development of models of social process.[21] In order to explain change we proposed a new metaphor to make possible the articulation of the behaviour of individuals with the institutions and other higher-level concepts that were the bases of social science thinking. We adopted the imagery—as a metaphor— that had proven so successful in the biology developed by Charles Darwin in his *The Origin of Species* (1859).

Darwin had turned the attention of biologists away from typological categories—the species that had previously been their focus—to the characteristics of the organisms whose variation was the stuff of his concept of reality. Diversity and variation appeared in a unit now called a "breeding population" that consisted of a group of individual organisms in sufficient contact and interactions with each other so that the possibilities are greater that they will mate with each other than with other organisms of the same type. One consequence of this, as Mayr observed, is recognizing that all

> organisms and organic phenomena are composed of unique features and can
> be described collectively only in statistical terms. Individuals, or any kind of
> organic entities form populations of which we can determine only the arith-
> metic mean and the statistics of variation. Averages, however, are merely
> statistical abstractions; *only the individuals of which populations are composed have
> reality.* (italics added)[22]

Some of the individuals in a breeding population are better able to utilize
the resources of their environment than others, making it possible for them to
produce more offspring compared with the other members of the population.
Over time, this differential reproduction results in a shift in the average characteristics of the population. This, in the Darwinian view, was the process by
means of which evolution occurred. In it individual organisms are assumed to
be goal-directed as they strive to acquire resources and to reproduce. Higher-
level units, such as populations and species, do not have goals but rather are
statistical abstractions taken from the behaviours of individual organisms.

Using this as our metaphor, we attempted to formulate a new way to conceptualize social processes and social change. Although still interested in
society, culture and institutions such as religion, politics and economics, following the lead of the Darwinians, we chose not to attribute to them reality in
their own right. Instead, they were taken to be statistical patterns abstracted
from the behaviours of the members of a specific population. What previous
students of social phenomena had assumed to be real and the objects of investigation were for us *the results of more fundamental processes that generated the
patterned regularities while also explaining the changes that transformed them.*

The individuals whose behaviours we studied were assumed, as with
Darwinian populations, to be found in groups, the members of which have
sufficient contact with each other and to interact to such an extent that the
probabilities are greater that they would interact (directly or by means of symbolic intermediacy) more with each other than with the members of other
populations. As they strive to attain their individual goals they make decisions
and choices that lead them to behave in given ways. If we focus on any specific
goal, or set of interrelated ones, we see that not everyone in the community will
try to obtain it (them) in the same way. If we count the behaviours selected by all
members at a particular time, we would obtain the statistical frequencies of the
range of decisions and choices made by all those seeking a given set of goals.

The most statistically numerous outcomes turn out to be the institutional forms described and examined by our colleagues. But in contrast with other studies, we also would record alternative patterns.

The goals[23] humans seek differ from those of the organisms studied by biologists in that in addition to those that are material, others may be symbolic, ranging from things as concrete as the shape or colour of carrying items to views of the afterlife. Given the arbitrary relationship between the physical representations of symbols and their referents, if they are to be used, transmitted to and received from others, they must be shared.

Symbolic ability enables humans to contemplate events and situations other than the ones they experience directly. As a result,

> they can invent and fantasize situations and behaviors to perform in them. They also can define symbolically what for them will be a reward. More importantly they can conceptualize what may be thought of as sets of alternative means for the attainment of what they define as goals. They can 'think through,'...in the abstract, as an exercise or problem, alternative ways in which the goals or rewards they wish might be obtained. They can select from the range of alternative possibilities they see the one that, in their best judgment and evaluation of the situation, given the information and knowledge they have, most probably will enable them to obtain the goal.[24]

Humans seek goals in diversified areas defined by terms such as faith, music or affective relationships. They may seek goals not valued by other communities. Like all other goal directed behaviour, human decisions are made in specific settings, but given their symbolic ability alternative options are available to them, depending on the knowledge an individual has and his judgement of the situation.

New goals and the means to attain them, analogous to mutations in biology, may be "invented," spontaneously by single individuals at any time, and then copied by others or discarded. Ends and means also may enter a community through contact with the outside, as for example, through newspapers, movies or radio and television programs. When goals are introduced intentionally, as in development programs, the means for their attainment may be presented along with them.

Goals new to a community may be consistent with those previously sought by its members, or they may differ and even contradict some or all of them. When they are not the same as those whose selection forms a dominant pattern, they may be debated as individuals examine the benefits each offers them. At times, new goals, and the means for attaining them,' may be viewed as deviant by those who value the old ends, leading to possible conflict and animosity between those who strive for the new and supporters of the old. The transition from one set to another, or from one array of means to a new one, may at times be marked by discord and hostility.

New means may enable the individual selecting them to obtain a goal, also desired by others, more easily or in greater amount. Following the Darwinian analogy, we may say that his choices are more adaptive than alternative ones. But again, given their symbolic abilities, others can recognize this and select the more adaptive choices the next time they find themselves in a situation where they seek the goals in question. Information obtained from outside also may enable some to make more adaptive choices. Given this, over time the frequencies of behavioural choices made by the members of a community may change, expressing themselves in new frequencies of choice and perhaps new (preponderant) patterns. This would be an instance of change in the institutions of the community.

Unlike standard decision-making models, we do not assume that there are right and wrong choices for any situation, only more successful ones. In the absence of in depth research outsiders may take no one set of goals as more important than any other. Though in our 1981 paper these points were made in a footnote, I now believe they should have been underscored in the text.[25]

The model is non-directional since the outside observer has no way to tell what goals are being acted on and which choices will be more adaptive in obtaining them. This rules out knowing if there will be a change in the frequencies of decisions made and, if so, the direction they will take. What the model provides is the ability to observe and examine the diversity of patterns of behaviours resulting from the decisions and choices of individuals and the ability to track them over time so as to document changes in statistical outcomes that reflect institutional change when it does occur.

Greed and Security in the Choices of the Poor and the Implications for Models of Development

In a 1971 article in the *Journal of Developing Areas*, I used the oriental fable of the monkey and the fish, previously employed for the same purpose by Don Adams (1960) and again by George Foster (1962), to emphasize the importance of understanding "the culture and social structure of both the donor and recipient societies cooperating in programs of development."[26] The fable read: "Once upon a time there was a great flood, and involved in this flood were two creatures, a monkey and a fish. The monkey, being agile and experienced, was lucky enough to scramble up a tree and escape the raging waters. As he looked down from his safe perch, he saw the poor fish struggling against the swift current. With the very best of intentions, he reached down and lifted the fish from the water. The result was inevitable."

Development programs have injected goals, and means for attaining them, into a large number of what are called target communities, or for our purposes, small groups of primarily poor people at the lower end of complex, highly stratified national social systems. Single goals, or small, interrelated sets of goals, that offer economic opportunities when introduced reflect images of development as conceptualized in the world order established at Bretton Woods. To succeed, the projects require people to behave in compliance with a constellation of interdependent behavioural patterns that are consistent with the model of modern, market-oriented capitalist society. Far too often specific projects, in their desire to "kick-start" development, lose sight of the fact that the fiscal and other stimulation of demand by governments to build and stabilize the nations of the world and prevent future depressions depends on the majority of their citizens' choosing and attaining goals that result in the patterns of family, education, politics, and other institutions that characterized the societies directly involved in World War II. The truth is that many people, such as those in Latin America, at all socio-economic levels, make choices that result in multiple, seemingly contradictory, patterns that combine market and patrimonial principles. Can new governments successfully stimulate demand when so many of their citizens choose to attain their economic goals by means of patronage and clientage? Could it be that the IMF and World Bank frustration that led to the Washington Consensus was due in part to the use of its loans to fuel chains of patronage and benefits? For many, not only those connected politically at the top, the patrimonial system may offer better strategies for the attainment of their goals than market forms. The poor, who are the primary targets of development programs, at times may find traditional means better enable them to attain their ends than those offered by the development workers. Perhaps they may hedge by accepting opportunities made available to them while also maintaining or seeking new ties of patronage and clientage. The implications of this possibility, with respect to the opposition between opportunity and security, with special emphasis on the poor, must be explored.

The capitalist market system offers opportunities to individuals, but has never been strong on providing them with economic security. Workers have gained better wages, job security, pensions, health care and a variety of other benefits only when they have banded together against those who own and manage the companies that employ them and form labour organizations. Similarly, small-scale producers have joined cooperatives to gain protection from their larger and more powerful economic rivals. By the end of the twentieth century the multinational corporations that produce most of the world's goods and services have gained the upper hand. Supported by a new generation of voters who, having experienced only prosperity in their lifetime, seem unable to relate to the prevention of unemployment and depression that motivated the representatives at Bretton Woods, they have broken or greatly diminished the ability of unions to provide security to workers. In their efforts to dominate markets, the multinationals have gobbled up co-operatives along with competing producers. The abilities of the organizations that traditionally have provided security for workers in the capitalist world are now greatly diminished.

In the more than half a century since World War II, technological advancement has made possible, for the first time in human history, the production of goods and services in sufficient quantities to provide for the basic needs of humanity. The multinationals, owned and managed by small numbers of North Americans and Europeans, control the new productive technology and with it the ability to supply the increased volume of goods and services and the distribution of this potential abundance. These items will be placed on the market with the expectation that they will be purchased with wages earned by individuals holding jobs. We already know that the role of labour in the productive process will be greatly reduced while output grows. As more and more people in the developing world are being induced to choose "modern," market-oriented behaviours by well-intended programs, there will be a reduced need for their labour. In spite of becoming educated and skilled, already employed individuals will see their jobs taken by others "willing" to work for lower wages elsewhere and there will be fewer jobs overall for an expanding workforce. A greater share of the income in the nations of the world already is going to smaller percentages of the population while the poor are receiving increasingly less, not just in wages, but also in security. We know the depravation suffered by those who seek jobs and are unable to find them over long periods. The poor in Latin America who are choosing both the opportunities offered by developers while also continuing their participation in relations of patronage and dependency are making what for them are rational decisions. This is at odds with the goals of development programs whose implicit intent is to end the dependence of patronage. Can development, as it is presently conceived, work when the choices people make in their best interests produce behavioural outcomes at odds with those assumed in, perhaps required by the extant model? If the answer is no, and developers continue to stimulate changes in this direction, moral and ethical questions must be raised leading, perhaps, to the model on which development is based being reconsidered.

My hope is that Michael Rosberg's insightful reintroduction of the populational decision-making model into the literature on development, with its emphasis on individuals making choices that form patterns that can be measured statistically, as opposed to focusing on institutions that grow, will encourage more thinking at the level of people and their choices and behaviours. While it may not provide all the answers, it at least would make it possible to recognize the existence of alternative patterns that, where statistically significant, would have to be acknowledged. Their recognition, and the reasons for them, would be a major step in the rethinking needed to answer why development has not worked.

SIDNEY M. GREENFIELD is Professor Emeritus of Anthropology, University of Wisconsin-Milwaukee, and Co-Chair, University Seminar on Brazil, Columbia University, NYC.

Acknowledgements

I am indebted to Conrad M. Arensberg and Karl Polanyi, my mentors at Columbia University, for helping me to appreciate and frame in comparative perspective many of the issues raised in this essay. For all our lively and compelling debates that helped me to clarify these issues my thanks to my classmates, friends and colleagues, Arnold Strickon and Morton Klass.

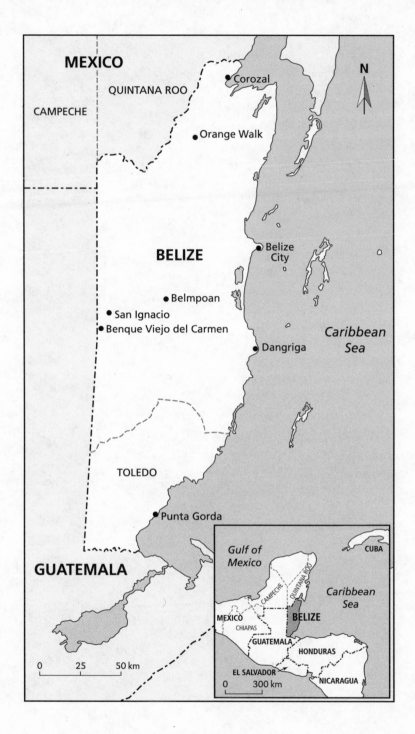

MEXICO

CAMPECHE

QUINTANA ROO

● Corozal

● Orange Walk

BELIZE

● Belize City

● Belmpoan
● San Ignacio
● Benque Viejo del Carmen

● Dangriga

Caribbean Sea

TOLEDO

● Punta Gorda

GUATEMALA

0   25   50 km

Gulf of Mexico

CUBA

Caribbean Sea

CAMPECHE

QUINTANA ROO

MEXICO

CHIAPAS

BELIZE

GUATEMALA

HONDURAS

EL SALVADOR

NICARAGUA

0   300 km

Morality is Blinding Us

THERE IS A SCREW MISSING. It ought to have been sunk through the aluminium window frame at the front of the bedroom of our new house up the coast from Belize City, with its thick little flanged head driven securely into the cement wall. There was supposed to have been a set of matching screws driven into the other holes around the frame. They were supposed to have worked together to anchor the window frame to the wall and to keep my wife and me safe during hurricanes. But they are missing.

I discovered their absence during Hurricane Keith. Sunday night, when my wife and I lay in bed, I heard a noise over a froth of wind whipping at the window and howling through the shutters. It was an irregular squeak and thump, three or four times a minute. The squeak was the metallic complaint of aluminium rubbing cement objecting to being bullied by that gale. Irritating, but endurable. The thumps that followed were another matter—a heavier thud following each squeak. They sounded like trouble. I lay there for hours, it seemed, trying to identify the sound. Yet all the while I knew exactly what was wrong: *a window was ajar!* My wife and I were going to die in our ridiculous king-sized mahogany bed; crushed like roaches on designer sheets. That window with the louvre cranks was about to skewer the two of us neatly to our oversized mattress—nude, and pinioned like insects to a cardboard science project on a seventh grade classroom wall. Horrible. The two of us killed. And ostensibly because Keith didn't have enough snakes and 'gators to destroy in the mangrove wetlands that surrounded our house.

But Keith wasn't the enemy. That window wobbled because the workmen wanted a way to finish the installation ten minutes sooner and get home. Plastic grout would never do the anchoring work of a gang of screws; but I'm sure they cared nothing for our security in a hurricane. They must have assumed we would never know—before we died—that we were skewered (or maybe screwed) by their slovenly workmanship.

With Keith approaching and the eerie sky gone yellow, I had got shutters onto most of the other windows late Sunday afternoon. A few, like the one at the front of the bedroom, remained unprotected—the hurricane came on so fast. Standing on tippy-toes atop a waving ladder over the second-storey windows, the corrugated shutters luffed and sliced my hands. I had to quit; the front bedroom window was left exposed. A likely death was the price we were to pay. Monday morning, I confirmed my suspicions: the entire window frame was rocking loose in its cement socket, preparing to burst inward and obliterate the two of us in a gale.

"Why would somebody do a thing like that?" my wife, who has a knack for putting the screws to one, innocently asked.

"Why indeed?" I muttered and cursed, and impotently wedged a couple of screwdrivers between the wall and the rocking frame.

The game of "what happens next" should have been within the capacity of those workmen. Shouldn't they have known? Squalls are frequent along the Mosquito Coast, hurricanes not unknown. The plastic goop they carelessly smeared around the rim of our window frame would hold no better than chocolate icing, or soap. They must have known. When you glue a large window into the face of a hurricane, what happens next is that it blows in and kills the occupants! We were about to be swallowed by the Gulf of Honduras.

Why indeed would somebody do a thing like that? A lack of concern? A lack of responsibility? A lack of empathy?[1] Everett Rogers, the anthropologist, defined ten characteristics of peasants; one of them is supposed to be lack of empathy. But even if this is true, it explains nothing. For one thing, these workmen may never have been peasants, even if they never cared about our safety. Anyway, Rogers was only describing peasant behaviour, whereas my wife wanted to know why it happened, and I for one, wanted to know *how* to make it stop.

There isn't always a lack of empathy when people are poor. In fact, there's often plenty of altruism: once, a raggedy Mexican fellow in Quintana Roo walked several blocks out of his way to help me get a heavy suitcase to a hotel. He refused a tip. I never saw him before or since. Another time, a lady in Southern Florida came out of her house with a baby to warn me out of her "bad neighbourhood" because the teens on the next block had a habit of robbing passers-by. She didn't have to do that either.

But these workmen were irresponsible. We were involved in a business transaction with them; yet, they were taking our money and giving us less than our money's worth. If they weren't altruistically doing their best then where was the foreman? What were his standards and why wasn't he doing his job? And where were the government inspectors? Evidently the foreman was no more motivated to hand over a quality job than the workmen. It wasn't just the people building our house. It was all over town, all over the country, and according to what I keep reading and hearing when I travel, all over the developing world. It was at all levels from window installation to the management of governments:

> The US Virgin Islands—St. Croix, St. Thomas and St. John—are at a delicate stage.... [Y]ears of official mismanagement and bloated public payrolls have left the US territory's government all but bankrupt, sparking talk of a federal takeover. Graft is common; just last month, the US attorney for the islands announced a major campaign against it, saying the "biggest priority for the Virgin Islands is public corruption." The Islands' economy is moribund, despite a program to lure investment that involves aggressive tax exemption.[2]

An opinion from another Belizean paper concurs, although what any of the Belizean papers say must be read with a goodly pinch of salt, given their tendency to reflect extreme partisan positions. Sometimes the presentation (or even the misrepresentation) of facts makes out one political party to be better than another. I'm not quoting these articles and letters to endorse them as truth, but to show that residents of developing nations—of Belize at least—think such things are true but haven't found effective ways of changing them:

> The recent Declaration of Monterrey, resulting from the Presidential summit
> in that city earlier this month, has devoted ten paragraphs to the problem of
> corruption in government and how to combat it....
> With dramatic impact the countries of the Americas are coming together to
> root out one of the biggest impediments to progress in the hemisphere—the

endemic use of corrupt practices by people in government for personal enrichment.

In the 22 1/3 years since independence corrupt practices have grown out of control in Belize. It is a problem which few in government are prepared to acknowledge. But recently Mr. Assad Shoman, former Foreign Minister and High Commissioner to London, writing in the December issue of *Ideas*, published by the Society for the Propagation of Education and Research (SPEAR) made the following observations:

"What can a politician do except work on ways to get money undercover and use some of that to help his/her constituents and the greater part to feather his or her own nest?

"The current state of the State and of politics that naturally flows from this is a recipe for corruption and bad governance...."

Belize has already tried the Contractor General Act, the Ombudsman Act and the Prevention of Corruption in Public Life Act. Singly and collectively they have not had the slightest impact on the sinister and cynical growth of corruption "in high places."[3]

The streets of Belize City are filled with potholes because the contractors—so everybody claims—make deals with the politicians to slip some of the government road construction budget into their pockets, and spend less than they should on the roads. Kickbacks. The same thing goes on in Colombia, for example. There was an editorial in El *Tiempo* in Bogotá when I lived there in 1965 comparing the streets of the Colombian capital to the surface of the moon and the explanation was the same: kickbacks. People out in San Andrés Island, Colombia, said the new hospital buildings were falling apart before they were finished for the same reason. In both locations they say that essential supplies and equipment are needed in the schools and hospitals, but there's never enough money in the budget because of "leaks." In Indonesia (as in many other nations) the government hires agricultural extension and health extension workers, but there are insufficient funds to get them to the rural communities. Or if they get there, the workers are under-trained, the data or statistics that have been gathered are insufficient, and not enough money has been allocated for operations to be effective.[4]

The donor nations have never met their target of 0.7% of GDP as a contribution to international development. But when corruption in developing nations is rampant, even an increase in badly-needed funding will not resolve the problems, as many nations mismanage what they currently have. David Shrock, of Canada's Mennonite Central Committee, connects the negative impact of international loans to Third World nations on the poor:

Most people acknowledge that much of the money that was borrowed was stolen by corrupt government officials, spent on poorly designed economic projects, or used to support military forces that propped up dictatorships and suppressed political dissent....

When loans were flowing into poor countries, people with personal, family or ethnic ties to government and military officials used their connections to get cheap loans and government jobs. When heavily indebted countries began to restructure their economies, these same people used their connections to buy government owned businesses for "cents on the dollar." Large landowners sold their land to multinational corporations or began to grow crops for export. Merchants prospered by selling imported goods...countries have focused on short-term survival....

Indebted countries cut their budget for developing the roads, bridges, ports, phone systems and power systems that are necessary for either domestic or international businesses to make productive investments in their country....

This money is most often a "foot-loose" form of capital that does not make local investments in bricks and mortar, enjoys long periods of exemptions from taxes, takes its profit out of the country instead of sharing it with a local partner, and continually puts their workers in competition with workers in other countries. This drives wages down to the lowest possible level, and adds little to the local economy.[6]

Just about anybody you talk to in Belize or many other developing countries eventually complains about irresponsibility and sloth in government and in the general population. Nobody I've met is happy about it, as a letter to the editor shows:

Dear Editor,

Another month has come and gone and with the very hard rain, our peninsula road is very dangerous again! The tourist season is upon us and many of us have purchased new bikes for guest use; however, we are afraid to let them use the bikes on the dangerous roads....

Any visitor driving down is faced with very dangerous conditions. Any vendor or supply truck, bus or private vehicle is faced with high repair costs, maybe impassable sections of deep mud, with not much help if the vehicle breaks down or gets stuck....

We collect and pay a lot of taxes—hotel tax, sales tax, and let's not forget all the gas tax our tour guides pay. Surely with this tax money we should get a paved road.[7]

But the situation doesn't change fundamentally. That doesn't seem rational, but that's the way it remains. Bridges get built and fall apart quickly, roads get paved and disintegrate inside a year, new laws get passed and enforced while foreign funders finance development projects. "New Year: New Law" the cynics in the Caribbean say. For now in Belize we are observing the traffic cops' new slogan: "Click it or ticket!" But in a year we'll be into another campaign, few traffic cops will be handing out tickets and few of us will still be using safety belts. At the same time the gap between rich and poor remains pretty much unchanged and so does productivity per capita.

Under the British, there were enforced standards in Belize and the other colonies that helped to keep poor folks polite and to extract labour of acceptable quality. One time, an old Belizean hotel gardener leaned on his rake to tell me about how much more he liked life under the British. Things were supposed to have been dependable in the old days; you could prop a stick against your front door and walk away. When you came back you'd find your possessions as you left them. People spoke to each other with respect. The whole village raised the child and workmen took pride in their work.[8]

Such is the collective memory and a good portion of it is likely true. Except for a few old-timers, little of that decency and pride of workmanship seems to have been internalized; I suspect it never was, except by a few. As the authoritarian colonial era ended, the self-regulation evaporated.[9]

If people in the post-colonial economies were internally regulated it seems to me they would have had more success rejecting corruption and sloth when these showed up. Decent politicians would have invested more of the national budget into productive strategies that would have improved the capacity of the population to produce. They would have equipped the hospitals and schools and paved the roads in more sustainable ways. Decent voters would have made them do it. But the whole idyllic edifice must have been built on an external system of intimidation and punishment for it to have crumbled so quickly. The great Britannic lion had played cat with the colonies to keep them in line and productive; most of the colonies probably played mouse. Now, the cat's away and as John Saldivar, the Shadow Minister of Economic Development for the United Democratic Party (UDP) in Belize writes,

> For a long time now our country has been bracing for devaluation. Those that are less knowledgeable about these matters might soon, if not already, start to think that the devaluation bogeyman is just that.... Yet, those who know of the functioning of an economy know that while it is the excessive bor-

rowing and sale of assets that has enabled this government to keep its foreign reserves artificially high and avoid devaluation thus far, it is the same two excesses that will make the economic crash even more painful and recovery so much more difficult. [10]

There is great unhappiness about the status quo and known ways of changing it are apparently inadequate.

The missing screws are realities that we cannot afford to ignore. Yet, I think that we who care about community development have tended to do exactly that—to let them drop into a sizeable chasm, and then be forgotten. [11] We need to search for them. The missing screws are the survival strategies utilized by the harried populations of the developing world and by those who harass them and profit from the interaction. In community development work, any behaviour we intend to change but fail to examine and comprehend, is a missing screw. The workmen who left my window unanchored and went home early, for example, were making use of some sort of survival strategy. And so were the foreman and the government inspectors. They were engaged in activities that I never examined originally, preferring to condemn them, to reject them, and ideally to replace them. Yet the origin, persistence and impact of such behaviours in the Third World need to be analysed.

The chasm where the screws go missing is something I shall call "The Valley of Means." By "Means" I refer to that complex and tangled web of alliances and factions that engages the minds and partially motivates the actions of those developing country populations, including both the victims and the victimizers. Within the murk of this Valley of Means I suggest lurk important transactions among rich and poor which merit more careful attention. The transactions reflect both the idealism and the opportunism of people intent on surviving and prospering if they can and generally doing so at the expense of others. In the Valley of Means and under some conditions we are observing rich and poor alike attempting to do well by doing others ill.

A successful fisherman in Colombia nicknamed "Mad Dog" [12] once approached me, saying, "I could buy you a beer, but just one." That seemed to me an odd way to socialize. To Canadian ears his manner was abrupt—a friendly offer, but more honest than expected as it called attention to the limit of his hospitality. Somehow it represented more of a business deal than a gesture of friendship. In Canada I don't think we're generally quite so bald about our intentions. We are perhaps more anxious than Mad Dog to make a positive overture to a friend, one that is affectionate. After all, if we invite a friend for a beer we intend to say, "I like you." If at the time of the invitation we announce the limit of our affection by quantifying the number of beers, we undermine the affectionate message with an economic one.

The behaviour of that fisherman contrasted sharply with that of an impoverished fellow named "Puppy" who sometimes went fishing with Mad Dog as an assistant, gutting his fish, scuppering the fish gurry out of the dugout floor with part of a plastic bottle and lighting his cigarettes. Puppy would practically force beers on me. That struck me as odd too because it felt like too much generosity considering the superficial nature of our acquaintance (not to mention my restricted tolerance for alcohol). If Mad Dog was too instrumental about our relationship, Puppy was too affectionate. Initially I chuckled and dismissed the oddity of these contrasting behaviours as examples of poor socialization. That was an outsider's conclusion: a value-judgement based, in this instance, on Canadian ideals. Instead of understanding what was happening, I passed judgement and felt superior.

Eventually the pattern was undeniable notwithstanding my nearly total cultural blindness. The behavioural distinction was consistent across richer and poorer fishermen in that area. And to the best I could discover the difference was a function of categorical options that differentiated richer and poorer fishermen like Mad Dog and Puppy. The more successful fishermen had direct access to fish, and hence to income because they owned their own dugouts and outboards. They were "Captains" with the power to provide employment or deny it. They had less need of anybody, including me, than the poorer ones did because they earned an acceptable income from fishing.

In contrast, social alliances were part of the poor man's economic strategy. Puppy had to rely on other people. He could not consistently depend on his own resources the way Mad Dog did. He was also more likely to raise a hog (a kind of living piggy bank) than the richer fisherman because he could sell it at times like Christmas when cash was needed. He was also more likely to keep boards (for a coffin) above the joists of his small cottage. In fact the fishermen without boats—the "Mates" engaged in a range of socio-economic survival strategies not needed by the Captains.[13]

Both fishermen offering me beers in the Valley of Means were employing economic strategies, even though they may also have been genuine gestures of friendship. It was hard to tell. Because of their social, economic and political circumstances, the strategies of richer and poorer fishermen differed markedly and with good consistency.

Puppy trolled for assistance from others and so Mad Dog covered his assets to protect himself from folks like Puppy. In an environment where people in Puppy's situation feel the need to take all they can and to offer little in return, limiting me to a single beer must have made good economic sense to Mad Dog. The situation demanded it. But if this is true, it meant that Mad Dog's behaviour was being controlled and shaped in part by ostensibly dependent people like Puppy. Simultaneously, it meant that the options of people like Puppy were being limited by the reactions of people like Mad Dog who controlled Puppy's access to income. It was a vicious cycle: because of his poverty, Puppy helped to keep Mad Dog a boss and because Puppy depended on him, Mad Dog was cornered into keeping Puppy in his place. An act of kindness by people in either category would result in personal disadvantage. Morality, when confronted by such costs and benefit realities, was being slighted. Moral choices could never be given their due unless one side was willing to suffer more so that the other could suffer less. It was a social stalemate, an example of class stasis[14] notwithstanding all the camaraderie that existed among the Captains and Mates on the beach.

That is how I began to suspect that the core of development's problems lay exactly within that frozen class dynamic. The social relations of production in this tiny corner of capitalism had made efforts to promote change impossible. Neither the Mad Dogs nor the Puppies on that beach were able to change their stultifying interdependence because they needed each other exactly as they were. An economic formula operated here that ensured inequitable interdependence. Unless a counter-strategy existed to address and adjust the formula, Puppy would remain subservient to Mad Dog or be by-passed for another equally unfortunate captain's mate. Mad Dog and the other Captains would ensure the continued destitution of the whole lot of them. Mad Dog was a Christian, but the actions of the other Captains and Puppy's the compliance of Puppy and the other Mates served to keep his hands tied. He was unable to be kinder to Puppy without depriving himself and his family. Morality in other words (i.e. what a good Captain ought to do) and social justice (i.e. what ought to unite oppressed fishermen's mates) had very little to do with what was actually going on, and personal advantage at the expense of others (what I call "greed" in this book) had everything to do with what I was witnessing.

There were other anomalous behaviours within this business of fishing in San Andrés Island, Colombia. On the beach, Puppy competed with other fishing Mates for a job in one of the dugouts. He was paid less in fish and cash by the dugout captain, Mad Dog, than he desired. However, if he was bypassed by all the Captains, he received nothing. The going rate paid by the Captains was of advantage to them and a source of irritation to the group of Mates who depended on them.

When at sea, however, Puppy was helpful and deferential towards Mad Dog. After all, that was necessary to gain his payment, and to gain an advantage over the other Mates. At sea, Mad Dog made efforts to conceal a school of fish if another dugout came over the horizon. Fishermen have to stand to pull in their lines hand over hand and if another dugout appeared while they were doing so, Mad Dog would sit down quickly, ordering Puppy to do the same—in the hopes that the other dugout hadn't realized this craft's good fortune. The two of them took advantage of other Captains and Mates.

Yet, should Mad Dog's dugout reach shore before the other dugout, he and Puppy would take pains to run across the sand and help roll the other craft up the beach on logs. In this instance, there was no distinction between Captains and Mates. This was a favour being returned. As they all said, "What go round, come round." Next time, it might be Mad Dog's dugout that was being helped by the other fishermen.

The set of economic behaviours just described was a missing screw. It was a range of inter-related strategies, an unexamined series of survival interactions that had everything to do with socio-economic development and with why it wasn't happening. Once I retrieved that screw from the Valley of Means and once I examined it, I was able to investigate the motivations that drove the behaviours of two categories of fishermen.

The operation of micro-economic forces that shape human interactions makes missing screws important for developers—and not just for Community Developers. What happens among individuals in the communities inevitably affects national development because local dependencies sustain systems of economic and political corruption and hamper economic growth. The principles at work in the villages and barrios of the Third World necessarily operate among some of the bureaucrats and politicians as well. After all, they derive legitimacy from voters and rich supporters. Ultimately what's happening in the legislatures and government offices is going to have an effect in the villages and barrios. There is a tangled web of social, economic and political interactions running from top to bottom and from bottom to top. If the "dynamic stasis" observed between Mad Dog and Puppy is replicated often enough then we have isolated a core phenomenon out of which much of the system of obstructed national development is spun. Beyond the national system there are opportunities for corrupt politicians, civil servants and entrepreneurs to engage in crooked deals with their counterparts in the more developed economies.

If this internal and international process of static class interdependencies and corruption is replicated across enough of the world, then maybe missing screws identified in the Valley of Means are somehow the core element of a strategy that allows us to make a dysfunctional system functional. Maybe this is true; maybe the idea is madness. Too little is known about the relationship between Mad Dog and Puppy to resolve the world's problem within the covers of this book. I shall only go so far as to suggest that greed and dynamic stasis are core phenomena which may have far-reaching implications for development above the community level.

However, in this book, I shall confine our discussion to an examination of local-level behaviours and of local-level development work. International tariffs and trade agreements, the investment and business behaviours of international business and industry certainly matter to development at the national level, as does globalization. Like the history of enslavement, the Middle Passage, the ensuing 100 years of debt peonage, modernization, the rise of labour unions and of the women's movement, Belize's participation in international trade in the face of growing globalization is a phenomenon that forms part of the context of pressures and opportunities within which the people of Belize must interact. These are all issues that will be addressed in the book because they affect the strategies that people like Mad Dog and Puppy currently employ. However, they will be discussed only as a formative context or framework for the behavioural analysis to be undertaken, and for the reconsideration of effective development strategies at the community level.

In many ways, the formative context for Belize is analogous to the contexts of inequitable socio-economic and political economic inter-relationships in all the locations where community developers are at work. I shall mention the reasons for my making this suggestion later in the book. This is because my hope is that the procedures used in the book to figure out more effective development approaches for Belize will enable others to test whether analogous procedures might not be just as effective in other countries where dynamic stasis occurs.

I shall speak of an "economic frame of reference" at the local level. By this, I refer to more than simply rich and poor fishermen and the cost of a beer. I include the cost or benefit of any aspect of culture-shaping behaviours in the Valley of Means among both the rich and the poor.[15] The task of understanding cost and benefit behaviours is one more naturally suited to Economic Anthropology than to Political Economics. The latter system helps explain the impact of current and historical forces upon people—that is, of everything that must be considered in the contextual framework within which Belizeans remember, learn and choose the way they interact with each other and with their natural environment. However, Economic Anthropology enables us to reveal these decision-makers as intelligent actors and not just victims of circumstance. A study of behaviours helps us figure out how decision-makers shape their environment and how they are affected by it. By watching the response of individuals to their environment and to each other, I believe we may learn much about the logic and purpose of people's strategies—those who have advantages and deal unkindly, and those who have few and attempt to make the best of their lot. In parts of the Caribbean you'll hear poor people say, "Make do with what you have, or do without" and I think they mean what I mean.

The knowledge we draw from the following chapters is intended to position us, as community developers, to interact more creatively, more purposefully and to greater effect. In the latter part of the book we will apply what we have learned to creating sharpened community development interventions. I even go as far as suggesting that the very oppressors of the oppressed—the landowners, industrialists, bureaucrats and politicians—can become integrated into the development process and become allies.

Social history and change are frequently viewed from the perspective of the historical forces that shape and constrain the choices of humankind, a perspective that I believe has handicapped international developers. An inherited conceptual framework limits our perspective to our understanding of injustice and poverty and consequently has restricted our development options. By adding a reversal of this perspective; that is to say, by also looking at the impact of social interactions on culture, society, economy, politics and the environment, I think we liberate ourselves and our work from a number of serious constraints that I discuss later in the book.

I speak here as though only a single approach to development has been taken. Very broadly stated, I would say there are at least two approaches, with great variations within each and with some overlap across the two. And there are probably undertakings that do not fit comfortably within either of the two categories I have in mind. The two approaches are apparently as antithetical in their ideas and methods as bank guards and bank robbers. The first general category can be called the establishmentarian approach.[16] The proponents of this approach recommend improving what exists and they identify institutional deficiencies and faulty or destructive practices in public, private and civil institutions in the developing countries.[17] Establishmentarian developers seek increased transparency, accountability and efficiency, and they try to reduce practices that destroy a range of fragile systems, both human and ecological. They work through those institutional representatives already established in positions of authority, believing that improved structures and procedures in target countries will benefit all their inhabitants. Some, but not all, of their methods are didactic by nature because there is an urgent need to identify destructive practices, and to teach better ones.

Developers associated with the establishmentarian approach would likely predominate within governmental community development agencies both in the post-industrial and in lesser-developed and low-income nations. One might also expect to find them in the international UN-related agencies and banks or attached to larger, more conservative non-governmental organizations (NGOs) in richer and poorer countries. Given their primary focus on getting systems to work correctly, and their tendency to be involved with larger, more conservative institutions, establishmentarian developers work at least as often with national and regional level community development projects as with local level ones.

In contrast to the first approach, the other can be called anti-establishmentarian.[18] Its proponents reject the appropriateness of those institutions and systems that do exist—they even reject the whole mode of production, together with its social relations and means of production. Anti-establishmentarian developers are those who oppose an entire international system of injustice and exploitation. They look to the systemic causes of suffering and seek to establish egalitarianism across class. Anti-establishmentarian developers gravitate towards the grassroots. They emphasize participatory methods to distance themselves from the authoritarians who enforce compliance with the status quo and they are vociferous about respecting and deferring to people with the lowest prestige. Employees and volunteers attached to many—but not all—smaller NGOs in rich and poor nations promote an anti-establishmentarian agenda.

At the grassroots level, anti-establishmentarian developers engage the perceived victims of injustice in a consciousness-raising dialogue about social injustice that originates in the post-industrialized nations and that creates the injustices in their own environment. They offer community development education to citizens of such environments to promote awareness of the destructive practices. They also dialogue with them about the type of corrective action that is needed. Anti-establishment proponents often promote and engage in boycotts, sit-ins, protests and demonstrations.

The establishment/anti-establishment dichotomy is not entirely discreet, either. Within developing countries, proponents of either approach may offer farming, small-scale manufacturing or productive credit extension services and both may adopt some participatory methods. Both may teach local populations community health, micro-lending or village-based and small-scale production. Still, the fundamental difference between repairing what exists and replacing it is clear enough, I think, to make the two categories useful. To take an example: infant mortality in Bangladesh is undeniably high when compared to that of Norway. In moralistic terms we can confidently observe that high infant mortality is a bad thing. A useful response to this deplorable state of affairs may be attempted from an establishmentarian as well as from an anti-establishmentarian perspective. Even though developers from either perspective seldom agree with one another, I think they will agree that their development work is intended to reduce the level of a bad thing (infant mortality) in Bangladesh.

The establishmentarian developers would see that infant mortality owes its prevalence to the inefficiency of health service institutions and to the ignorance of mothers regarding low-cost, life-saving measures. For them, the logical course of action[5] would be to bring the institutions to a greater level of efficiency at national, regional and/or local level. They might also attempt to achieve a higher level of transparency in the health delivery institution(s), supposing that corruption is part of the defined problem.

The anti-establishmentarian developers—whose data suggest a causal connection between dying babies, inefficient health services and the ignorance of mothers—will also feel a responsibility for finding effective ways to get mothers to change their practices. However, they will also be concerned about the mothers' deference in the presence of imperious bureaucrats, and will want to change that injustice. They may well be concerned with the way international capitalism ultimately reduces the entire class of women to poverty and helplessness and keeps them there. Because of this concern, mothers need to challenge the health delivery system at a local level at least. If the anti-establishmentarian developers are able to organize it, mothers from many localities will be encouraged to unite to challenge the inept health system regionally and even nationally. Ideally, the whole miserable system of international capitalism should be destroyed and replaced with something more concerned about ending the injustices affecting people's human rights.

For adherents to both perspectives, what is happening locally is wrong and must be changed. In quite distinct ways, both sides attempt to supply change, but unfortunately their respective approaches unintentionally put developers in awkward opposition to what health organization personnel and mothers of dying children are doing. This happens because what mothers and health workers do hurts babies, whether through malice, ignorance or neglect. To be fair, both establishmentarian and anti-establishmentarian developers generally make Herculean efforts to do something useful about the situation. At least one set of developers sees a need to raise the consciousness of the mothers, and both establishment and anti-establishment developers want to get present behaviours to change. What local people are presently doing contrasts sharply with what both types of developers think they ought to be doing, based on what they know harms and helps children. From this perspective, it would be fair to say that both types of developers are opponents of what they find target populations and suppliers of alternatives are doing. Is it therefore stating the situation too strongly to say that developers become the antagonists of the local population—both humble and powerful?

Let's conceptualize the situation: normally, a division is drawn to cut verti-

Figure 1.1
Approaches to Development

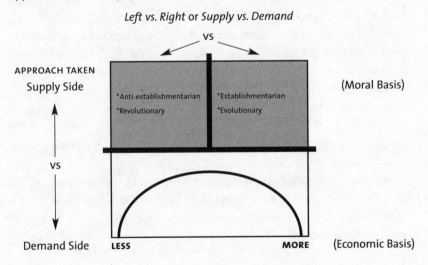

cally between an establishmentarian frame of reference on the political right, and an anti-establishmentarian one on the left (see Figure 1.1). This distinction serves to accentuate a difference between an evolutionary and a revolutionary approach. But making such a division ignores a supply-led approach to development that is actually common to both perspectives. As suggested, the supply-side approach (whether establishmentarian or anti-establishmentarian) places developers in opposition to the populations they target for change by offering the mentality, the values, the objectives and/or the methods that they think the target population ought to adopt. This is a great obstacle for community developers, who are clearly put at a disadvantage by this situation. For one thing, establishmentarian and anti-establishmentarian development workers are made out to be competitors. For another, developers are pushed into the confines of a moral perspective—a moral frame of reference if you will. Offended by the evil consequences of inequitable social relations of production (like those between the fishing Captains and Mates), developers from the left and from the right are immediately drawn to the business of supplying corrective measures. In the midst of the "busy-ness" of picking mates and catching and selling fish, this moral fixation with injustice blinds all of us to the other phenomenon at work: the economic (i.e. cost and benefit) interactions among rich and poor—which I was first able to understand by observing fishermen like Mad Dog and Puppy, notwithstanding my own cultural biases.

These economic interactions include issues of credit and debt. But they also include personal, familial and collegial interactions (e.g. gender-based, tribal, religious, party-based, ethnicity-based, skin colour based and age-based) and the interactions relate to access to money, land, water and even love (or to lovers at least); indeed to any objective a person could value. Furthermore, the many bases for social interaction, including one's political affiliation, religion, and so forth, may under the right circumstances serve as the grounds for unity, notwithstanding other divisive differences such as status, class, gender. So sometimes, Mad Dog and Puppy may have reason to unite. If they can get the government to agree to a raise in fish prices, for example, both of them stand to gain.

In contrast to supply-led development (offering solutions based on the developers' ideas of what target populations ought to be doing), I will use this book to explore a demand-led development approach (having developers respond to the agendas of the target population). The demand-led approach does not require that developers have to oppose what is valued locally, as the supply-led approach does. Instead of making a vertical division based on the political differences of the establishmentarian and anti-establishmentarian development approaches, I wish to draw a horizontal division in this book to distinguish between development perspectives that are either moralistic (see the top half of the Figure 1.1) or economic (see the bottom half of Figure 1.1). Furthermore, I will be recommending the advantages inherent in an economic approach.

Rather than our having to focus primarily on the social injustices of the current mode of production, I think the economic frame of reference will allow us to pay greater attention to local survival behaviours and objectives. These are issues we need to understand better to achieve participatory planned change at the community level more effectively. By making this shift in focus, however, I am most emphatically not recommending that we accept injustices like high infant mortality in Bangladesh, or sweat shop conditions in Malaysia, to take another example. Malaysian workers are not content without bathroom breaks; Bangladeshi women are not unconcerned with the death of so many of their babies. We can see that these injustices are the by-product of inequitable interdependencies of rich and poor and we can see how people suffer as a result. Even if the poor were content with their lot, the shocking gaps between rich and poor in the areas of health, longevity, maternal and infant mortality and so forth would demonstrate unacceptable injustice and cry out for correction. And cumulatively, poverty is demonstrably harmful at the national level and a phenomenon that threatens the survival of us all.

The question that concerns me—and the one which I think should concern us all—is not whether we should be good moralists and fight for social justice. We should. The question I ask in this book is whether, through moral methods, we as community developers are using the very best means to do so. The Nobel laureate, Amartya Sen, uses national economic indicators to remind us that development is a broader concept than national economic growth.[19] I like the way he takes us back to the original definition of economics as a technical means to human ends and the way in which he criticizes development economics for having made a developmental holy grail of economic growth. I also admire the way he demonstrates that economic growth is seldom achieved unless citizens of poor nations gain political freedoms such as increasing social facilities, transparency guarantees, or protective security. By tying these gains to economic growth, he demonstrates that Freedom at last is Development. Sen demonstrably links moral values to development; what I undertake below is an examination of how we might do better at making it happen.

There has been something of a knee-jerk reaction, I believe, to the issue of human rights in development. The United Nations adopted the Universal Declaration of Human Rights in 1948.[20] Forty-nine years later, in his 1997 Reform Proposal, the Secretary General of the UN called for all UN agencies to mainstream Human Rights in all their activities.[21] The NGOs immediately saw legitimization of something they had understood for years, but in response to this call from the UN, a moralizing strategy for developers has been created that is based on a moral frame of reference that is, in turn, based upon structural analyses of social change and history. The moralizing strategy has guided the type of action we are to undertake. Claudio Schuftan's position for the NGO community represents this approach:

> 61. **The role of civil society groups is to, among other, act as pressure groups.** Therefore, to guarantee gains, civil society will have to continue its strong socio-political mobilization effort in a bid to hold national and international institutions with obligations in the realization of Human Rights accountable. (8)
>
> 62. Civil society will thus have to oppose development activities that are ill conceived and even counterproductive in Human Rights terms. **Ergo, development agencies will need to fix their sights more on the Human Rights dimension of their work and civil society will have to create and sustain the pressure for this to happen.** (31)
>
> 63. The NGO community can indeed play a major role in this. Among other, they will have to: keep asking the right questions that seek information on violations/fulfillment of Human Rights, submit written statements (plus photo and video documentation when appropriate) to authorities and **to watchdog groups on their assessments and findings, follow up on corrective measures taken (or not taken), detect bad faith in the implementation of Human Rights obligations, and publicly denounce this fact.**[22] (emphasis added)

Moral indignation is frequently the departure point of many efforts to make development happen. Fifty years after development became a conscious undertaking, we can find any number of books and articles on international development that begin with observations about our alarming rate of project failures and provide the dismal statistic to substantiate this claim.[22] Brinkerhoff and Goldsmith, for example, report the depressing results as follows:

> The enormity of the sustainability problem is suggested by two recent stud-
> ies. One, done by the World Bank, evaluated some 550 projects. Nearly half
> had sustainability difficulties; 15% were rated unlikely to be sustained; 9%
> marginally sustainable, and 24% uncertain. Only 52% appeared to have suc-
> cessfully achieved sustainability (World Bank, 1990, p. 32). The United States
> Agency for International Development (USAID) conducted a separate study of
> this issue (Kean et al. 1998). It used a different methodology, so the results
> cannot be compared precisely to the World Bank's examination. But the con-
> clusions were even more damning. Two hundred and twelve project
> evaluations were reviewed. Twenty-six percent of the projects earned strongly
> negative ratings, 56% got marginal marks, and a mere 11% of the projects were
> considered to have strong prospects for being sustained after the termination
> of US assistance. [24]

Many of those writers who report our failures, like Brinkerhoff and
Goldsmith, think we ought to be doing much more of what has already been
done. They offer extremely sensible experience-based advice for achieving sustainability in development-oriented institutions in the Third World, such as:
secure internal commitment, pick feasible objectives, choose the right moment
for strategy formulation, build alliances, differentiate between perceived and
actual payoffs, offer long-term overseas training, and set extended planning
horizons. [25]

I too am concerned about the paucity of our achievements. But unlike many
who recommend repeating or intensifying our actions, I suggest a different
approach because I think that something goes missing when we repeat or
intensify our efforts. Given the presence of inequitable interdependencies and
resultant social stasis, we need advice on how to carry out the actions they recommend when the political will to undertake them is so evidently missing and
when low levels of trust and high levels of individualism make these actions
nearly impossible to apply.

We saw these difficult conditions when considering the plight of Puppy
and other Mates within his economic class. We understand that Puppy will pay
a heavy price if he tries to organize a union within those who share his class
interests, since the Mates who share this interest are the very ones trying to take
his place in Mad Dog's dugout. Yet many scholars seem to ignore this reality.

In the face of all the pragmatic behaviours swirling below us in the Valley
of Means, we redeploy moral development strategies. The pragmatic behav-

iours are evidently unseen transactions; or if they are seen, are undervalued. The evil brilliance of immorality must simply blind us.

Those of us who wish to be good and to see the world to become better have been—without necessarily realizing it—responding to a nearly irresistible urge to leap righteously from disapproval to the supply of interventions. Consequently, many or most local opportunistic behaviours in the Valley of Means (e.g. those of Mad Dog and those of Puppy) are discovered to run counter to our well-meant initiatives. Mad Dog and the other Captains, for example, should pay Puppy and the Mates more. Puppy should unite with the other Mates against the meanness of the Captains.

Even if the community development project measures undertaken by some developers are intensely participatory, they will necessarily find themselves assuming an adversarial posture vis-à-vis their community development targets. Until the oppressed are assisted to stand up and fight oppression and until those doing well at the expense of the majority fall to the will of the oppressed, participatory developers—and indeed all other developers, too—must never desist from getting other people to do what they should. They must never condone what they are doing instead. Participatory developers evidently know enough about social justice and class exploitation to see what is wrong and needs to be corrected. Consciousness-raising is necessary so that those enduring "false consciousness" may see what the developers see. The participatory processes are not used to determine what is to change nor to determine what is to be achieved. For such community developers, participatory methods are merely about letting oppressed sisters and brothers choose the weapons of conflict.

The macro-economist, Robert Klitgaard, understands the futility of using a moralistic approach in development. In suggesting his original remedies for corruption in the public sector, Klitgaard makes the following observation:

> But notice that none of these [i.e. Klitgaard's remedies] immediately refers to what most of us think of first when corruption is mentioned—that is, new laws, more controls, a change in mentality, or an ethical revolution. Laws and control prove insufficient when systems do not exist in which to implement them. Moral awakenings do occur, but seldom by the design of our public leaders. If we cannot engineer incorruptible officials and citizens, we can nonetheless foster competition, change incentives and enhance accountability—in short fix the systems that breed corruption.[26] (parentheses added)

I have characterized the interactions between rich and poor in Belize, the

Caribbean, and even the Third World chasms in rather opportunistic terms that frequently apply to many—though not all—people and not in all circumstances. Later, I review the formative history and cite a number of examples drawn from Belize to reveal the logic of such behaviours and to show why the Belizean strategy is so likely to reappear elsewhere in the Caribbean—indeed wherever pronounced socio-economic inequalities exist. If I'm correct about the unsuitability of our approach to development in the face of the opportunistic behaviours we encounter, I think we can say that we are witnessing a juxtaposition of Third World of pragmatic adaptations (i.e. theirs) with Community Developers' world of idealistic interventions (i.e. ours).[27]

An experiment reported in 1999 distinguished between individuals who considered themselves more competitive and those who considered themselves more prone to sacrifice for others. Both types had the opportunity to earn profit by investing either with their group or individually. Investments occurred when the group was acting alone, but also when the group was investing against a competing faction. Results were as follows:

> The competitors used individualistic strategies against other members of their group. But when the group was competing against another faction, the competitors switched strategies, attempting to profit by investing through their group.
>
> In contrast the sacrificers tended to forego maximum personal gain for the sake of seeing everybody in the group do better.[28]

The results suggest that cultural values as well as changing opportunities shape our strategies, and the data presented in chapter 3 suggest that conditions of unequal distribution of resources and imposed scarcity favour the development of high levels of individualism and the pursuit of immediate gratification. Under certain conditions, Third World people are evidently more akin to the individualists in the experiment and developers are more like the sacrificers. We may unwittingly assume that ours is the appropriate way and proceed with our development work in quite ineffective ways. To be more successful as community developers we may need to adjust our approach in ways that are better suited the predispositions of those we target.

If the idealistic strategies are part of our own baggage, our development failures result from our attempts to project our own valuations upon others. We do admire self-sacrifice and some delay of gratification for the sake of equity and social betterment. We do accept lower wages for ourselves and we are remarkably dogged about pushing for results. So in consequence, do we also expect that the values of our development targets ought to be in accord with ours—or at least that their behaviours ought to change for what we consider to be the better? At some level, do we disapprove of the egoism and impatience for gratification exhibited by people like Puppy whenever they ignore their family, beat their wives or spend what little they earn on the lottery and on drinks carelessly shared with friends? But do we know whether the lottery is the poor person's stock market or whether the drinks cement affective links that can be used later when people like Mad Dog take another Mate and go off fishing? If these factors matter, how should they affect the way community development interventions are designed and implemented?

Fifty years of unassessed reactions to knee-jerk morality, to a loosing of development missions upon the wrong targets or in the wrong manner and, consequently, to a falling short of the betterment we seek, should be enough to encourage us to take a fresh look at the problem. To do so, I think, we may have to temper our nobler urges. But there ought to be enough development disappointments now to convince us that neither fixing what exists nor smashing it has been sufficiently effective. The third option offered below may work better.

I use an economic frame of reference in this book to consider this alternative perspective on community development and to work out what I call pragmatic interventions for community development. The categories of moral and economic frames of reference are not of my own invention and have been in use since the 1960s among economic anthropologists, but I am applying them to these reflections on community development as a way of suggesting a means of proceeding that may bring us greater satisfaction and at the same time offer the developing world greater justice and comfort.

Economics is often understood in narrow terms as a sphere of activity relating to capitalism, business, industry, taxation, international trade and so forth. Because many economic behaviours of this sort bring much misery to the poor, the term itself has many negative connotations for some developers. That is unfortunate, because the same word *economic*, when used in the phrase an economic frame of reference and when contrasted with a moral frame of reference is intended to convey the broader sense of the term economic. Indeed, in the manner of Amartya Sen, I intend it to refer to economics in its broadest sense. I want the word *economic* to call to mind the whole realm of costs and benefits, and the realm of the considerations of producers and consumers of any conceivable good or service (e.g. food, a healthier environment, quicker arrival of the police in the slums and ghettos)—about what is being demanded, and what, therefore, is to be supplied. Below, the sometimes narrow concepts are going to be applied to issues of culture, justice and responsibility in addition to economics. All manner of considerations are constantly shaping the choices being made by rich and poor alike. The realm of options and choices has practical potential for developers. Therefore, I am hoping that readers will be willing to look past the destructive associations of the word and concepts related to it.

I have observed the role of values in human decision-making and think it important to dwell a bit upon this point. The human and natural environments within which any of us live do not completely motivate our actions because actions are also shaped by our ideals, that is, by internal, historical factors and by the opinions they have formed within us. We are not Pavlov's dogs. If you present meat powder, we, like they, may involuntarily salivate. But unlike his dogs, we may choose to remain vegetarian, or to defy Pavlov because he keeps us caged, or because we simply reject manipulation. Decision-making really means calling upon all our human gifts, including our valuations. People die for causes, whether true love or liberty, and that includes a few of the opportunists in the Valley—though many developers may wish more of them shared our idealism. A decision-maker, therefore, is not a person whose choices are limited to achieving the greatest success, earning the most money, or winning over the most attractive lover. Decision-making may include issues of reputation, honour, the survival of one's people, or any combination of the above.

Wishing to see our community development targets become more responsible means wanting them to do what is best for others or for the environment rather than being governed by greed. However, R. Butler makes a sobering point when discussing environmental protection and peasant behaviours. He argues that our idealistic expectations are improbable if they favour social ideals over survival needs:

> This park approach [restricting access] can be short-sighted because people—peasants, not indigenous peoples—living around the forests are often among the world's poorest and depend on unsustainable harvesting from the forest. Designating an area as a park does not mean the people in the area will have their immediate needs satisfied.... **Local inhabitants depend on the rainforest for their survival and until other means become available, will continue to use the forest for immediate gratification in a non-renewable fashion.**[29] (emphasis added)

Local counterparts, whether from the villages and barrios or from government offices, are sometimes said to be hesitant to volunteer and remain active, or to change systems since doing so may incur the wrath of a politician or a key individual in government. In fact, one of the persistent criticisms one can hear about people from developing nations is that too many of them are so cautious as to be unoriginal, too tied to traditions, routines and regulations. There are complaints about their lack of individuality and lack of commitment to a goal or a vision. Or the opposite explanation—that the individualism of the poor prompts them to seek immediate gratification—may get developers to the same point.[30]

Sometimes developers sound as though they want target populations to exhibit more selfless energy, leadership and responsibility—perhaps more than they expect from the rest of us. Certainly, this is the opinion of the Bangladeshi adult educators quoted below:

> Today, especially in Bengal, things are going terribly wrong. Many people believe it is because of the moribund bureaucracy—government, institutional, private...whatever—that is responsible for this unacceptable state of affairs.[31]

The implication above is that such developers need target groups, political leaders and the wealthy to be idealistic. For development efforts to succeed they must focus on those ends the developers consider important. Then target people will begin to strive towards the changes considered critical by the developers. David Korten is so bold as to suggest that, "The foremost development priority of the 1990's is to transform the ways in which people perceive their world, use its resources, and relate to one another as individuals and nations."[32] Morality's handmaiden is evidently guilt, which is used to motivate action. Consumerism, which elevates our wants, must then be demonized so that the importance of moral action can be given greater value. As Korten sees it, we must literally change the minds of adults even though Butler suggests good reasons why the chances of broad success with such an approach are slim.

The following quotation from religious-based developers is a clear example of the moral frame of reference in use. Not too surprisingly, it has a belt-tightening, almost sermonizing, tone to it. It is certain about what other people ought to do. The moral righteousness is evident. It is not clear that the targets of community development are specifically addressed. They are not specifically excluded, however:

> Although not commonly discussed in relation to the challenges of environ- ment and community development, there are current in the world certain

trends—including the widespread lack of moral discipline, the glorification of greed and material accumulation, the increasing breakdown of family and community, the rise of lawlessness and disorder, the ascendancy of racism and bigotry, and the priority given to national interests over the welfare of humanity—all of which destroy confidence and trust, the foundations of collaboration.

The reversal of these destructive trends is essential to the establishment of unity and cooperation.[33]

There is little tolerance here for the "foolish ways" of the world—ways that have pragmatic value to Mad Dog and Puppy and to others who employ them. If people, both in the Valley and above it, emphasize a pragmatic focus on the present and on themselves over an idealistic vision of the future and the general weal, we have, I think, to relate to that orientation in some creative manner. If they are useful to survivors and opportunists, these foolish ways won't go away even if they are immoral, corrupt and able to generate class stasis and to retard development.

I therefore propose that we make use of greed rather than ignore or fight it. Such an approach does force our faces into something of a paradox: the world must at last change to improve. If villagers or office workers in the Valley resist change, wouldn't serious-minded developers not have to help them? Shouldn't developers therefore identify the improvements desired and invent tactics to move target populations off dead centre? This is what we've been at that for a half-century and it barely appears to work. This paradox between needing to see change effected and rejecting supply-led community development must be resolved. To win at basketball for example, you have to understand the other team's strategy. Once you see how they gain an edge, you have to take advantage of their game to win your own. But in this book I am suggesting that community development from an economic frame of reference must be different. To win at community development both we and our "opposition" need to be playing on the same side—engaging in community development work without having to take an adversarial position, either towards the targets or even towards those who currently prosper at their expense.

I think we have been too quick to dismiss the legitimacy of local attitudes, opinions and behaviours. You'll sometimes hear that what members of the target population do want for themselves (e.g. a pair of Nike shoes; a bigger boom box) are irrelevancies—trivial pieces of false consciousness engendered by capitalism and worthy of scorn. Better, we are confidently assured, to help such people understand that their wants are contrary to their class interests; in other words, that they ought to do less well for themselves in order to do greater good for others. Our attention is being called back, I assume, to the effects of capitalism and to our need to destroy it.

In contrast, I suggest that deprecating the lust of target people in favour of getting them to reject capitalism is counter-productive. Lust after all, is a potent force; it is a mechanism that already exists and already motivates individuals to change their present condition. I suggest it has genuine community development potential and explore that possibility in this book.

So what if selfish lust were not automatically worthy of scorn? What if, in terms of community development tactics, Nikes and boom boxes were the ideal aspiration for community development targets, and for developers, the most effective and quickest pole to vault populations onto a more egalitarian platform if the conditions were right? What if the pragmatic alliances already existing across classes were of more utility than the dysfunctional ones within them? And what if class unification were an idealistic pipe dream of less benefit to community development than to community developers?

As far back as 1966, John Dewey argued that the generalized ends keep changing as we deal with the means at hand and that nothing is fixed.[34] Moralizing is static because it has set notions about good and evil. In contrast to static moralizing, Dewey's remark is profoundly dialectical. Dewey implies that there's no necessary advantage in making Nike-lust and boom box-envy into absolute evils and refusing to deal with them on that account. Nor is there particular advantage to swearing undying opposition toward capitalists. Individualists in the Valley of Means already appear to know quite a bit about this. Dewey's remark tells us that our valuations generally depend on the next best move. Perhaps this fact is a good thing—or a useful thing at least.

Of course we don't want to be working towards the death of Bangladeshi children nor towards the continued denial of bathroom breaks to Malaysian sweatshop workers. Morality has something to do with community development work and we know this. Dewey is reminding us that the ends we and our community development targets think we're after constantly shift because our current situation is fluid. He also reminds us that we developers can do better if we pay attention to the fluidity of the situation. People may have good reasons for engaging in behaviours which moralizing developers may find distasteful. Better, perhaps, to assume that development targets know what they're about and attempt to comprehend before offering "better" methods or "raising the consciousness" of others. Otherwise, we ignore the missing screws.

Perhaps we should operate with a more fluid understanding of allies and opponents and objectives so that we can factor those missing screws into a more iterative development calculus. In other words, we may need to think in terms of better and worse instead of good and evil and to focus less upon the behaviours we dislike and more upon the contexts within which such behaviours make sense and upon those that call for behavioural shifts. In dysfunctional situations, moral behaviour may be suicide. Developers have been asking target populations to discard the baby with the bath water. In this instance, I think that the bath water is the set of damaging social consequences that cause suffering in the developing world and the baby is an individual's lust to do better. Greedy personal impulses are healthy, but under certain circumstances they may have negative socio-economic effects. It is therefore those "certain conditions" that must become the focus of our interest.

From the perspective of contexts and adaptations we can see that underdevelopment is not simply a phenomenon imposed on nations like Belize from the outside even if colonialism and international capitalism helped engender and perpetuate it. An injustice like slavery once worked upon a population establishes self-replicating, destructive and self-preserving social dynamics. Mad Dog and Puppy showed us an example of such dynamic stasis in their Valley of Means. It was full of busy-ness and full of barriers to improvement.[35]

A system of economic distortions, political favours, power dependencies, opportunistic alliances and competitive factions, as well as theft and embezzlement operates in the Valley of Means. Neither Mad Dog, nor Puppy, nor anybody in that Valley may love it and it clearly benefits very few. The system primarily functions to damage everybody in the Valley. The poor can't get ahead because of it and therefore hate it. Those who are powerful can take advantage of others but can also be skewered by their resentment just as the window installers very nearly skewered my wife and me during Hurricane Keith. The very people who suffer from it sustain it. To survive, it is necessary for individuals to work the system in which they live, yet in contexts of class and economic difference the very act of doing so retards improvements. Contractors, importers, politicians, government bureaucrats and window installers are locked into complex networks of favours and obligations that result in the late delivery of shoddy products and services, in double-dealing and in embezzlement. Multiplied across a whole economy, this cycle yields restricted national productivity, inferior products and insufficient tax revenue to deliver effective health and education or useful infrastructure. This is a poor calculus for community development and hardly better for national development. The inter-linkage of distortion reaches as low as the inefficient worker and as high as the corrupt politician, the importer and related foreign industries. It's a single smothering cloth woven of a multitude of opportunistic strands.

Yet all the while workers, entrepreneurs, bureaucrats, politicians and foreign industrialists have been responding to detectable sets of opportunities and all have been avoiding threats to their personal or professional survival. Most do not know how to make the opportunity context serve them better because experimentation carries high risk. Furthermore, there has been very little research by the community developers on how to make the contexts serve the majority better.

The work of this book is to find and investigate some spontaneous examples of positive, inter-dependent, demand-led development relationships—conditions where we can see greedy behaviours producing positive socio-economic consequences. It is also to figure out how we and the targets of community development might deliberately negotiate our way into such relationships without marketing morality to the poor and their oppressors.

The usual definition of demand-led development supposes both an ability and a willingness for those making demands to pay for what they want.[36] This will require that we figure out how development by demand might still be relevant to populations that apparently possess neither the desire nor the resources to pay for what might be offered.

Belize is used here as a case study and a real set of survival behaviours is analyzed without betraying the confidences of the persons involved. In the real world, the cobweb of survival transactions is admittedly complex—and that includes Belize. There are jungles in Belize, offshore cays, coastal towns built out of the boggy wetlands, inland villages and hills in the sub-tropical rainforest. There are Spanish/Indian Mestizos in the north and west, Mayas in the west and south, black/British Creoles in Belize City who were subjected to slavery and figured out how to endure, and Garifuna (St. Vincent Arawak/Carib people mixed with escaped blacks) who never had to endure slavery, in fishing villages on the southern coast. There is a smattering of East Indians in Belize City on the coast, and a few Taiwanese everywhere. There are free trade merchants, and drug dealers, shrimp aquaculturalists, chicken pluckers, unemployed hip-hop youth, computer repairmen, ministers, psychiatrists (two, I think), drainage ditch cleaners, social workers, and a number of crooked politicians and sunburned tourists.

But in the whole country, there aren't more than a quarter million citizens and residents, and only a hundred thousand tourists who mostly arrive on cruise ships and stay for a day. If ever there was a place both complex and intimate, a place where, like my wife, you could ask, "Why would somebody do a thing like that?" and hope to get anything approaching a sensible answer, Belize would be that place. Some of the behavioural complexities in this humid Valley can be defined and tentatively mapped, perhaps. A few of the social and economic webs can be untangled to reveal the rewards accruing to different strategies in use and the associated costs that are paid.

Understanding the survival game in Belize might allow us to design appropriate non-adversarial development interventions for one location that make use of the games, and might teach us how to go about dealing with the unique challenges elsewhere. If a procedure can be worked out for Belize, and if there are important similarities to be found in the rest of the Caribbean and in other nations marked by inequitable relationships, then there is hope that analogous development strategies can be worked out elsewhere. We must, I think, find these missing screws and use them effectively. After all, screws are meant to close gaps.

In the middle of Hurricane Keith I managed to wedge two screwdrivers into the wall and the menacing window held for the duration of the torment. For some time afterward, I had wanted to get even with the workmen. But I think I've come up with something better than revenge. I've decided to write a book.

Decision-Making and Responsibility

Ultimately, man [sic] should not ask what the meaning of his life is, but rather he must recognize that it is he who is asked. In a word, each man is questioned by life; and he can only answer to life by answering for his own life; to life he can only respond by being responsible.[1]

Irresponsible Choices And Stasis

WRITING FROM A NAZI death camp, the existential psychotherapist Viktor Frankl observed that responsible acts and the devastation worked by irresponsibility are central to our being. People need a reason to live. Without one, they die spiritually. Here is his description of the existential vacuum that accompanies irresponsibility:

> No instinct tells him what he has to do, and no tradition tells him what he ought to do; sometimes he does not even know what he wishes to do. Instead, he either wishes to do what other people do (conformism) or he does what other people wish him to do (totalitarianism).... [He is] doomed to vacillate eternally between the two extremes of distress and boredom.... Moreover,

there are various masks and guises under which the existential vacuum appears. Sometimes the frustrated will to meaning is vicariously compensated for by a will to power, including...the will to money.... Existential frustration often eventuates in sexual compensation...[and] the sexual libido becomes rampant.[2]

Frankl was therapist to Viennese clients following World War II. I am in a poor position to suggest what frustrated their will to meaning. But I think that in the post-colonial world, much of the source of that frustration is patronage, which is a system built upon extracting and extending favours in a context of inequity. Patronage, in other words, has to do with compulsion and with limitations on freedom and I believe that irresponsible behaviour has a great deal to do with the frustrations associated with such limitations.

Another word for patronage is "clientelism" and this is the term I prefer to use here. The former term focuses on those who dole out privileges and favours. The latter pays attention to the clients who depend on the patrons. I use the latter term because the clients of post-colonial nations are the "target population" of interest to community developers. Furthermore, I think that the frustrated behaviour of target populations (i.e. the lust for power and money, or the sexual obsessions) in turn frustrates the efforts of the developers.

J.D. Martz defines clientelism as follows: "Clientelism involves sets of patrons and clients cooperating with one another to retain maximum benefit for themselves from all assets which any of them handle by personally exchanging these assets among themselves."[3] The patrons are those who control the resources and sometimes make use of gatekeepers to control the flow of clients making demands. The clients are those without resources of their own. They must reach the patrons to survive. We have seen that the dugout Captain, Mad Dog, was a patron to his client, Puppy. The other fishermen's Mates were sometimes competitive clients who helped keep wages low and helped keep people like Puppy deferential towards the Captains. However, sometimes Captains were competitive with each other and sometimes everybody—both the Captains and the Mates—would co-operate. For our purposes, this element of dynamic and inequitable exchange under conditions of coercion (by force or because of need) should therefore be added to the Martz definition of clientelism. Among economists, inequitable and coerced exchanges are known as "rent extraction."

In *Money for Nothing: Rent Extraction and Political Extortion*, Fred McChesney considers the ability of politicians to demand favours as well as to supply them.[4]

D. Schansberg summarizes the political rent creation and rent extraction behaviours discussed by McChesney:

> Rent creation is an attempt to gain political favor, whereas rent extraction is an attempt to avoid political disfavor.... If demand is relatively inelastic, rent creation will occur; if supply is relatively inelastic, rent extraction. The decisive question is, Which group does the politician have more completely over the barrel? [5]

Brusco, Nazareno and Stokes offer another definition of clientelism that limits patronage to the political arena:

> We define clientelism as the exchange between politicians and voters of material private goods for votes. Under clientelism, electoral support is the sole criterion on which politicians give goods to voters. This exclusively electoral criterion distinguishes exchanges from programmatic exchanges, in which the beneficiaries are defined by more universalistic or generic categories. [6]

This second definition excludes any inequitable exchange that does not involve votes for politicians. For several reasons, the "material goods for votes only" definition is less appropriate for this study. For one thing, the "votes only" definition does not cover cases like those of Mad Dog and Puppy who are engaged in inequitable exchanges outside the political arena. For another, the definition doesn't cover cases where politicians are required to grant favours to receive political financing from interest groups or rich entrepreneurs, or vice versa. For example, if such an entrepreneur wished to assemble a strip of land along the waterfront where the mangroves are protected by law, he or she would have to offer enough of a material or financial payment to make the appropriate politicians and civil servants agree to look the other way while the landfill comes in and the fencing is erected. Such action can distort general infrastructural development planning. Exceptions are made because special favours are granted. The action can also have negative impacts on the natural environment.

These four sorts of distortions (services for votes, political favours for cash, material goods for political favours, and inequitable and extra-political exchanges) may each relate to that sort of clientelism that affects development in low-income countries. We want to examine such rent-extractive exchanges within clientelism. In such conditions, socio-economic dependencies can keep blocs of voters silent in the face of injustice when protest would motivate change. Possession of material resources can buy special favours either within or beyond the social arena because Smith's hidden hand cannot correct economic skewing. Material goods can purchase favours, as a result of which both skewing of income and the natural environment may be worsened and the opportunities for responsible behaviour become diminished.

In a different study, Paul Yoo Hyung-Gon contrasts the case of South Korea (what he calls "good" clientelism) with that of Kenya. He recognizes that in countries where productivity is insufficient for patrons to satisfy the demands of clients, clientelism can degenerate into escalating authoritarianism. Hyung-Gon also adds an additional jarring element to the rent-extractive definition and argues that clientelism can be good for development:

> Broadly conceived, political clientelism is 1) based on an imbalance of power 2) existing in the context of personal, face-to-face relationships that 3) encompasses a wide range of political and economic forms of exchange, and 4) is distinguishable from politically and economically negative corruption or corruption outright....
>
> Whether or not patron-clientelism is positive or negative depends on the circumstances under which it operates. Patron-clientelism can be positive as long as the national pie is large enough. Patron-clientelism involves a favoured sector of the economy and non-favoured sector(s). As long as the favoured sector produces enough surplus, the state can use some of the surplus to buy off discontent and garner legitimacy for itself. This is the golden rule of clientelistic development: the misallocations of resources and patronage are outweighed by the economic and political benefits gained from patron-client politics. However, if the favoured sector cannot produce enough surplus, the entire system is put in jeopardy. The situation degenerates into politics of the belly, where the instability and discontent created by the lack of patronage leads to greater competition for the remainder of the national pie, and greater incentive for the patrons to engage in rent-seeking behaviour. A patron, given the choice between using patronage for himself or the client, chooses himself. [8]

It is these cases where there is an escalation in the level of authoritarianism that interests us here. [9] However, unlike Hyung-Gon, I do not think we have to separate rent-extractive exchanges within clientelism from destructive social and/or environmental consequences and irresponsibility.

The Westminster model parliamentary system operating in Belize is essentially the same as the one in Jamaica. Carlene J. Edie has described Jamaican clientelism as follows:

> Patron-client ties are among the most conspicuous features of political behaviour in Jamaica. Hundreds of demands are made daily on public and political

figures in the urban areas of Kingston and the rural parishes. These demands are met largely through interventions of the elected officials in the affairs of the municipal bureaucracy, whereby bureaucratic elites are instructed to dispense resources to reward loyal party supporters.... Democratic politics in Jamaica is maintained by state-controlling party elites who grant patronage resources in exchange for party support. Internal political order hinges on the political directorate's ability to obtain international capital transfers.[10]

And here is Agere's explanation of political institutions in the Caribbean. In a sense, Edie's description of Jamaica can be generalized to the region:

> In the Caribbean these institutions were planted in soil where no strong competing culture of political organisations existed and they appear to have developed deep roots—in some territories over a period of more than 300 years. It is doubtful, however that British influences have in fact permeated all strata of West Indian societies to the extent generally assumed. Indeed, at certain levels the influence [i.e. British institutional form of government] is at best superficial, and political and social life is characterized by an inarticulate and apathetic public opinion, apathy and nonparticipation of the masses, and authoritarian/submissive attitudes reflected in a dependency syndrome. These attitudes, originating perhaps in the heritage of the plantation and colonial society, are not consonant with the attributes of British or Western-style democracy.[11]

Figure 2.1 below summarizes the relationships that occur within a clientelist environment.

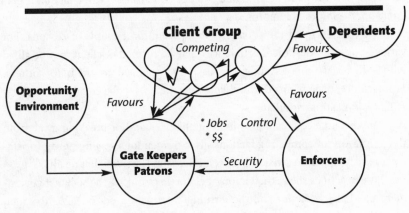

Figure 2.1
Strategic Alternatives for Clients (Generalized)

Clientelism ties *Have-nots* (i.e. clients) to *Haves* (i.e. patrons) in an unequal distribution of desired or required opportunities. The *Haves* derive legitimacy from the *Have-nots*. That gains them access to the supply of opportunities (the opportunity environment). So long as the patrons distribute adequate opportunities to the clients, the patron is sustained—and where support falters, the patron can turn to the enforcers (e.g. the police, the courts, the prison) who are usually able to forestall forced change emanating from the client group, and to maintain dominance.[12] Competing patrons (not shown) vie, therefore, for the support of a constituency. In such a situation, no ambitious neophyte politician, for example, will be able to receive constituency support without distributing opportunities to him or her. For this reason, *alliances* among patrons with varying levels of access to opportunities become attractive unless they are independently wealthy. And for this reason also, *factions* among various patron alliances become inevitable as they compete for access to the pork barrel.

At the same time, the *Have-nots* obtain opportunities (e.g. job, cash) from those they legitimize with votes and favours. As a result, the relationship among clients is unstable. They compete for the attention and support of the client, and pass favours to those dependent upon them (e.g. family members, girl-friends), often extracting favours in return (e.g. pin money, food, shelter, drinks, sex).

Clients may form temporary alliances with other clients, and do their best to blockade competing client alliances (i.e. factions) from gaining access to patrons. The client alliances, however, are fragile. When necessary, alliance members may break away from one alliance and affiliate with a faction if personal opportunities are improved by doing so.

The complexity of the situation is increased for a couple of reasons. For various opportunities, distinct alliances may be formed. A client may be allied with individuals for certain resources, but opposed to them for others. Furthermore, dependents of the clients may themselves be engaged in making and breaking strategic alliances.

The dynamic of creating or joining alliances and of breaking away from them in favour of competing factions gives tremendous staying power (or stasis) to the inequitable division between *Haves* and *Have-nots* that results.

Edie describes the perpetuation of clientelism during the socialist government of Michael Manley and the ensuing free market era of Edward Seaga. Though supporting diametrically opposed political philosophies, neither Prime

Minister was motivated to dismantle clientelism. Edie's observation implies that the phenomenon is a key ingredient for successful management of Jamaica. It allows the political system to shift and the political actors to change, while the class system remains essentially untouched for the following reason: where resources are scarce (e.g. food, water and sanitation, shelter, income-generation opportunities, information) clients will support those who have access to resources (i.e. patrons and their gatekeepers). They will compete with their peers for preference by patrons, and they will punish inferiors to exact obedience and optimize access to patrons. Disunity among peers will remain great, thwarting their ability to negotiate with patrons for better opportunities or to rebel against them effectively. Client loyalty will perpetuate the advantageous position held by the patrons. Patrons must, given inter-patron competition and the need to maintain status difference with those below, devour most of the opportunities themselves and leave little to share among the clients. Resources will thus remain scarce. In this manner, the cycle will be repeated.

In a clientelistic system, every action, every selection, is politically loaded. The opinions of politicians and of the government in power are of great importance and are at the forefront of everybody's mind. The government is the poor person's major lifeline and even the biggest entrepreneurs engage in their projects in close conjunction with government. If a "tourist village" is built to receive the tenders filled with cruise ship tourists, to dispatch them to the offshore cayes in water taxis, or in buses to the Mayan ruins in the forest, the investors have to collaborate with government to obtain the waterfront property and capture the business of tourism. That's not going to happen without a close relationship with politicians.

"The reversal of these destructive trends is essential to the establishment of unity and cooperation," the Baha'i Community told us about the irresponsible actions they observed in an increasingly amoral Third World. People need to step forward for the sake of societal betterment but apparently don't do so often enough. Either debt and obligation constrain them, or the fear of debt and obligation does so. Ironically, many of the poor already help others achieve their goals at the expense of their own—the rich force them to do it. The result is an existential vacuum for the person on the bottom and non-development, or social stasis, for society. Oddly, those whose goals are nothing more substantive than material possessions, power and sex themselves fail to escape from the hole. Following Frankl, we have called it an existential vacuum, but I am inclined to think we have returned to the Valley of Means.

If existential hollowness appears to be universal in clientelistic states where there is rent-extraction and social stasis, who among the population will know something is amiss? If they are aware of it, will not many—perhaps most—attribute the gap to American TV, Colombian drugs and foreign tourists, or perhaps to the departure of the British? Susan Sontag says people who experience new and disagreeable situations blame others.[13] Populations that function within a context of dependence and imposition might just as easily assume the blame for their pain or seek alleviation of pain through the purchase of lottery tickets, through bouts of ecstasy inspired by music or evangelism, from the numbness of the bottle, pill or injection, or through a resigned effort to be good now and to receive glory in heaven over the damned. In a context of ubiquitous poverty and inequity one would behave as others do—unhappy perhaps, with the status quo, but aware of no possible alternative.

Towards the end of 2002, a popular American song in Belize and throughout the Caribbean explained that the artist and a neighbour were "banging on the bathroom floor" when they were discovered by his girlfriend. But in the chorus he denied responsibility: "It wasn't me," he said. So far as he could understand, external and irresistible forces had brought him low. That's the poor man's fate where constraints are great. And not just the fate of the poor man. I say this because I have heard of an expensive boat, fast enough, I believe, to outshine most other boats. In self-deprecating irony, the name is, It Wasn't Me! Now, in truth, I know nothing about the boat, save for the way its name tickles my imagination. Nonetheless, a witty phrase like that gives you invitation to wonder.

The attitude apparently taken by the Artist was that the game was set by others before his time and without his consent. He's only a poor man doing what he can. The moves he makes optimize his opportunities. This time fate got him and his neighbour as far as the floor and then fate brought around his girlfriend at just the wrong moment. What more can one expect in this life? For all I know, the same thing may be true of the rich fellow in the speedy boat: I imagine he has the craft, the drinks and the "bling-bling"—that is, the flashy appearance of wealth—to attract the ladies, though the truth may be quite different. If that isn't true of the actual owner of It Wasn't Me, it is certainly true of many other people in Belize. The poor guy on the bathroom floor admires people who have the flash and the possessions to attract women and who go for that sort of thing. But Lord knows what people like that have to do to get and keep what they have and to get some more. It's just life. It's bigger than anybody in Belize and there's nothing anybody can do about it. After all, there's nobody you can trust. You just play the game.

From the perspective of the average citizen within a clientelistic state, the surrounding societal and environmental conditions determine the limits of one's choices. A person's choices vary with the situation. Whether on the yacht or the bathroom floor, one makes the most of one's little opportunities and exclaims with some degree of sincerity: "It wasn't me!" Deals can be made, women (or men) targeted like quarry and brought down—but societal change is not within the conceivable realm of possibility.

To the moral developer, the facile excuses and the unquestioning acceptance of the status quo may be repellent. It's easy to conclude that "They ought to try." But the general belief of populations within clientelistic environments is that they cannot. Frankl used therapy with clients who were intent on defining personal meaning in their lives, on finding a reason for existing and for making a responsible contribution to a formerly impressive society that was reconstructing itself after anti-Semitism and war. But in a clientelistic world therapy is inadequate. There is no acknowledgement of personal emptiness, nor much desire to fill it. The cyclical excitement of the yacht and the bathroom floor replace linear ambitions towards change. Emotion appears to have flooded responsibility and what people ought to try is simply not relevant.

In Belize and in the Caribbean, and perhaps throughout much of the developing world, we observe pervasive vacillation between boredom and distress, lust for power and money, and rampant sexual libido. Hope is apparently futile and as we'll see below, it is probably unrealistic to assume that, given a history of slavery and oppressive colonialism, the majority of people in clientelistic states would be positioned to begin the post-colonial era (only in 1981 in Belize) like the Übermenschen lionized by Nietzsche. How could they emerge from degradation as confident and self-reliant Dionysians, strong enough to throw off the bonds of history and culture and eager to take responsibility for creating their own reality? It surely takes time to regain one's traction. To make the situation worse, the interactions engendered by the past create their own, current context and additional reasons to refrain from changing the current modi vivendi.

To shirk responsibility is to abrogate power. The existential vacuum is not and cannot be one's own fault. To fill the void in the Valley is therefore not one's duty and anyway, given the context, is pointless. When the workman ducks the chore of installing screws he depends on the foreman to catch him. He is not controlling himself; de facto, it becomes the other fellow's job to be sure all the gaps are sealed. The workman plays the role of the child and defers responsibility to the foreman for the adult tasks. The child's task is to gratify the child.

We could say that a split occurs in the personality of such people: the id functions ("I wanna..." or "I don't wanna...") take control and the superego functions ("You hafta..." or "You can't do that...") are left to the boss, or to the preacher, or to the cops, or maybe, to the military. Except that when clientelism is at work everything depends on the patrons. Everybody does what the person above him or her wishes to have done, including the authority figures who, very unheroically, behave like everybody else. They take advantage of the opportunities presented to them by virtue of their positions regardless of the consequences to society, and regardless of their official responsibilities. They defer to those above and exact obedience from those below: kiss up, kick down. Together they all engender and sustain an authoritarian universe. The choice between ethical behaviour and personal survival or advantage within a clientelistic society is obvious: when thrown upon the seas of survival, try to swim.

Clientelistic people shirk responsibility because they don't have to take it on (i.e. won't get caught or can't be held responsible) or because they can't afford to be noble. One can know the right thing to do but decide against suffering the consequences. As contradictory as this may sound, there are many hills upon which to die in the Valley; wise warriors pick an appropriate one. A person in a clientelistic state can rant about the loss of backbone and the erosion of values—as people indeed constantly do in the local papers—but the one who rants isn't the one about to die (or suffer, at least) for a bad choice made on an inappropriate hill.

An abrogation of authority to somebody else can be a voluntary or a life-or-death kind of abrogation, but it's an abrogation nonetheless. The basic argument is that somebody else must do it; somebody else must take the responsibility; or somebody else holds all the cards and, at this moment, much as I would like to, I just can't do the responsible thing. The individual who shirks responsibility (that is, who defers to somebody else) is an individual who feels powerless. She or he may be boastful or belligerent, but somebody else, now living or formerly threatening, is perceived to be in charge. The person who shirks responsibility is a person who accepts the status quo, who leaves things the way they are, who does not take responsibility for changing things and who does not help development to happen.

Shirking responsibility is a survival stratagem (if you're poor) or otherwise a ploy to solidify or increase your advantage. The ability of an individual to contribute to development is a function of his or her level of self-esteem. And the level of self-esteem is proportional to a person's economic, physical and/or mental independence. Shirking responsibility isn't just a moral issue, therefore; it's also an economic one.

Responsible Choices And Change

It is an observable reality that not everybody crumbles—not even every citizen in clientelistic states. There are occasional and memorable acts of bravery and defiance, conscious choices to resist and to create in the face of overwhelming pressures to conform. Belize, like each of the former slave economies of the Caribbean, has a history of rebellions—brief and ultimately unsuccessful, but nonetheless terrifying to the slaveholders.

Heroism happens everywhere and at all times. The Bible is filled with heroes. Miriam questioned Moses' marriage to a black Kushite woman and was turned white with leprosy by Moses' protective God. Judith slew Holefernes to save her people. Mattathius, the old temple priest, was killed because he refused to bow to Hellenistic paganism. His sons, Judah Maccabbee (i.e. The Hammer) and his brothers responded to their father's defiance by carrying out the first recorded uprising for religious freedom (against the Seleucid Tyrant, Antiochus IV, 175–163 BCE). They used guerrilla tactics and established the Hashmonean dynasty in Judea that produced a sporadic reign of cruel and incompetent rulers, the last of whom was the wife of Herod the Great. The original Maccabbees, however, had chosen to be heroes.

Whole populations may see its constituents making the choice to arise in defiance. The legendary Thracian gladiator, Spartacus, led such an uprising. He escaped Roman captivity in 72 BCE and was joined by an army of 70,000 slaves who preferred to defy the Roman Empire and die rather than to endure slavery. Much of India chose to back Ghandi and to defy British colonialism. In the United States, Nat Turner rebelled against American slavery in August of 1831. More than 40 slaves in Southampton, Virginia chose to fight for freedom by his side.

Within a few years of emancipation in 1836, tiny Belize could point to an individual who broke away from the behaviours of the rest of the pack and who distinguished himself. Isaiah Morter became Belize's first black millionaire. Then, along with Marcus Garvey of Jamaica, he invested his fortune in the development of the United Negro Improvement Association (UNIA) in the United States and brought the movement, which was the forerunner of the NAACP, to Belize. Thousands of New World Africans joined the movement— some of them from Belize.[14] More recently, the African American population in the States united under the Reverend Martin Luther King in the 1960s and broke the segregation barrier.

Within the context of clientelism, the Übermensch will be the exception and outright collective rebellion a rarity. Notwithstanding the disapproval of others, the expected mode is irresponsibility. It seldom makes sense to assume responsibility when the conditions are wrong. Yet heroes struggle to shape destiny, to function either as isolated individuals or as part of a whole social movement in the face of the majority's preferred course of action. Heroes may not even act on the side of tolerance and goodness; for this discussion the point is that, singly or in groups, they take action to change history. The degree of heroism exhibited by a range of beleaguered individuals will vary. There is a series of possible defiant acts that extend from total capitulation through bad-mouthing opponents behind one's hand or spitting in massa's soup on the kitchen side of the door to open rebellion.

Inevitability Or Choice?

Inevitability implies a brainless, inflexible sort of stimulus/response relationship between external conditions and human behaviour. Inevitability in humans would mean they are as predictable as rats. The responses of individuals in any society are constrained and encouraged by the conditions they encounter and consider, whereas rats are not expected to reflect on preferences, to weigh short- or long-term pay-offs against each other, or to draw upon experience in the way that humans are perfectly capable of doing. In fact for humans, it is choice that is inevitable. We can know what we're doing even if we choose to ignore it. Any action, even the choice to take none, represents the behaviour of a sentient being.

The choices people make can range from irresponsibility (i.e. short-term and favouring the self over all others) to responsibility. Irresponsible choices are just as economic as responsible ones, though their frequency may be much higher, and though the calculus used and the end sought by the decision-maker will differ. One's immediate personal objective may just as well be death through self-immolation with a longer-term objective of social betterment, as immediate, increased wealth through bank robbery. One may also choose to do nothing. It's still a choice. The occasional responsible choice is the individual's to make, and, like common, irresponsible action, the individual is making that choice on the basis of expected costs and benefits. Both the most popular choice and the exceptional choices need to be understood in dialectical terms. Conditions influence choices but choices also change conditions. As developers who employ an economic frame of reference, we therefore need to comprehend both the modal and exceptional choices as well as the formative and current conditions that shape them. We need to do this neither to laud nor to denigrate the modes and the exceptions but to comprehend their logic and to consider the conditions under which such behaviours make sense. Personal choice can be related to institutions:

> It is up to individuals to choose to, for example, practice family planning or adopt modern agricultural techniques. But whether they make these choices and can carry out their decisions depends, partly, on the presence of institutional mechanisms to provide the necessary technical advice and physical inputs. Without effective institutions, people cannot easily maintain forward momentum to correct the social and economic deficiencies they face. [15]

But it is equally true that without making appropriate choices, individuals will be left without the effective institutions they require. Where there is social stasis, irresponsible choices are being made by enough people to distort the functioning of the institutions that affect society. The distortion, in turn, frustrates individuals. That reifies the logic of counter-productive behaviours. And that's the dialectic of socio-economic stasis where there is clientelism and underdevelopment.

The paradox is that the dialectic sustains a reality that is both undesired by the individual and counter-productive for the society and its economy. Plenty of married couples are locked into that kind of dialectic. For example, she criticizes his behaviour. He acts that way because she's so critical. What is she to do but criticize? If it takes a really good marriage counsellor to get them to interact in a whole new way, what would it take to make a sick society well?

Moral developers may pin all hopes upon the fact that individuals can choose to defy the odds and be heroes. If enough people agree to change their behaviour in the right ways, institutions that now cause grief can be changed and good things can then begin to happen. That would be development, the end all of us desire.

People who are already making responsible choices by trying to make a contribution to society do not need developers to identify a target for change or an appropriate strategy (although developers' funds could help them to try to convert a critical mass of their peers). However, irresponsible people, those seeking personal benefits, who use short-term survival strategies that have negative long- or short-term impact on their peers become attractive to developers because they are seen to be part of the problem.

So the establishmentarian developers make conditions to elicit change (i.e. providing rewards for local project executors if the developers' conditions are met). The anti-establishmentarian developers try consciousness-raising (i.e. engaging in an exploration of the status quo with the target population as a way of ridding them of false consciousness and of discovering class interests). This is supposed to elicit a voluntary behavioural change. Other strategies are attempted as well.

However, I believe that pinning hopes on people's ability to behave altruistically is an unrealistic expectation for community developers, notwithstanding their awareness of injustice. For the people who are expected to take action against injustice, the survival realities of the target group and the general despondence may simply be overwhelming. Only heroes risk all. They surface infrequently, seldom amass much of a following and seldom engineer sustainable rebellions that open fresh opportunities for egalitarianism and mutual aid. If once successful in eliminating their persecutors, the new leaders tend to replicate the systems they attacked: trust is low, authority is centralized, power is grasped, disagreement is quashed and finances are incompetently managed. To invest development monies on igniting an anti-establishmentarian sort of alternative is to bet against staggering odds.

Unlike pragmatic politicians, idealistic developers may not even know the magnitude of the forces with which they are attempting to compete, nor the risks they are asking target populations to incur once they abandon the traditional patrons. In too many cases, the developers are simply failing to compare their wares to that of the competition. What they may do instead is to pass judgement on the behaviour of the people they are attempting to rescue.

Is Something Wrong With Third World People?

The psychiatrist, Thomas Szasz, called "mental illness" a destructive myth that discredited psychiatry, threatening to put it on a par with astrology.[16] He argued that unless there are physical disorders there is no illness per se, only adaptive behaviours to extraordinary circumstances. Psychiatrists who made "illnesses" out of adaptive behaviours were no better than witchdoctors, he argued. In the 30 years since Szasz wrote his groundbreaking book, scientific advances have revealed a host of mental diseases of physical origin that Szasz couldn't have known about. Nevertheless, his general observation still has validity. Atypical behaviour may not reflect madness but may simply be the result of an encounter between mad experiences and mad conditions. New situations press old buttons and old defensive behaviours reappear.

I think that Szasz's observation is still valuable and valid for community development. The clinical model of therapist (i.e. the developers) curing "patients" (i.e. reforming anti-social behaviours) doesn't necessarily suit reality. Many of the behaviours we disparage (e.g. the widespread lack of moral discipline, the glorification of greed and material accumulation, the increasing breakdown of family and community, the rise of lawlessness and disorder, the ascendancy of racism and bigotry, and the priority given to national interests over the welfare of humanity) never did require treatment anyway. They had always been rational given the options available to the people using them. In truth it would be mad to abandon those desperate measures and take some of the bait offered by developers, or to join the vanguard of those intending to fly in the face of the status quo. Only a hero would do a thing like that and few of us would step forward and be heroes. The same is true for members of a target population and we are misguided to ask them to do so.

It is best to avoid the assumption that the people who are the targets of community development somehow differ from the rest of us because their preferred strategy differs from ours. The target peoples with whom developers work may stubbornly stick to the tried and true in the face of the "better" alternatives proffered by those who may understand very little about the reasons behind the stubbornness. That obstinacy may give rise to the assumption that peasants, First Nations peoples and slum dwellers are different from more educated people in more sophisticated environments—that is, from people like us. Many people have made such assumptions. For instance, in 1852, Karl Marx characterized peasants as "a sack of potatoes."[17] Others have argued for a "culture of poverty"[18] or for "present-orientedness"[19] as the cause of patterns of distinct behaviours among the poor. Emile Durkheim made distinctions on the basis of culture, contrasting mechanical solidarity (e.g. that of African tribal members, or maybe The Borg in a *Star Wars* episode, each of whose social segments purportedly behave exactly alike) with organic solidarity in a modern society (i.e. a complex division of labour within a social organism where different classes contribute variously towards the harmonious operation of the whole).[20]

Another way of explaining the failure to make rational choices is to posit racial or gender distinctions. Such arguments say that for genetic reasons, or for reasons of natural selection, people whose behaviour differs from ours are just too dumb to be original, too cowardly to make the obvious choice, have brains that are too small for their bodies, or genitalia that are too large.[21]

None of these arguments works well. People who don't make the choices we value make choices important to themselves. When they fail to respond to our incentives it's precisely because they're responding to a different set of incentives that work in their context. Performance comparisons made across races and used to demonstrate the inferiority of one race are drawn in a context of pervasive racism. Therefore, there's no way to keep racism from contaminating a performance comparison. No significant difference has been found between head sizes and intelligence.[22] Other than the fevered report on race and genitalia by Captain Sir Richard F. Burton in the late 1800s, which is quoted by Kinsley and Masters, I don't know that anybody has confirmed a link between how much is up above and down below.[23]

If Dr. Szasz was right about mad conditions explaining mad behaviours, then there isn't anything uniquely venal or greedy about Third World people. Irresponsibility is universal. It's found in the countries at the top of every list. In Canada, for example, you will find newspaper reports of special deals made between private contractors and government employees, elected representatives or political appointees, or embezzlement of government funds by public servants. A newspaper editorial from the director of FAIR (the Federal Accountability Initiative for Reform) describes corruption in government, its sources and its impact on Canadian civil servants in terms used to characterize the dysfunctionality of the Caribbean civil service[24]:

> Lavish spending of taxpayer dollars by senior bureaucrats and politicians is nothing new.... Despite the escalating erosion in Canada of democratic rights and freedoms, there has been no political revolt. Like eunuchs, too many members of the governing party have abandoned serving the public in favour of loyalty to their own political power and comforts.... The inner operations of the entire public service is no better, long deviating from its obligation to serve the public in favour of service to the masters, the senior bureaucrats and their

political friends.... Fear and intimidation have become management's dominant tools in cultivating a compliant and submissive workforce.... Creative thinking, professional analysis and independent thought are increasingly crushed by oligarchic and power-hungry bosses whose careers have been built not on loyalty to the public but rather sycophancy to the bosses.... Any credible vision of freedom of expression as guaranteed in our Charter of Rights necessarily includes the right for employees to blow the whistle on illegality and wrongdoing that threatens the public interest.[25]

The existence of elaborate auditing measures to ensure transparency in post-industrialized countries is evidence of their indispensability. There is always somebody ready to favour himself and eager to avoid the practice when other factors keep him from doing so. Similarly in the North and the South people are equally able to internalize conscientiousness, thoroughness, honesty or altruism and to yield to or resist our instinct to survive. We can all choose to be generous if the cost isn't too high. In certain circumstances the cost of generosity or nobility is too great for all but a few of us.

False distinctions between "them" and "us" are not required although the literature on Third World people is filled with that sort of dehumanized description: "we" are modern and decent whereas "they" are backward, primitive, mechanical, Gemeinschaft, proletarian, have low need for achievement, suffer from external locus of control and have an image of Limited Good that necessitates greed. The person making the observation establishes a kind of hierarchy and with few exceptions, the people who are being described are found lower on the hierarchy.

However, we benefit by refusing to accept the essential imperfections of others. If the difference does not lie within the population, there must be a difference in the contexts within which they act. An advantage of this shift in focus is that when we come to make community development happen we are more likely to tinker with the context than with the people who inhabit it. Another advantage is that we can assume equal intelligence everywhere and approach target populations as colleagues and peers. If their behaviour makes no sense to us, the onus falls upon us to figure out how to use it. Acceptable action varies with the situation.

The ability to be greedy may not distinguish nations and populations because greedy folk are everywhere. But you may find differences in the intensity and frequency of greedy acts, in the awareness and responsiveness of institutions to the public agenda and maybe in the number of checks and balances operating or in the vigour of their implementation. It may be possible to demonstrate a positive relationship between the frequency of anti-social acts (e.g. civil service embezzlement) in a society and the number of people in it who believe in stern punishment for robbers. The less a population is able to behave itself the more the members of that population will want the authorities to keep people in line and the smaller the internal peacekeeping force per capita, the less need there is for its people to be kept in line.[26] That sounds like what the Belizean gardener was saying about societal disintegration and about wanting the British colonizers back. This positive relationship between the under-development of a nation and the apparent tendency for its inhabitants to behave irresponsibly and to want somebody else to set things right becomes an almost irresistible invitation for developers to scramble for solutions. However, if the solutions include reforming Third World people, I think we will scramble into failure.

Judging Morality

Developers who condemn sloth, deceptiveness, evasion, or irresponsibility (I'm obsessing about the window installers again) never move beyond excoriation and the satisfaction of a good tantrum. It is perhaps better to try understanding the context that prompted the irresponsible behaviours and the history that contributed to the choices. Behaviours exist in a vacuum when we moralize. "Don't tell me about unhappy childhoods," the moralist is saying, "just tell me who did what and I'll tell you who's naughty and who's nice." Yet so long as behaviour is being judged and found wanting, opportunities, constraints and motivations are being ignored. On the contrary, judgement becomes irrelevant if the facts surrounding "bad" behaviour are examined.

Unfortunately the minute we try to understand behaviour or to seek motivation, things get complicated. Understanding behaviour requires that we acknowledge forces outside the individual or the organization that shape the behaviour of either. We enter a complex world where environment shapes behaviour and where behaviour shapes environment. This, in turn, suggests a need for us to think about two things at once—to chew gum and walk so to speak. Because environment and behaviour are interdependent no person is entirely in control of him- or herself. Additionally, understanding behaviour requires that we think about people's past experience because that's also going to affect the decisions that are taken.

Moral values are easy to deal with. Things are either good or bad.

Sometimes they're more good than bad; other times they're more bad than good. Yet once we know how things tend to fall, we know what to do. We can take sides, or be in solidarity with a particular side. In short, we know the enemy.

An economic valuation is a calculus. A calculus is a formula with a number of changeable elements. Given the right quantities of each element, the calculus of factors interact as desired and the equation works out properly. For example, a loan repayment consists of the "principal" borrowed (p), plus the "rate of interest" (r) being charged for the loan over a period of "time" (t). If the three factors (p, r and t) are known, the monthly loan repayment can be calculated. If a loan payment is missed, then p, r and t have to be recalculated to figure out the new (and higher) monthly repayment. The same sort of recalculation must be worked if the loan amount (p) is increased or if the loan rate (r) is increased or decreased. But the point is that when the quantities are known, the calculation can be worked out.

The same thing is true with an economic valuation of any social behaviour we observe within a clientelistic context. In such cases, we are not considering principal, rate and time, but rather economic, or socio-environmental, political, or cultural phenomena factors. Or even more confusing, our calculus involves any combination of the five factors. Thus, an economic perspective is more challenging than forming a bias on the basis of ungrounded—imported, and hence, culturally biased—valuations.

When looking at social interaction in economic instead of moral terms, we are no longer deciding who is right and who is wrong, but rather how various formative factors are affecting the behaviours we're observing. This complexity may in part explain the temptation to treat situations in developing countries as a doctor treats a patient; that is, by determining what's wrong and then prescribing. It is simply easier to decide what others "ought to do" if we never have to acknowledge the gritty choices those people have to make or have made for a lifetime or have inherited as part of their cultural baggage. And it's easier not to get into the consequences that flow from taking our advice. What poor people "ought to do" is probably an ill-afforded luxury when we begin to know something about their situation and is in all likelihood of little profit to the rich. In the end, after half a century of moralizing and then giving out advice, there is a growing realization that people are not much listening to us anyway.

Social Irresponsibility and Moral Developmental Failures

This is a world troubled by global economic and ecological distortions, by growing disparities between poverty and wealth and by widening holes in the ozone layer. In the face of all this, how much attention should we be paying to individual irresponsibility and the decision-making environment? Would it not make more sense to track the social and economic impact of globalization on poorer nations and on lower income populations, or to devise strategies for reforestation, or for targeting micro-finance programs at greater numbers of the poor?

That is of course what is being attempted with some success by moral developers. There are places where literacy rates have improved and where infant mortality is down; there are examples of improved herds and larger, better crops. There is also an increase in the number of micro-credit loans and some examples of high repayment rates.[27] Repaid loans in turn bring about a gratifying increase in family income. There are even examples of increased transparency in governance and of improved community development approaches by Third World governments, such as a shift to a community-based approach from a state-priority basis.[28]

But much, perhaps even most, of what moral developers have tried still doesn't work too well. Trickle-down assistance pretty consistently refuses to trickle.[29] National economies in take-off mode usually fail to do much better than the now grounded Concorde out of Paris and local irresponsible behaviours undeniably play a role in the failure according to many experts:

> Whereas private companies (particularly those traded on stock markets) are under constant pressure to prove that their investments are resulting in improved profits or growing market share, public enterprises in Latin America rarely report results of any kind. Even when they do produce an annual report, public services hardly ever disclose enough financial information to let taxpayers determine whether funds were spent efficiently or even if the service met its stated goals.
>
> Even in the poorest Latin American countries, billions of dollars are spent on public services each year. But without detailed information about the performance of these services, the probability that large percentages of those funds are misspent or siphoned off through corruption is very high. Financial record-keeping at many public services is so lax that it is impossible to determine exactly how the budget was executed in the previous year. On the rare occasion when audits are performed, they often reveal that practically all of a public service's budget is spent on salaries. Taxpayers, who see very little

benefit from most public spending, gradually come to the conclusion that all government services are inefficient and corrupt: "In many of our countries we do not have an evaluation culture," says Hamuy [Chief of the Government Programs Evaluation Department in Chile's Ministry of Finance], "and that is particularly true in the public sector."[30]

Fernando Carrillo-Florez, a former Colombian minister of Justice and a senior advisor in the Inter American Development Bank's State, Governance and Civil Society Division complains about "institutional weaknesses, judicial branches that are not independent, weak congresses, electoral systems that are not transparent, the lack of checks and balances for exercising control, and the absence of accountability by public officials to citizens."[31] The author of the article observes that "Public opinion surveys show that citizens have all but lost faith in political parties and public institutions. In some sectors people even speak with nostalgia of the days when a military junta ruled their country."[32]

Another IDBAmérica article rejects the notion that clientelism has value by saying that

> until a few decades ago serious academics argued that corruption was actually good for economic growth. At the time, the prevalent perception was that bribes helped business people cut through red tape, greasing the wheels of otherwise lethargic bureaucracies and offering public servants an incentive to work.... Since then, the world has taken a much less sanguine view of this phenomenon.... [It] can seriously hamper economic performance by discouraging investment, limiting growth and distorting public sector spending. Similarly, a country that succeeds in reducing corruption and polishing its image could reap substantial reward...a nation that moves up a notch on a corruption index where 0 is virulently venal and 10 is absolutely angelic could see its GDP growth rate increase by 0.25%. This may seem a small gain in a single year, but over the course of many years it can represent an enormous achievement.... Trade restrictions, government subsidies, price controls, multiple exchange rate schemes and legal monopolies have long been suspected of breeding bribery, embezzlement and favoritism.[33]

Privatization at first appears to be a route to development saving moral developers the pain of having to confront the issue of personal responsibility-taking. The objectives of privatization are to reduce the responsibility and cost of government, to take the means of production away from corrupt, incompetent and/or unmotivated bureaucrats and to put them into the healthier atmosphere of the free market. The hidden hand of capitalism can do the development work of making socio-economics work on behalf of its population. Private businesses can nurture the fortunes of the average citizen and help national economies to grow quicker. The businesses can then generate new ones in a ripple effect to employ more people and deliver more benefits nationally. However, a lot of the privatized businesses have proved to be no less corrupt than government nor any more able to respond to demands from the world market for raw and manufactured goods, or from their own people for food, shelter, water, sewerage or services. Newly-privatized companies in non-industrialized countries do little better and sometimes worse than when they were owned by governments and clumsily operated by the rule-bound civil servants. Formed from the sale of government corporations, they are frequently purchased by the more powerful politicians and their well-heeled supporters. They form legal monopolies that succeed in concentrating more wealth into fewer hands. In other words the venal, individualistic tendencies already at work in clientelistic systems re-emerge with privatization. Self-interest and opportunistic alliances effectively stay the hidden hand of capitalism.

The same has been the case in agricultural reform. Large blocks of under-utilized, privately held land may not be redistributed primarily to landless producers. They may be redistributed to agro-businesses owned by cliques of politicians and their financial backers, or purchased by multinationals. Even if they become productive their owners may channel earnings out of the national economy, or into the pockets of those who are already advantaged. The idea behind agricultural reform and privatization was not to contribute to what Engels had called "an ever thickening forest of ever thinning arms,"[34] yet all too often that has been the effect.

The irresponsible (i.e. short-term and personally advantageous) decisions made by rich and poor in the Valley of Means have the power to defeat development initiatives at whatever level of complexity and within whatever sector. Whether our interventions are intended to strengthen the economy, the physical infrastructure, critical institutions, agriculture, industry, service delivery, education, health, gender equity or class relations, moral development has been overwhelmingly defeated. Whether the strategies have been establishmentarian or anti-establishmentarian, they have been swamped by failure. Where stasis is engaged with moralistic development, I believe that economic transactions down in the Valley of Means have made moral development work all but irrelevant. And for this reason I think it is necessary to take a closer look at the uncomfortable way that idealistic community development attempts to fit into the pragmatic world of clientelism.

The Emergence of Expediency
in the Caribbean Region

ANY COMMUNITY DEVELOPMENT initiative must contend with the set of socio-economic behaviours that is already operating in an environment and that is practiced by target group members. Chances are greater that change will occur if the developer adapts creatively to local behaviours than if the developer attempts to make the target population adapt. Our intent in this book is to understand how to engage with existing behaviours productively. This chapter examines the historical realities people encounter in coercive environments and the behaviours they develop in response. The chapter will also try to understand how responsive human interactions can be so similar across many nations with colonial histories even though the particulars of their histories may be quite different. Historical data on sugar-producing and lumber-producing slave economies in the Caribbean will be used.

The immediate difficulty we encounter is that our understanding of history is shaped, in part, by the historical accounts available to us. In the case of the Caribbean accounts—indeed, the accounts of many post-colonial populations—the historians tend to encourage us to think of the historical actors in moral terms. During the colonial period, contemporary writers had frequently portrayed the colonialists as the people who wore white hats and tended to conquer the "savage races" and to "civilize' them. While many accounts still make buffoons of the "natives" or "locals," the reaction to this demeaning portrayal of colonized populations in the post-colonial period has led to a situation in which serious historians have tended to see greed and villainy on the side of the colonials; nobility and class struggle on the part of the colonized.

I call this side-taking tendency a "difficulty" because—to the extent that it is accepted without question by international developers—it encourages developers either to enlighten the innocent oppressed, or to join in solidarity with those who nobly struggle. Neither tactic has proved particularly effective.

I would therefore also like to use this chapter to demonstrate that even if we rely on the accounts of biased historians, we can find evidence that the historical actors (whether colonial or colonized) were about as likely to wear white hats as they were to wear black ones and also about as likely to betray class interests as to support them. This evidence leads me to conclude that we are on stronger ground as developers to assume that neither betrayal nor championing of class interests offers us a good enough understanding of actors. We do better to assume that individuals are decision-makers and that conditions shift over time. That being the case, the decisions made by a set of individuals at one time may be quite different from those made at another. Furthermore, not everybody within the set will face identical conditions. Therefore, within any typical "class" behaviour we are sure to fund sub-sets of atypical behaviours.

There are surely as many routes to survival expediency within clientelistic societies as there are clientelistic societies in the colonial world, and no two routes or resulting systems will be exactly the same. Below, I use a history of slavery to summarize the general formative pressures in the sugar-producing islands of the Caribbean and then highlight the unique factors that affect the population of timber-extracting Belize. Then I trace changing conditions through the post-slavery, transitional period of debt peonage to the emergence of class, politics and politicized ethnicity. I also briefly mention the forces of modernization and globalization. I do not focus on these periods per se, but use them to suggest what must have been the motive for employing certain survival tactics and behavioural adjustments in social interactions. This gives me an opportunity to demonstrate that whereas the particularities of survival tactics may differ from one situation to another, it is still possible to draw a general observation: when people's futures are threatened by other people, they will develop effective survival strategies to retain an advantage, to gain additional advantages and/or to keep themselves from losing whatever advantages they believe they presently have. Furthermore, within the generalized behaviours, it is possible to define important exceptions.

In the first chapter I had mentioned a hotel gardener who claimed that life under the British was better—there was enough security that propping a stick against your door would keep your home and possessions intact even if you were gone for six months. Nowadays, many neighbourhoods in urban centres of Belize are too dangerous to walk through come nightfall, and some are not very secure by day either. So in a way, I'm also using this chapter to understand what happened in the forty years since Belize achieved home rule in 1964 and connecting the Belize present-day community developers encounter to the two hundred years that preceded it.

In the foreword to Nigel Bolland's collection of essays, *The Struggle For Freedom*, the Belizean scholar, Assad Shoman, quotes Bolland himself in saying that "the struggle of the freed persons, in whatever arena it was played out, was ultimately meaningful for them 'precisely to the degree that it offered to the former slaves opportunities to gain some control over their own lives and their own communities.'"[1] This remark is complex because sometimes the opportunities available to the individual freed person to *increase* control over his or her own life are the very ones that *diminish* the opportunities of the class of freed persons to gain collective control over their socio-economy. In the next chapter of this book we shall examine situations where personal greed encumbers community empowerment. And we will later look for situations where personal greed actually facilitates community empowerment. For this reason, as we compare the histories of sugar and timber-extracting economies in the Caribbean, we will not only present moments when community and individual freedom were both being advanced but also find occasions where one struggle impeded the other. Ultimately, the intent of the chapter is to demonstrate that history has not only taught Caribbean people to struggle for a people's victory. More accurately, it has taught them to struggle as individuals to survive by any means possible. Uniting for the sake of advancing the welfare of the community is only one of the tactics employed, and one that is generally ignored when it is considered to be less rewarding to family and/or to individual interests and when other, better alternatives present themselves.

In preparation for our study of modern-day survival tactics, we shall portray the historical emergence of *a reliance on expedient measures* as the fundamental behavioural strategy of people within subjugated political economies, both colonial and post-colonial. In the next chapter of the book, and not too surprisingly, we shall see that many of the historical survival strategies continue to exist and that they continue to encumber community empowerment efforts. We will also suggest that, whether we consider this historical legacy an encumbrance or a boon to community development, we still need to comprehend it, engage with it and then utilize it creatively.

Belize (in the Yucatan south of Mexico) is thought by many to be like Guyana (on the edge of the Orinoco, south of Venezuela). Both are Commonwealth, Anglophone nations with colonial histories of slavery and extraction of wealth; both are located on the mainland and are surrounded by non-Anglophone nations and have coastal wetlands that fringe the forested interiors that are watered by many rivers and populated by "Amerindians." Nigel Bolland effectively contrasts the pluralism and politics of these two countries and Shoman observes that the key to understanding the differences (in political outcomes) lies in seeking cultural and racial/ethnic identities not as "given" social factors, but "as dialectically related with class formation and the political processes of emerging nationalism and state formation."[2] Apparently similar nations can develop quite dissimilar characteristics that are explained by the inter-relationship of historical structural factors. Predictably, the more closely Bolland compares Belize and Guyana, for example, the more different they appear in terms of the role of ethnicity in politics and economics.

The historical factors summarized below that distinguish Belize and sugar-producing parts of the Caribbean allow us to extract some of the defensive and offensive strategies that are still being used by its various populations. I contend that the general survival strategy observed in either situation is fairly common in distinct types of political economies. Similar adaptive behaviour becomes logical, necessary and reified across geography and history because critical characteristics of colonialism are universally present where there is inequity and coerced labour. But we will also see that the generalized survival strategies can become particularized to suit quite different contexts.

The Sugar Plantation Economy of The British West Indies, 1623–1775: Factors Shaping Survival Behaviours

Between 1650 and 1700, the British passed a series of Navigation Acts that levied shipping taxes on the goods exported by British merchants. Understandably, these taxes were unpopular with merchants in Britain, who argued that they were an anti-liberal interference with Smith's "hidden hand of capitalism."

But the wealth the taxes generated effected enormous changes in the British Caribbean, which until that time had returned limited benefit to the motherland. Privileged borrowers were able to make use of the wealth thus pooled by the British government to invest in new, more intensive (and taxable) forms of agriculture in the Caribbean for crops that could be exported to Britain—such as tobacco, sugar and eventually cotton. Throughout the Caribbean, the production of such commodities in profitable quantities relied upon forced human labour and it did not take long for a system of slavery to be introduced. The establishment of more competitive farming on one plantation exerted tremendous financial pressure on other plantations to follow suit and to introduce slave labour.

Richard Sheridan estimates that between 1627 and 1775 about 1,500,000 slaves were imported into the West Indies, most of them being retained for labour there.[3] According to Sheridan, one demographer conservatively estimated that 15 million Africans survived the horrific conditions of the Middle Passage between West Africa and the British Colonies in the New World between the 16th and 19th centuries.[4] He also cites Fage's estimate that an equal number of Africans died as a result of activities related to the slave trade, including warfare, the Middle Passage, and the "seasoning" of slaves. Ultimately, and concludes that "altogether, between twenty and thirty million souls were probably lost to West Africa which had a population that was unlikely more than twenty million at most [at any time within the four-century period]."[5]

Clearly such a vast number of slaves threatened the lives of white planters and slave-owners. Sheridan quotes from Ligon to show some of the ways in which slave owners in Barbados protected themselves from the fear of insurrections as early as 1650:

> If any tumult or disorder be in the Island...the next neighbour to it discharges a musquet, which gives the alarum to the whole Island; for upon the report of that, the next shoots and so the next and next, til it go through the island; upon which warning they make ready.[6]

Sheridan continues: "Other precautions included the policy of stocking plantations with blacks of diverse tribal origins 'whose different languages and animosities have kept them from insurrection and rigorously enforced slave codes.'" Insurrections, slave conspiracies and Maroon (i.e. escaped slave) wars occurred most frequently between 1685 and 1740 and were repressed through "furious vigilante hunts and a blood bath attended with all the horrors of a medieval torture chamber."[7]

Repulsive and inhumane as the practice may have been to any British gentleman educated in the philosophies of the Grecian democrats and the Enlightened British, slavery was nonetheless adopted and quickly justified because it was rewarding to the economy of Britain, to British investors and to West Indian planters. It was too costly an alternative to reject on mere moral grounds, given the competition offered by other nations, other British investors and neighbouring planters. Slaves on the plantations were used to carry out a range of tasks as it was cheaper to use slaves as skilled craftsmen than to depend on white tradesmen "despite the relatively short working life of the black hands. Rough calculations show that if a prime field hand in Jamaica laboured for twelve years he returned 6 per cent per annum, while fifteen years of labour yielded 9 percent, and twenty years nearly 11 percent."[8]

Sheridan quotes an anonymous Englishman in 1749 who asserted that "Part of our British Manufactures, are owing primarily to the Labour of Negroes." The writer concluded that the Negro trade, "and the natural consequences resulting from it may justly be esteemed an inexhaustible Fund of Wealth and Naval Power to this Nation."[9] Consequently, Sheridan observes, "West India plantations greatly stimulated the British and North American economies, since they were a key component of a market system that was self-generating and constantly expanding."[10]

Sheridan's analysis allows us to suggest that a number of pressures were exerted upon plantation populations. These pressures were important because so many of the modern survival strategies we discuss in the next chapter have, I believe, developed in response to them. These pressures include:

• the introduction of British taxes permitted concentrated investment in commercial and profitable export agriculture in the Antilles in order to benefit the British economy and privileged British investors;

• reliance upon imported African slaves by Antillean planters concentrated a productive population at minimal cost to the planters;

• the overwhelming presence of an enslaved and coerced Black African population encouraged the formation of colour-based alliances among whites for self-defence and reduction of slaves to a competitive faction;

• actions by white planters to achieve the atomization of the slave population on the basis of linguistic and competitive tribal affiliation, thus ensuring protection from organized rebellions;

• the differentiation of tasks across the slave population that created a range of coveted ranks and specialties with concomitant and inequitable survival opportunities. This provided motivation for those slaves who were of a lower status to undermine the reputation of more advantaged slaves in the eyes of masters and foremen, thus improving their own personal status and survival chances;

• intensified efforts across artificially differentiated slave populations to deepen individualized alliances with white masters and to engage in strategic and temporary alliances with other slaves and freed blacks, while attempting to rid oneself of dangerous and/or destructive alliances with other slaves;

• and, finally, an intensified effort among white planters to heighten socio-economic solidarities within their class and to seek socio-economic alliances in Britain with those who might be able to help fortify the institution of slavery.

From this list, we are able to propose a couple of the generalized survival behaviours that necessarily emerged from plantation slavery throughout the sugar-producing English Antilles. One of the tendencies made evident by the list is the emergence of colour-based social divisions within the general culture of the Antilles. For economic reasons, white skin became valued higher than black, and lighter skin, more greatly valued than darker skin.

A second observation is also based upon the economic forces at work. Once the new taxes were introduced in Britain to make the Antilles more of an asset, there was an almost irresistible pressure upon the Antillean planters to participate in slave-based commercial agriculture as a defensive survival behaviour. Moral objections, if there were any, simply collapsed in the face of the power of greed. Sheridan quotes the exceptional case of "John Newton, the master of a slave vessel from Britain who later became an Anglican clergyman and anti-slavery leader" and publisher of an anti-slavery book (*The Journal of a Slave Trader, 1750–1754*).[11] Newton, as an individual who rejected slavery on moral grounds (and survived through affiliation with his church) may fit our classification of a hero—one of the minority of individuals who rejects and opposes the status quo on moral grounds. However, such heroism among the white planters was evidently inadequate to derail the move to plantation slavery.

We may conclude that the behaviour of the planters was effectively shaped by their need to survive and their opportunity to improve their personal condition.

In later parts of his book, Sheridan presents the factors that gave rise to the abolitionist movement. Remarkably, the rise of the abolitionist movement was also inextricably linked to the economy of sugar plantation slavery and not solely to moral objections. The economic expansion and industrialization associated with the re-investment wealth generated by the enslavement of Africans supported the growth of the industrial sector in Britain and her American colonies. In part, their new-found wealth afforded many from the British upper class and emerging middle class the leisure time to cultivate the intellectual and philosophical convictions that opposed the institution of slavery. The abolitionist movement that rose to end the practice of slavery—at least in name—came about largely as a side-effect of the very system it intended to end. The abolitionists' objections to the institution of slavery were doubtlessly grounded in morality. But just as surely, the luxury of educated British and Americans who stimulated the rise of an abolitionism championing morality was purchased with the blood of slaves.

A third observation implicit in the history of slavery is the rise of defensive alliances. Whites established colour-based, sustainable coalitions for mutual protection against the blacks they themselves had made so dangerously rebellious. Factors that mitigated against a perfect solidarity among whites (such as land hunger in small Antillean islands serving to increase predatory competition among white planters) also operated but have not been discussed here; they were not adequate to destroy the institution of slavery. With the self-interested help of the British government and the presence of the military and the police to enforce racially-based inequity, the white planters generally maintained solidarity and successfully retained dominion over the black population for the most part. Whites could ally on the basis of skin colour with relative ease given the crisis of violence they had instigated.

The black population, both enslaved and freed, also resorted to the use of defensive alliances but with notable differences. Given their reduction in status under duress, alliances of the black population could not be so robust and sustainable as those of the whites. In part, this was because actions by whites had reduced many, but not all, to the very edge of life. For plantation blacks, observable differences in social status represented distinctions in survival opportunities. One black person's fortune was gained and sustained at another's detriment. The need to rise became as urgent for some blacks as the need to prevent others from rising became for those more privileged. Alliances across rank may have proved useful in destabilizing those of superior rank, but as in a game of musical chairs, there were more people looking for higher stations than available places.

As a result, trust across occupants of lower orders was fragile: their usual need was not to promote the social interests of class, but to promote their own survival as individuals. For blacks within a colour-sensitive sugar slavery system therefore, factors like gender, tribal origin, skin colour and unequal survival privileges all became factors that could be used both to create alliances and to suspect members of the alliance. The alliances tended to be dynamic (they existed only for the duration of their usefulness) and therefore fragile and short-lived—a phenomenon may have helped to undermine the ability of slaves to sustain their many rebellions. There would have been too many other alliances forming and dissolving within any rebellious group of slaves to permit an overarching alliance to remain solid. Certainly, the organized antagonism of planters, and of trained police forces and armies, did not make their attempts to sustain organization any easier.

Distinct Slavery, Similar Survival Behaviours in Belize

Belize represents an example of a non-sugar producing but coercive economy that allows us to compare the defensive responses devised by inhabitants of both types of slave economy. In the 1600s, the presence of logwood in the Yucatan peninsula (where Mexico meets Central America) permitted "some buccaneers [to change] from plundering Spanish logwood ships to themselves cutting the trees."[12] The purple dye used for the royal robes of Europe was extracted from the logwood and the Spanish allowed the British settlers in the Bay of Honduras (known as the Baymen) "to cut and export logwood and mahogany. They elected magistrates from among the wealthiest settlers, and the British government appointed a superintendent to act as the chief executive."[13] The British subsequently signed a series of treaties with the Spanish, who held the region around what became known as "British Honduras," in which the Baymen were forced to agree "not to build forts, establish any form of government, or develop plantation agriculture."[14]

A new form of slavery therefore emerged, based initially on the extraction of logwood trees and later, mahogany. The small logwood trees grew in clumps near each other, permitting men to live with their families in Belize Town on the coast. In contrast, the huge mahogany trees, which became economically more attractive to the colonialists in the 1770s, grew sparsely in the dense forests of the interior. The former crop was harvested by a Bayman and one or two slaves. The latter crop required more complex social organization that involved teams of slaves who had a range of skills related to the logging industry of the late 1700s. The mahogany camps were set up deep in the sub-tropical rainforests of British Honduras and a single white owner or overseer might remain isolated for months surrounded by a number of black slaves, many of whom were armed with guns and machetes for the purpose of clearing the bush and for providing the group with fresh game. Naturally, the authority held by any white over any black slave was diminished because he was outnumbered and because some of them were armed.

Some of the moderated attitude of the slave owners in the British Honduras may be reflected in a communication one of them sent to another. The slaves bore the brunt of the hardship of the 1760s and 1770s when logwood prices were depressed and mahogany production hadn't yet predominated. The suffering led to a succession of slave rebellions in 1765, 1768 and 1773.[15] There was another rebellion in 1820 about which one white colonial drew a surprising conclusion when he wrote that "the Negroes who had first deserted and had excited others to join them, had been treated with very unnecessary harshness by their owner, and **had certainly good grounds for complaint.**"[16]

Relative to the sugar producing islands of the Caribbean, constraint was evident among the slaves of British Honduras as well as the white masters. Despite their rebellions, slave resistance was constrained partly because the men were separated into small groups far in the forests and were away from their families for prolonged periods of time. The opportunities and the motivation for escape and rebellion were reduced by access to refuge in the forest and by the restraints imposed on slaves through separation from their families. An additional factor that obviated the need for frequent or sustained slave rebellions was the fact that it was relatively easy for slaves to escape to neighbouring Spanish territories (present day Mexico and Guatemala) and to form independent communities in the forest.[17] Therefore, the distinct social and economic characteristics within which slaves and masters operated in British Honduras served as a moderating factor for the behaviour of both groups.

Other factors helped to shape survival strategies in Belize. Because of the 1876 agreement, settlers and slaves were largely unable to establish permanent provision grounds and Belizeans were consequently dependent on imported food (which is still the case today). In contrast to plantation slaves, Belizean slaves had allowances for food, tobacco and pipes, and clothing. Extra labour would sometimes be paid for by masters in cash. Saturday labour belonged to slaves and could be purchased by masters at 3s 4d per day, or £8 13s. 4d. annually.[18]

During Christmas—their only leisure period in the year—dory or pitpan races were organized on the Belize River. Dories could be large and manned by twenty to forty paddlers. Each dory's paddlers were uniquely dressed to represent the rival mahogany extracting firms to which they were attached and both blacks and whites bet money on the races.[19]

Freedmen and slaves identified with members of their own tribes and even went so far as to group in tribes and nations and to select their own kings. Obeah, inherited West African magical practices, were outlawed on pain of death by the magistrates, but were never effectively suppressed and were even practiced by some of the whites.[20]

Families were affected by seasonal separation, but families were seldom divided by sale of members. Kin and kin networks remained fairly stable. Families were expanded by the inclusion of whites, so that a single Creole culture gradually emerged and English Creole became lingua franca in Belize.[21] Enduring families elevated the focus on family as the inner circle and basic unit of trust, but prolonged separation because of seasonal logging operations of the men threatened the conjugal bond. Power and prestige struggles based on confrontations employing the threat of force and use of verbal denigration undermined trust and promoted a more individualized and expedient use of family linkages. Males relied on individualized and expedient measures to achieve harmony within small crews of fellow-workers.

Bolland concludes that conditions in Belize Town "offered opportunities for African continuities while, at the same time, providing a context within which Creole institutions and culture were created among blacks and whites, enslaved and free."[22] For the most part, European-derived institutions (economic, political, military, legal, religious and educational) formed the core of Belizean society, although these were mixed with African ones. In 1830, the *Honduras Almanack* allowed "free blacks to organize their 'nations'" and "uphold their original systems, prejudices, superstitions, and amusements" only as far "as they can be allowed consistently with the regulations of civilized society," that is, within the limits imposed by the colonial administration. This was also true with regard to slaves.[23] By the end of the nineteenth century, the emerging Belizean cultures had been "transformed to a largely Creole community in Belize Town."[24]

The structure of the society in Belize and the consistent pressures that were exerted on slaves and on the white settlers elicited strategic responses from both sides. The relationship white settlers had with their slaves was not protected by force so much as it was on the plantations and required increased reliance on informal negotiation over formalized and enforced regulation. Over time, a Creolised value system gradually replaced distinct British and African cultural and external systems of sanctions and obligations and both settlers and slaves increasingly relied on amoral expediency to achieve results. Relative to the insular sugar plantations, there was reduced and sporadic reliance on direct confrontational measures in favour of the formation of expedient alliances or withdrawing from confrontational situations.

Belizean and Sugar Plantation Slavery Survival Strategies

White settlers on the sugar plantations of the English Antilles were less vulnerable than those who settled in the forests of the southern Yucatan behind the Gulf of Honduras. As a result, whites on the islands maintained greater colour distinctions and greater colour-based solidarity and relied mostly on external force to maintain these distinctions in their society. There was less negotiation across the insular racial divide and the level of social and geographical insularity, coupled with the intensity of oppression experienced at the hands of whites, allowed for the formation of fragile though effective alliances among Antillean slaves. This resulted in the outbreak of frequent and violent rebellions, although the intense lateral competition among slaves reduced their ability to establish enduring alliances within their community.

In British Honduras, there was greater opportunity for slaves to reduce and abbreviate the intensity of white settler violence perpetrated against them and to erode the magnitude of the racial divide. At the same time, the conditions of enslavement among the Baymen undermined attempts by the slaves to establish and sustain affective class solidarities. Instead, the promotion of opportunistic alliance-building and withdrawal from situations that elicited confrontation became logical strategies. Unlike the sugar economies, there were occasional alliances between both slaves and freed blacks and the white settlers in British Honduras. Cross-gender alliances were not threatened so much by betrayal, but they were weakened by male absence and slaves and freed blacks had better opportunities to maintain tribal alliances. Towards the end of the slave era, this relatively greater latitude made the gradual evolution of a Creolised culture that stretched across classes a possibility. Put in a different way, even though higher status was ascribed to white skin than black, in British Honduras ethnicity was not the only basis for creating opportunistic alliances for survival purposes.

What seems to be common to the survival strategy of plantation whites and slaves and the population of British Honduras was that expediency and temporary alliances became accepted survival strategies in both societies. Despite the differences that can be noted in the nature of the alliances that were formed, both these coercive economic systems required the development of refined negotiation skills.

Caribbean Nation-Building Beyond Slavery

Within the context of the struggle for freedom among Caribbean blacks, Nigel Bolland writes that "former slaves, like their masters, brought a whole complex of attitudes, values, self-images, and notions of rights and entitlements out of slavery, but the meaning of freedom, which was dialectically interconnected with the system and experience of slavery, was different for ex-slaves and ex-masters."[25] Bolland's remarks here are important for the distinct way in which slaves and masters emerged from the slavery period. That distinction would also determine the way in which they then related during the post-slavery period. Bolland presents a generalized distinction between the white and black perspectives, but that bifurcated vision may be flawed to the extent that it compares differences of perspective and behaviour across two categories of race without taking account of additional and equally important differences within each category.

These internal distinctions also matter. The slavery period established complex internal struggles and alliances both within and between members on either side of the racial gap and across the genders. To cast the whites as villains and blacks as heroes is to tell an oversimplified truth and for the purpose of understanding modern behaviours, such a simplification either makes it difficult to explain some of today's non-heroic accommodations or encourages us to ignore them. They tend to fly in the face of our inherited idealism about oppressed peoples and about the right way to do community development.

Bolland convincingly argues that the tactics in British Honduras and the English Antilles differed, but that the intent across the two regions of the Caribbean was identical: the planters and the British Government wanted to maintain planter (i.e. white) domination over labour and over the means of production, and the blacks wanted to achieve independence (after their own definition of the concept) notwithstanding the counter-pressures exerted by whites. But for our purposes as students of community development, I believe we need to define more articulated strategies than the generalized behavioural "norms" among whites and blacks only. We shall look more closely at the subtleties later in the chapter.

Nigel Bolland provides the evidence that demonstrates that emancipation did not end the nearly total control by whites over the black labour force, and that the latter group attempted to improve their quality of life. With the end of slavery,

> the locus of authority and social control passes from an individual master to the state, as personal relations of domination are transformed into a bureaucratic structure of domination.... The former masters conceived of market relations as compatible with...their own personal freedoms, including their freedom to hold and dispose of private property and to hire and fire labor power without interference. But it would be naïve to assume that former slaves shared this liberal-bourgeois concept of freedom. [26]

For the ex-slave, Bolland argues, ownership of land had significance far different than for whites, and far beyond the values of liberal-bourgeois notions. Since the slaves had been deprived of land and family, personal autonomy had to be defined in terms of the creation and maintenance of "such a network of ties and mutual obligations.... In this vision of society, the principles of mutuality, cooperation and interdependence, in contrast to social hierarchy, competition, and the dependency of subordinates, are deemed [by the ex-slave] to be the very fabric of society itself." [27]

The factor determining whether ex-slaves had been able to move beyond estate labour dependency would be the availability of land. [28] Then Bolland carries out a "comparative study of transition from slave to wage labor, in terms of varieties of labor control, as an aspect of the transformation of systems of domination." [29] The observation he makes from his comparison is important:

> It is an undeniable fact that planters were able to continue to control labor in Antigua, St. Kitts, and Barbados to a much greater extent than in Jamaica, Trinidad, and Guiana. The ascendant explanation of this fact identifies the availability of land as the crucial factor. [30]

Continuing his bifurcated comparison of European and African ideas of freedom in the Caribbean, Bolland argues that the case of British Honduras, where land was plentiful and where the Europeans also remained ascendant, suggests that other factors can be at work, and that population density alone does not determine the availability of land. Undue abstraction of concepts (e.g. labour, freedom) from their social context is not warranted.[31] He suggests that labour control must be understood by examining a range of factors including

> wage/rent systems, the advance and truck systems, contracts and taxation, sponsored and indentured immigration and restrictions on emigration, vagrancy laws, and the role and function of the magistrates, police, and prisons. In addition, the structure of the political system, with its restricted franchise and colonial administration, and the ideological role of ministers and missionaries in churches and schools should be examined.[32]

Bolland has increased the sophistication of historical analysis by increasing the number of factors we need to consider when understanding the perspective of Europeans and Africans in the Caribbean. He says that beyond the availability of land, five or six instruments were available to the handful of landowners in the former British Honduras (i.e. Belize) and used to retain the benefits of slavery to them for a hundred years after its abolition in 1836.[33] These authoritarian measures included criminalizing breaches of labour contracts extended to the former slaves and ensuring debt peonage through a pair of systems locally called "advance" and "truck." [34]

In the British Honduras, labourers were kept indebted and so, with the assistance of a stern judiciary and police force, they remained available to the lumber barons. In addition, the schools and churches canonized the values of humility and deference to one's social betters, rewarded rote learning, and punished questioning and individuality.[35]

Land, ownership of which could function as a means for improving one's class status, could legally be sold to the freed blacks in British Honduras, but access was limited: it was costly for them, tangled in red tape, and required the approval of the British Governor. Even after 1981, when the English left and Belize was independent, most of the arable and non-reserved lands were owned by foreigners and a few Belizeans who either lived in the towns or left to earn a living in the United States.[36]

Bolland comments on the pivotal role of the state in maintaining the status quo following emancipation in the Caribbean. He argues that control over land and labour were functions of the power of planters within colonial rule, and that "On issues of wage rates and rights of occupancy to houses and grounds, the ex-slaves faced not only their employer-landlords but also the power of the colonial state."[37]

Magistrates in British Guiana were empowered to stop a convicted labourer's wages, to set direct tax rates and import duties, to require licenses for porters, hucksters, and shopkeepers and poll taxes. Massive immigrant labour schemes were also proposed by plantation owners and supported by governments.[38]

Belize has always needed to supplement its workforce. Labourers have mostly come from other countries in Central America and Mexico, although there were some indentured labourers from India. Resultant ethnic and regional competition has served as a further method to divide the labourers—an advantage to those wishing to retain privileges of class.

Finally, Bolland observes that the role of race as a mechanism for denying power and rights to former slaves, and of maintaining the dominant structure needs to be understood. These aggressions were opposed by ex-slaves by "a variety of techniques of withdrawal from and resistance to the coercive system, in the form of task-work gangs, strikes, absenteeism, non-cooperation at work, and the creation of mutual aid societies, "free villages," and independent peasantries, and even emigration."[39]

All of these data help support Bolland's contribution: to understand the general opposition of Europeans and Africans in the Caribbean, we need to look at a range of factors beyond the availability of land. But to understand modern day survival strategies for the purpose of devising effective development strategies it is necessary to look beyond the general division between the races.

Survival Strategies that Emerged after Slavery

As the era of slavery drew to a close, white planters still needed to maintain dominion over a slave population that formed the majority in most of the Caribbean. On the whole, their survival needs led them to adopt more conservative social and politico-economic structures that help to explain the legislative, religious, educational and racist means that were used to perpetuate the plantation system. But this doesn't explain the behaviours that seem to contradict this post-slavery conservatism, such as métiage (that is the costly and counter-productive system of having larger—usually white—landowners in the Lesser Antilles grind the cane of small—occasionally black—landowners), incremental pay raises to black plantation labourers, or minor legislative adjustments that ameliorated labour conditions. More informal contradictory behaviours included participation in the christening of the children of ex-slaves, charitable donations to impoverished labourers, and participation by whites in Obeah practices. These anomalies must be seen either as affective alliances without any economic motivation—indeed, which fly in the face of economic motivation—or as strategic alliances to bolster the other coercive measures employed. But either way, they represent behaviours that cut across the division of Europeans and Africans in the Caribbean and that open members of either group up to a range of strategies that may advance personal opportunities at the expense of race or class solidarity.

In this same period, freed blacks were very much in the minority and had only a tenuous hold on freedom. They necessarily inclined toward the standards, manners and beliefs of the whites (on whom their continued freedom depended) and distanced themselves from the slaves' values and behaviours that represented everything they had escaped. This strategy on the part of freed blacks surely did not sit well with the slaves who were ambitious to achieve their own betterment and who were frequently forced into competition among themselves. However, freed blacks were also related through one parent—frequently mothers—to ex-slave siblings and relatives. In many instances, friendly relations would have been retained across the gap—especially since advantages beyond affection (e.g. free or low-cost labour, social access to freed blacks and whites with jobs) could be obtained by nurturing such affiliations.

After emancipation, the situation for ex-slaves would have remained more complex than for either the whites or the freed blacks. There would have been some attraction to two contradictory behavioural strategies. On the one hand, there was a need to hold onto whatever values and practices were not taken from them by the white planters and, as a way of improving their situation, to maintain a rebellious posture whenever possible towards whites who coerced behaviour and who had previously claimed ownership of slaves and freed blacks.

At the same time, whites typified independence and power and the behaviour of slaves was professed (by whites) to represent something less than human. Moreover, operating as they did within the confines of slavery, ex-slaves often competed amongst themselves for preferential places. This certainly eroded trust and increased antipathy among ex-slaves, so there must have been some pressure among these people to nurture the very values and behaviours of whites, as they seemed to symbolize freedom from the miseries of peer group conflict.

As the whites continued their struggle to maintain dominance over ex-slaves, a host of contradictory pressures must therefore have beset ex-slaves.

Such pressures would have included a need to fight whites and freed blacks for control over their own labour, the need to form solidarities with other similarly coerced ex-slaves and to compete with ex-slaves for coveted advantages. They also needed to form alliances with strategic whites and freed blacks, distance themselves from competitors, and imitate legitimized (i.e. white) lifestyles.

The plight of ex-slaves was yet more complicated. In addition to the contradictory pressures to rebel and to ally with members of all three groups, there must have been a consistent need to create original behaviours that represented their ideals of freedom and family solidarity.[40] Bolland observes that "the former slaves recognized, as surely as did their former masters, that the struggle for political power was a collective struggle and that a person's or family's security and freedom depended very largely on the outcome of this struggle."[41]

But if this recognition had been impressed among ex-slaves in terms so black and white, they could have simply accomplished their objective by means of a single, protracted labour strike by a union of ex-slaves that would almost certainly have broken the power of post-slavery planters and their governments. Ex-slaves could then have successfully gained the labour advantages, the land and access to credit, the educational opportunities and the family security which they so dearly sought.

That such simple victories were not achieved suggests that the brutalities of slavery and the subsequent authoritarian colonial measures that held sway after emancipation left the bulk of the Caribbean population atomized (i.e. not united as a class) and perpetuated dependent relationships for income. The ability of the ex-slaves to undertake effective measures of rebellion and self-reliance were therefore somewhat limited and their revolutionary activities were undermined by their individualistic ones.

Bolland himself admits that reality for ex-slaves was complicated and sufficient to frustrate class action:

> The features of a plantation system (which include monocrop production for export, strong monopolistic tendencies, a rigid system of social stratification, which includes a high correlation between racial and class hierarchies, and a weak community structure) conspire to ensure that estate labor will be casual and seasonal, poorly paid, closely supervised, socially degraded, and hard to organize.[42]

Expressed in reversed terms, the reliance among ex-slaves on individualized strategies of deference and accommodation to the status quo served to undermine the class struggle for social change. However, such strategies were employed because they were important and frequently critical survival measures.[43] They were necessarily employed more frequently than the occasional examples of united effort to achieve class solidarity because they were almost constantly called for. They represent another important missing screw—something that needs to be confronted and understood in our contemporary efforts to do developmental work. These strategies are as important as the heroic acts: heroic acts explain the intermittent struggle for justice through equity; the actions of the ex-slaves represent the continual struggle for daily survival.

The principal behavioural strategy employed during the period of slavery—that of maximizing individual gains and minimizing losses—retained equal utility in the post-slavery period, both in the English sugar Antilles and in British Honduras where hardwoods were exported. It worked in both settings because the ex-slaves had a need to ally at one moment with other ex-slaves, and at another, to ally against them with family members, with whites or with freed blacks, to the detriment of other ex-slaves and their class-based interests.

This is not to argue that class-based interests weren't of undying and critical importance. Bolland has provided us with convincing data to the contrary. Neither is it an argument to say that the oppression of planters and their governments were unimportant factors for the disorganization of ex-slave attempts to correct the inequalities or to withdraw from them. Bolland's archival work should also provide adequate evidence of the unrelenting and negative pressures exerted by planters and governments, and of their general effectiveness. The very recognition of their effectiveness demonstrates that class-based initiatives by the ex-slaves were not implacable, were sporadic and were generally unsuccessful. Again Bolland admits that, "these market forces and colonial laws of the British Caribbean in the mid-nineteenth century helped to perpetuate the poverty and powerlessness of the ex-slaves and their descendants, who were denied the civil rights of liberal society for over a century."[44] There is also recognition by most students of this period that the alternative strategy to rebellion (or withdrawal) by the ex-slaves was accommodation.

The accommodation measures had to be non-rebellious in nature and had to assure the continued survival of the ex-slaves—as families if at all possible, or as individuals if the situation deteriorated to that extent. Furthermore, in the absence of benefits flowing to united peer-groups of ex-slaves, the accommodation strategies had to be worked in every conceivable direction. This required alliances wherever an opportunity could be detected, notwithstanding the position held by the target of assistance in class terms. The cost of this kind of transient alliance-making may have contributed to the powerlessness mentioned by Bolland; it surely contributed to the erosion of class solidarity among ex-slaves and to their fragmentation. But it just as surely contributed positively to the enduring presence of the ex-slaves and their descendants.

The Rise of Fragmented Nationalism Throughout the English-Speaking Caribbean

Bolland emphasizes the defensive struggles that slaves engaged in to gain a freedom after their own definition of the concept (i.e. control over one's labour, ownership of land and hence, stability of one's family). In contrast, Franklin W. Knight observes that nationalism and class consciousness were slow to appear in the English-speaking Caribbean and black populations showed enthusiasm for education and for co-operative associations, whether religious or agricultural in origin between the 1840s and 1950s.[45] However, the dearth of economic and popular support made it impossible for workingmen's associations to survive and so, "although Marcus Garvey enjoyed spectacular popularity throughout the region, his attempt to mobilize the Jamaican masses into a political party in the 1930' was far less successful than his efforts in the United States."[46] These failures may be due to the antagonistic behaviours of whites, but to a fair measure, they should also be attributed to the complex, dynamic and individualizing tensions within the black community and across the genders that emerged from the slavery period along with the shared determination to gain freedom.

Nevertheless, Knight remarks, nationalism and class consciousness grew with the return of Caribbean soldiers following World War II as the returning soldiers agitated for change.[47] Similarly, a number of Caribbean ex-patriots gathered political experience during the Harlem Renaissance in the United States, gaining perspective about the role of the Caribbean in world affairs. The Caribbean press and Caribbean writers too began to reject European romanticism in favour of examination of the Caribbean and its classes.[48]

Labour riots occurred in the Caribbean between 1919 and 1929. That was followed by the diminution of the export economy with wages almost disappearing and foreign labour markets (US, Panama Canal) closing to black labourers. By the late 1930s, labour unions appeared in Jamaica, Trinidad, Barbados and British Honduras. Political parties were spawned by the unions,[49] including party creation in British Honduras and the pressure for independence spearheaded by George Price.

Shoman says Belize is an economic satellite of the industrialized countries, feeding them what raw products it has (i.e. hardwoods, and more recently, shellfish, citrus, sugar, bananas and tourism), and purchasing manufactured goods from them. Those inheriting the reins of government from the British were not encouraged to make changes in the authoritarian system because the foreign industrialists benefited from having things remain essentially as they were. The Belizean leadership that assumed power from the colonials needed to maintain socio-economic disequilibrium.[50] There were also advantages for the Belizean import-export bourgeoisie if class relations remained unchanged and there were concomitant privileges and opportunities for the politicians and managers who replaced the British and who accommodated themselves to the local moneyed class. Disadvantaged Belizeans, by virtue of their supplications to the politicians for assistance and special favours, helped to ensure the continuation of the economic and power systems.

Shoman describes other events that helped shape the modern two-party clientelistic system, including the emergence of the labour movement and political parties and the exacerbation of ethnic and regional differences to undermine class-based interests and to elevate loyalty to either of the two parties above everything meaningful. Shoman claims that the pointless competition between the two major parties, together with the small size of the population, reduces all debates to a trivial competition among potential leaders based on scandal and defamation of character.[51]

Gordon K. Lewis includes two chapters on "The Federal Venture" in *The Growth of the Modern West Indies* [52] —that is, on efforts to create a federation of the many British Caribbean territories that currently exist in what Franklin Knight calls "fragmented nationalism" in the title of his book.[53] Efforts to devise a confederation of the Caribbean appear as early as 1860 and reappeared through 1947.[54]

Knight observes that the English Antilles admired the Cuban model as the "centrifugal winds of political decolonialization" swept through the world because it was viable and in many ways applicable to their condition. However, the British colonies in the Caribbean did not control the political apparatus and "to secure the nation, it was first necessary to constitute the state."[55] Knight argues that since "the middle of the nineteenth century...British officials were looking for some way to reduce the mounting administrative costs and embarrassment of small colonies which seemed economically unviable."[56] Attempts to achieve incorporation with Canada failed. And then the federation itself lasted only four years (1959–1962). British Guiana and British Honduras remained on the sidelines. The larger powers in this confederation of ten former British colonies included Jamaica, Trinidad and Tobago, and Barbados. When, in a referendum, Jamaica voted itself out of the federation:

> Prime Minister Eric Williams of Trinidad had made a laconic prophesy of axiomatic political astuteness: "One from ten leaves nothing," meaning that the defection of any of the ten member states would destroy the federal idea. The West Indian Federation collapsed in 1962.[57]

Reasons cited by sympathetic and hostile analysts for the failure of the federation are listed by Knight and include insular political squabbling among the politicians, the weakness of the constitutional structure, the great distance between the islands, the inability of West Indians to rule themselves, and the alien imposition of the political form itself.[58]

Knight's study focuses on the efforts of Jamaica and Trinidad to develop a diversified industrial base because of bauxite and petroleum deposits and efforts to protect their new industries, and he describes the victory of pragmatism over idealism in the following terms:

> In short their insular economic interests took precedence over their sense of common identity...both islands [insisting] on measures that would limit the power of the federal government to impose taxation on their incipient industries...[and efforts by Trinidad to restrict] the free flow of citizens of the federation from one region of limited opportunities to another of less restricted opportunities.[59]

He then offers an observation about post-colonial nations that sounds very like the observations I have been making regarding the individualized survival strategies of Caribbean peoples during and after colonialism:

> So the very fears which had caused British Honduras and British Guiana to sit on the sidelines led to the creation of a weak federal center where **each unit tried to yield as little power and autonomy as it could in order to retain as much as was possible.**[60]

Knight includes Gordon K. Lewis' analysis of the failure, saying that:

A federation, therefore, "was in itself a grossly misconceived structure to impose upon West Indian society" because "it assumed the almost permanent divisibility of the society".... The assumption should have been that the regions comprised one unit, and a political prescription should have been made for a unified state. Such an assumption, however, could only have been generated by a people with more *conciencia de sí* than was evident in the British West Indies between 1944 and 1962.[61]

I endorse Knight's remark because I think the need for individuals to employ a strategy of heuristic and expedient alliances precluded the emergence of more nation-based *conciencia de sí*, and continues to impede the emergence of that kind of strong nationalism.

Bolland presents the evolution of a complicated series of events in British Honduras that followed the decline of the timber trade in the 1850s and 1860s and that included a brief boom in chicle exportation, which benefited Maya, Mestizo and Garifuna populations, the impoverishment, unemployment and social dislocation of urban-based Creoles (which was worsened by the Great Depression and falling sugar prices and a catastrophic hurricane that destroyed Belize City in 1931). Demonstrations and strikes followed and unions were formed in the mid-1930s and 1940s.[62]

Consistent with an argument that says Belizeans, like other Caribbean populations, have found it valuable to engage in heuristic and expedient relationships with others, Bolland says that "many Belizeans not only practice or participate in more than one cultural tradition but are also coming to share an overarching national identity as they interact with people of different ethnic groups.... Political affiliation constitutes an identity that often cross-cuts rather than reinforces ethnic identity because party politics is not organized on ethnic lines."[63] He concludes that "The Belizean independence movement emerged initially, therefore, as a coalition between a broadly based trade union and a group of educated middle-class Catholics"[64] and then adds that true to the pattern of short-term, pragmatic and shifting alliance-making a subsequent "series of rivalries and splits between the politicians badly divided and weakened the labour movement with the result that constitutional rather than labour issues came to predominate in Belizean politics."[65]

In Belize, there is an idealistic African-consciousness movement among Belizean Creoles that traces its roots back to a 1919 protest by returned ex-servicemen. They protested racial discrimination and, under the leadership of Samuel A. Haynes, founded the Universal Negro Improvement Association

(UNIA). There was also the existence of the Garvey-inspired Black Cross Nurses Association (1920–1970), the black Power-inspired movement of UBAD founded by Evan X Hyde in the 1960s (who is still active through the *Amandala* newspaper), and KREM radio and TV stations. There are also cultural revivalist efforts by the National Garifuna Council and among the Yucateca, Mopan and Kechi Mayas by the Toledo Maya Cultural Center which may be considered equally idealistic.[66] Nevertheless, Bolland concludes of Belize that

> with the decolonization process since the 1950s no single cultural section has taken the hegemonic place of the British, though the Creole and Mestizo groups may each fear that the other will do so. Ethnic groups in Belize do not organize or interact qua groups in the political system, nor are the political parties mobilized or oriented primarily on an ethnic basis.[67]

This phenomenon, I suggest, is assisted significantly by the alliance-building and rivalry from competing factions and may, in fact, principally account for the pattern of sustained class stasis and suspended class struggle in which the Have-nots fail to gain traction or move towards parity with the Haves, notwithstanding their ability to benefit as individuals from short-term favours granted by those who control access to resources. The internal competition is certainly sustained by the external pressures, but they are the mechanism of dynamic stasis.

Bolland dedicates the latter half of the same essay to a study of the ethnic politicization of Guyana, the former British Guiana. We need not enter into an examination of many of the details, but Bolland's conclusion is valuable for our purposes. The deliberate political moves by the British government and colonials in Guiana's history, essentially to protect the safety of whites there, account for the emergence of a very politically racialised environment. In that setting, intra-ethnic alliances were called for, exactly in contrast to the cross-boundary alliances required by the population of British Honduras. In a real sense, however, the end result is the same: in any of these locations—Belize, the former British Antilles or Guyana—populations emerging from slavery and colonialism find themselves needing to negotiate the continual creation of opportunistic alliances and the dissolution of other alliances for the purpose of maintaining status and income, or of advancing their position; in other words, for the purpose of survival. In Belize, alliances are often made across the divides of race and gender; in the Antilles, race is more of a barrier; in Guyana, race is a major factor in establishing alliances. But in all cases, the individualized and frantic process of making and breaking fragile alliances either takes the place of or hampers the advancement of class struggle and the result is dynamic class stasis throughout the region.

Belize as Nation State: Independence vs. Individualism

In the 1947 elections for Belize Town Council (the major forum for debating national issues), representatives from the St. John's College alumni group won four seats. These were an educated elite from Belize's leading Catholic school, all of whom had studied abroad and who rejected colonial rule. Additionally, Philip Goldson, a like-minded politician turned journalist, was assailing colonialism from the newspaper, The Belize Billboard.[68] In 1950 pro-British politicians were stoned and there were massive demonstrations (in one instance 10,000 people in a nation of only 90,000) such as the one on 12 February at Government House to protest a visit of Princess Alice, and one at Battlefield Park where the police used tear gas on the crowd. Princess Alice's visit was cancelled.[69]

Assad Shoman quotes an article in The Belize Billboard by Leigh Richardson, who was then studying in London:

> Mental slaves are slaves in the most profitable way, doing their master's bidding without hope of reward and without desire for flight and insurrection. This is the form of slavery that Britain maintains in her colonies, subjecting them to patient waiting for constitutional progress at her leisure and encouraging the inevitable boot-lickers among their inhabitants to foster among their fellow citizens a distinct feeling of inferiority and utter dependence on Britain, both of which elements are then combined and presented in a compound called loyalty to Britain.
>
> To free ourselves from colonial status we must have national unity against mental enslavement and to achieve that national unity we need a national party....[70]

While Richardson identifies the British as the impediment to independence, he also identifies "inevitable boot-lickers among [Belize's] inhabitants" as the cause of low self-esteem and dependence on Britain among the majority.[71] The cure, he argues, is national unity, which can be gained through the creation of a national party. Richardson fails to examine the apparent contradiction of relying on a national leadership to replace the British as a way of moving beyond issues of self-esteem and strategies of dependence. After all, expedient dependence on those with access to desired opportunities was already the prevailing general strategy employed by Belizeans. This piece of patriotic idealism from Richardson was doomed from the start. Short term unity had proved effective in the past and was proving to be so again. But becoming and remaining united simply wasn't the Belizean way. Better personal opportunities would almost surely pull apart alliances.

The People's United Party (PUP) was formed on 29 September 1950 with John Smith as the leader, Leigh Richardson as chairman, George Price as secretary and Philip Goldson as the assistant secretary, but this alliance did not last long.[72] In 1948, the Governor had appointed members to the Blood Commission. Shoman writes that their 1951 report represented a "perfect mimicry of the colonial policy of gradual tutelage" when it said that democracy could be best protected by avoiding any "premature extension of political responsibility" in Belize, a multi-ethnic country with 42 per cent of the population being "Amerindians" and 22 per cent Caribs (i.e. Garifuna people). The Commission, representing the professional Creole middle class, was "more concerned with protecting its own class privileges than with developing a nationalist movement."[73]

The PUP attacked the report, called for immediate elections and refused to refer to the colony as "British Honduras," using the name Belize from then until official change was sanctioned in 1973.[74] But almost immediately, the PUP unity began to reveal the fissures in its make-up. The Belize City Council, dominated by the PUP, was dissolved in July 1951 by the Governor for refusing to fly the British flag or display a portrait of the King. Before September, the PUP Leader, John Smith, resigned when the PUP refused to agree to fly the British flag at public meetings. The National Party opposition accused it of harbouring pro-Guatemalan sentiments. Shoman suggests that the opposition party, consisting of pro-Creole "'respectable' allies" had been cleverly co-opted by the colonial government.[75]

The British Honduras Federation of Women (BHFW) was a charitable organization of middle class Creole women that targeted working class women and also had some connections to the National Party.[76] They were approached by the Citrus Company to recruit women workers and they published an advertisement,

> inviting 150 women to work in the citrus canning industry in Stann Creek at a minimum daily wage of $2.00 with quarters and sick benefits.... [The General Workers' Union (GWU), with the same leadership as the PUP party] already had unionized that factory, however, and since the women targeted were in fact members of the GWU, it was a clear attempt to undermine the authority of the Union.... At the same time, however, the GWU agreement discriminated

against women, their pay being $1.80 per day as against $2.25 for men. [77]

When the government agreed to allow talks, all employers except the Belize Estates and Produce Company (BEC) agreed to negotiate. The GWU and much of the general population attempted to hold out against them, but were eventually forced to capitulate. Only 70 of the 268 men laid off were rehired, but the GWU membership grew from 1,000 to 8,200. [78]

The GWU/PUP's militant wing organized a "domestics wage drive"[79] calling for only $5.00 a week. The drive did not succeed, and Anne MacPherson ascribes this to a large female unemployed pool and to PUP/GWU preoccupation with impending general elections: [80]

> [T]here was no significant support from either party or union men. Like the leaders, they very likely saw women in the role of supporters and may not have considered female wages worth their time, energy or resources. [81]

Here again we witness expedient alliances being organized across solidarities of nationality (National Party and the British), gender (BHWF women and National Party men), and class (BHWF women and working class women). Also, within the nation of colonized Belizeans, factions can be seen to be competing (National Party and BHWF women empire loyalists versus independence-minded members of the People's United Party and General Workers' Union). And orchestrating this confusion, the ever pragmatic British forestalled independence by offering incentives that encouraged an ever diminishing portion of the population to work against the majority.

The general elections of 1954 were overwhelmingly won by the PUP/GWU and an uneasy truce existed for the next seven years between them and the colonial government. Richardson and Goldson sought co-operation with the colonial government; Price did not. The former promoted association with the proposed West Indies Federation; the latter, and most of the Belizean population, refused. At the September 1956 annual PUP convention, Richardson, Goldson and ten other officials resigned. Price held the support of the party rank and file. Price was elected party leader and remained so for 40 years. [82]

As a result, the GWU also suffered a split and the PUP formed a rival Christian Democratic Union. GWU membership fell from over 10,000 in 1954 to 700 in 1956. Shoman says "the trade union movement never recovered sufficiently from partisan manipulation to achieve anything like the tremendous impact it had in political developments in the early 1950s."[83] It is worth observing that for the trade union movement to have lost its power, there needed to have been individual maximization—what Shoman calls "partisan manipulation." People had decided in favour of personal opportunities over group benefits.

At meetings with the colonial government in London, the British accused Price of selling out to the Guatemalans (who claimed all of Belize as one of their provinces) and dismissed him from the Executive Council. Local PUP opponents exploited the charge, dividing the people.[84] In 1958, they charged Price with sedition for allegedly making anti-royalist remarks. A jury acquitted him and his popularity soared. Under Price's leadership, the PUP won their most solid victory of the next four victories, defeating a merged National Party and the Honduras Independence Party (led by Goldson and Richardson). Goldson became leader of the opposition party, the merged National Independence Party (NIP). Assad Shoman's summation of George Price's stature is that "there is no doubt that of the early PUP leaders, all from Belize City, Price was the one who was most committed to a truly national vision, to breaking the monopoly of power that resided in Belize City and to bringing the people of the out-districts into national politics."[85]

With the victory and a new constitutional system and greater powers for the elected leaders, Price, "the one who was most committed to a truly national vision," made a breathtaking compromise with his lifelong foes, the British colonial government. Price accepted "step-by-step constitutional decolonialization." The new ministerial system was dominated by the Creole middle-class (with the needed administrative and technical skills) whom he had to win over. He also needed time to gain the approbation of the public.

In 1961 Hurricane Hattie caused severe economic damage and utter destruction of Belize City and Dangriga to the south.[86] The British responded with significant aid for reconstruction and for the construction of a new capital inland:

> Price's dream of building a new capital in the middle of the country had to do with this political strategy; he wanted to look symbolically in toward the country, to bring the administration closer to the people and to break with the past of Belize City as a refuge for pirates, colonial administrators and bootleggers. The fact that the British agreed to make this dream a reality no doubt ameliorated Price's earlier hostility to them. This was also the time that the British had reopened negotiations with Guatemala, and Belizean representatives were being taken along. All this meant that Price had to work very closely with the British, and the British embrace tightened.[87]

There can be little doubt that the Belizeans, like the quarry of any coercive colonial regime, had learned the pragmatic survival games as well as their oppressors. It is clear that the political leadership was making and breaking alliances, fighting and joining alliances, and changing immediate priorities to gain longer term objectives. Equally in Belize we can see factions of class, ethnicity and gender making use of exactly the same behaviours. This is neither the behaviour of buffoons nor of heroes, though Belizeans have been capable of adopting such roles if it suited their purpose ("play fool to catch wise," as they say). Clearly this is the adaptive behaviour of survivors.

Shoman quotes "the Caribbean anti-colonial activist and writer," Frantz Fanon, who makes the pragmatic claim that:

> in the thick of fighting more than a few militants asked the leaders to formulate a dogma, to set out their objectives and to draw up a program. But under the pretext of safeguarding national unity the leaders categorically refused to undertake such a task. The only worthwhile dogma, it was repeatedly stated, was the union of the nation against colonialism.[88]

Shoman had observed that because most Belizeans were too poor to maintain national unity following colonialism, and were deeply divided also on the bases of gender, ethnicity, religion and class differences, "the PUP's [postcolonial] answer was to bring in more foreign investment."[89] The PUP was adapting to survive. Then he adds this observation:

> With its leaders divided and confused, it could not be expected to build up a cadre of conscious, revolutionary militants, nor did it seek to do so. It relied instead on the vain hope and a mere changing of the guard, from British to Belizean rulers, would provide the distributive justice it proclaimed as "its most sacred political and industrial principle". People were made to believe that self-government would bring real social and economic change benefiting the majorities.
>
> When this did not occur, it inevitably led to disenchantment and bitterness.[90]

The leading politicians had shown themselves capable of making any alliance, and of adopting any ideology (save that of putting themselves beneath their peers). In like manner, the Belizean population had proven themselves equally capable of supporting an independence movement which appeared capable of winning and capable of obtaining distributive justice for them as a class. They also showed themselves capable of abandoning the leadership they followed and then attaching themselves to it once again, depending on the waning and waxing fortunes of that leadership and of their chances of benefiting as individuals.

I suggest that this history reveals two organizing principles at work: First, class idealism (whether based on racism, classism or gender exclusion) is a force that unites. The second force—the more pragmatic and immediate interests of the inner circle, of family, even of self—is ready to deviate from class-based solidarities where these do not appear to be functional, and equally capable of assuming them when convenient. Only the blindness imposed by idealism could prevent one from recognizing the existence and value of the second operating principle.

When the "disenchantment and bitterness" of being abandoned by its leadership is great enough, other pragmatic solidarities will be established, because of necessity. If the resultant atomization of class, of physical security, of the level of personal trust is the undesired but necessary by-product, than this is the price that will be paid. One can lament the dearth of idealism, or castigate post-colonials for their lack of it. Like anybody, the post-colonial population is quick to take the moral high ground when attacking their opposition—even if they are working their own pragmatic strategies when doing so.

But moralizing advice, it would appear from our examination of Belizean history, is the last alternative that a political party in Belize, or the population of Belize would adopt. For them, survival has seldom been achieved through idealistic solidarity but rather through heuristic opportunism, through greed. Though no party would admit it, nor hardly any Belizean, the people of Belize have found a way to endure.

Increased Global Dependencies in The Post-Independence Era: Erosion of State—Growth of Crime & Violence

Between 1962 and 2003 a number of proposals to resolve the Guatemalan claim on Belize have been attempted and have failed. In 1991, Jorge Serrano, the democratically elected President of Guatemala, recognized the independent state of Belize and established diplomatic relations.[91] However, boundaries have not yet been fixed. Shoman argues that "such independence as was gained in 1981 [from Britain] has been and continues to be eroded, not by Guatemala [i.e. the territorial differendum], but by other powerful governments and international organizations such as the International Monetary Fund (IMF) and the

World Bank, as well as by multilateral corporations and foreign investors."[92] Among these losses of sovereignty Shoman includes:

• Government economic policy [conformation] to the dictates of the IMF and USAID [in the 1970s]: a reliance on largely unregulated market forces, privatization, trade liberalization, the encouragement of foreign investment and export-led growth;[93]

• an increasing reliance since 1985 on tourism that "is dominated by foreigners, and does little to stimulate the productive economy, since most of its inputs are imported. Tourism is also notoriously vulnerable to recessions in the USA and Europe";[94]

• The privatization, since the mid-1980s, of banana plantations and much of the patrimony (including Belize Telecommunications Ltd. [BTL]; the Belize Electricity Ltd. [BEL]; and the Port Authority). Other holdings slated for privatization include the Airport Authority, the Belize Marketing Board and minority holdings in Belize Sugar Industries and government-owned land.[95]

Shoman observes that "the effect of privatization so far has been to remove assets from government into the controlling hands of a very few investors; lack of local capital willing to invest also means that control of privatized industries shifts to foreign investors."[96] The "controlling hands" have included Belizean entrepreneurs and elected Belizean officials who found opportunities to benefit individually at the expense of the national interest.

Furthermore, he says, "the decision has been taken to eliminate all [import substitution sectors—industrial goods and agricultural food production protected by high import tariffs and quantitative import restrictions]" and predicts that the resulting downward economic spiral will increase unemployment.[97]

As government's revenue base has shrunk, a 15 per cent value-added tax (VAT) was introduced on selected items in 1996 "to recoup the revenues lost through the scheduled reductions in customs duties and the elimination of revenue replacement and stamp duties."[98] With a change in government in 1998, the 15 per cent VAT was replaced with an 8 per cent sales tax, and the number of items taxed greatly broadened, and broadened again in 2004.

Shoman correctly observes that the centre of power has moved upward from the slave owners to the state, and thence, to the level of global capitalism. In this process, especially during the growth of the globalized economy, Belize as a nation has lost investment opportunities of potential benefit to its people as a result of the private deals made in benefit of a few insiders in government and the private sector, and as a result of the dictates of foreign economies, the World Bank and the IMF as globalization proceeds.

Shoman laments this "shrinking role of the State"[90] as though peoples of the Caribbean were somehow in better hands when the slave owners ruled, or the colonial governments, or when the post-colonial leaders scrapped for power and the international economy had less impact on the local ones. Shoman laments the erosion of the "former role [of the police functions of the State] of protecting the poor and providing comprehensive social services"[100] apparently forgetting that the State's police functions had always been skewed in Belize towards controlling the poor and allowing the rich, whom it protected, to benefit. Shoman looks to government for leadership and for defence of the exploited poor. In Belize's history, government has played that role poorly and some other strategy may be necessary.

Where Shoman is doubtless right is where he observes that organized rebellious actions taken against slave masters, colonial rulers and post-independence politicians of the past are nothing compared to those that would have to be taken to defeat the forces of global capitalism. The assumption made, of course, is that rebellion is the appropriate strategy. Shoman accurately states that:

> When governments cannot protect the people, they have to seek alternative means of survival. One of the symptoms of the failure of the economy to satisfy the needs of the population has been the growth of what is called "the informal economy"—activities that take place outside the pale of governmental regulation or supervision.[101]

The most notorious of these activities is the illegal drug trade...[in] cocaine and crack.... Although the major beneficiaries of this trade are a few foreign buyers and their local agents, money from the trade circulates in the economy and reaches a number of people.[102]

There is broad belief in Belize, and some anecdotal confirmation by community workers, that "money from the trade circulates in the economy" because there is a lively business in drug sales locally involving those who obtain drugs from the local agents, deliver quantities to gangs in tough neighbourhoods who in turn hustle and sell drugs to the local population and to tourists; that there is a concomitant need for guns so that local hustlers can protect turf from other gang members; that some members of the police force engage in drug and gun sales; that larger drug dealers purchase police and political protection; and that some campaigning politicians use individual police officers to pay gang members for peace or disturbances according to their needs.

If such accusations are true, then, in moral terms, some members of the communities of business people, the politicians, police and gang members in low income neighbourhoods are tied into "unholy" alliances that introduce increasing levels of crime and violence to the people of Belize. But an important point here is that throughout its history, the various governments of Belize have never been able to protect the interests and needs of the Belizean people. What we now call the "informal economy," the "activities that take place outside the pale of governmental regulation or supervision," have always existed side-by-side with the historical class struggles which Bolland, Shoman, and many other students of capitalist history have taken pains to lionize.

I think that the authors cited above are correct when they argue that the action of forces and people external to the Belizean population were responsible for the chaos and poverty that is now experienced by so many in this country, and for the enormous benefits accruing to so few. They have acknowledged in passing the necessary "accommodations" of those cornered by the actions of more powerful groups and individuals. Examples of such accommodations would have to include acts of disloyalty by individual slaves to the class of slaves as a way of obtaining personal advantages from the slave master—actions which have had the effect of undermining the class struggle itself. In moral terms this suggests that we should laud the rebels and damn the majority of slaves bent on survival through "accommodations." The complication here is that depending on the circumstances the very slaves who sometimes engaged in class-based rebellion, more often made pragmatic and more personal accommodation to their masters and to the institution of slavery. The accommodations have value as great as the heroic behaviours, perhaps even greater value in that they preserved lives.

The same writers have generally neglected to explain that there was also need for the more powerful groups to make "accommodations" on the grander stage where they competed. An example would be the need for white planters to convert to plantation slavery when the Navigation Laws were passed and it became clear that land farmed without slaves could not be long retained against other planters converting to slave labour. Because the bind forcing the planters to engage in slave labour is not mentioned, one is given the sense that blame

85

should only be assigned to those whose immoral and cruel actions resulted in injustices perpetrated upon the slaves, that is, that we should sympathize with the slaves but not with the land owners.

The negative social consequences resulting from the "accommodations" made by many of the slaves are seldom described. The historians seem to be exclaiming on behalf of the poet on the bathroom floor: "It wasn't me!" and then refusing to make similar excuses for the rich fellow with the same graffiti on the side of his boat.

It is the need to take sides and to blame to which I take exception because it takes us away from understanding accommodations. Among community development activists, this traditional response to oppression has been adopted: one is expected to blame the rich first, and then to work on target populations to abandon their apparently futile and self-interested behaviours in favour of more idealistic, class-based alternatives intended to bring down the wicked.

Close inspection of the interaction between individuals will show why there may be greater utility accruing to community developers who choose to analyze self-interested local behaviours with a view to engaging with them productively. Perhaps development at the level of collective action should be more like Kung Fu than Boxing. In the latter sport, opponents attack each other directly and the tougher boxer wins. In Kung Fu, each opponent turns the very force of the enemy against that enemy. In Kung Fu, the smarter opponent wins.

Clientelism Versus Moral Community Development

THE DISCUSSION OF THE historical context of the Caribbean and in particular Belize showed why it was logical—no, necessary—for its inhabitants to develop highly adaptive responses to a series of very unreliable environments throughout the era of slavery, as well as during colonialism and the modern era. Conditions were simply too unreliable to permit stubborn adherence to the tried and true. For the slaves, power was in the hands of the colonial masters. For the colonial masters, power was dependent upon the support of England. Over the decades and centuries, power moved from the hands of the masters and the Empire to the level of global capitalism.

In the old spaghetti westerns the villain shot bullets at the feet of the hero. The hero—logically—danced. The culture of people subjected to the political and economic whims of colonial history and its ensuing events has become as lithe as the dance of the cowboy. At times, the culture evoked acts of friendship and solidarity; at others it necessitated acts of betrayal and re-alliance with former foes. Slaves seldom cried like heroes for "Liberty or death!" because you could bet the choice would fall on death. When the situation called for it, the slaves danced in tune. Yet when united rebellion was possible, they seized upon that heroic opportunity just as readily as they chose to perform acts that protected family at the cost of class or to undertake more desperate acts that only protected the individual. It is impossible to reduce the cultural core of the oppressed slaves to valiant notions of constancy, loyalty or dogged stubbornness. Instead, the circumstances of history necessarily evoked a cultural centre that was brilliantly flexible and pragmatic. In modern times, the former slaves have retained the qualities of flexibility and pragmatism in order to survive.

To expose people's survival strategies is like playing with fire because it reveals the very deepest level of a population's culture, the very root of their being. Some writers describe culture as a complex thing made up of various layers. One such writer, Edgar Schein, suggests that culture can be seen through a number of layers. The top layer consists of the "cultural artefacts" (things made or produced by a people such as their pottery, mode of music, dance, religion, daily gestures and modes of interaction).[1] Underneath this layer we find a second layer that can be thought of as the layer of espoused values and ideologies. These values and ideologies may not correspond exactly with observable artefacts, but can allow practitioners to suggest why certain things are done the way they are. But to get to the core of culture, Schein suggests, we have to go down one more layer. This third layer contains the shared, tacit assumptions about how things are in the world and how they should be. This layer includes language and other methods of communication such as body language. Schein suggests that core assumptions are born out of a shared history of experience and that they are taken for granted by members of that culture. The core assumptions operate outside of awareness and are a defining property that allows for differentiation between groups. It is often awkward to talk about these basic assumptions and any discussion will generate a defensive posture, but ultimately, the core values are self-reinforcing (our successes prove their worth).

And yet, to create a community development strategy that can become more effective than those employed by the establishmentarian and anti-establishmentarian developers, I think that we have to expose these survival strategies and find out more about the culture that drives them. An orientation that is so integral to the being of populations within clientelism is not easily rejected. Perhaps for that very reason, when altruists (including community developers) tell people who have learned tried and trusted methods of survival to sacrifice their best chances for the sake of others in the face of conditions that call for self-interested opportunism, they are consistently ignored. This is because the altruists fail to respond to the population in a way that is relevant to the way they see the world. If we want to offer appropriate (i.e. attractive and effective) opportunities, we first have to understand how the population perceives the world by observing their interactions.

One of the most effective ways I know of to present some of the interactions I have come across is to present them as anecdotes. These anecdotes will help us to create behavioural categories that occur locally in Belize and that are not too different from what one might observe elsewhere in the Caribbean. It is easy to see that these behaviours are continuations or variants of the aggressive and defensive actions elicited by historical pressures.

But before we can look at the anecdotes in more detail, let me recap some of the characteristics of these behaviours we are about to witness. In any given situation, a particular behaviour offers some advantage to the person making use of it; the chosen behaviour puts another person, or people, at a relative disadvantage reduces interpersonal trust, weakening the foundation upon which institutions that can provide social benefits can develop projects. Even so, passive/aggressive strategies may at best improve survival opportunities. They may at least prevent existing opportunities from being eroded.

These strategies are called minimaxing strategies. Minimaxing appears in many areas of life in the developing world and form a very fundamental, deeply rooted part of one's culture.[2] Rose Ngugi describes the phenomenon among users of public health care facilities in Kenya:

> Cost sharing resulted in a drop in the use of public health facilities in Kenya. But, these facilities continued to take a high priority among the other alternatives when sickness befell. Shifts across the facilities indicated a search for health services that yielded utility equivalent to the fee charged, while demand for services across the alternative sources reflected complementarity in consumption. Several factors influenced the observed pattern: direct and indirect costs, income base, satisfaction with services received, and demand level in the household. **As rational agents, users of health care services aimed to minimize costs and maximize their satisfaction.**[3]

This defensive/aggressive tactic has the advantage of protecting what one has while trying to increase what one needs or wants. It does not differ from what every vendor does when deciding whether to sell a bunch of carrots. There is a need to seek a point of transaction that is optimal for either side. Nothing more can be gained without giving up too much of something else.

Before we look at some of the minimaxing interactions I have observed, I want to state, in the strongest terms possible, that the brief, negative behaviours presented in these anecdotes are not included with malicious intent. Their purpose is not to make buffoons or caricatures out of complete and complex humans, nor to make objects out of intelligent, sentient decision-makers. Let's remember that the same people who here have to endure the revelation of an embarrassing moment are equally capable of behaviours that are noble, honourable and self-sacrificing. Belizeans don't just engage in selfish behaviours. There are plenty of occasions that allow for kindness. Belizeans pay visits to the sick and offer pleasant greetings to one another all day long. They bake Christmas cakes for friends, deliver messages and packages, raise children for kin, and offer coins to beggars in the market. And they do plenty of these things.

One can find greedy motivation in these acts, I suppose. A cynic can find greed in mother's milk, or in a soldier's sacrificial death on a live grenade. When Belizeans are being nice, I think it's simpler to understand that they're acting as genuinely good-hearted people. Freud may have had that kind of pragmatism about behaviour. "Sometimes," he is reputed to have said, flicking his ashes with a twinkle, "a cigar is just a cigar." The simple truth is that under different circumstances I have seen that every Belizean I am about to describe behave in kind and generous ways.

That brings me to another point: where there is poverty all about and where the ability to depend on others is quite variable, the circumstances are highly changeable. So it would be unfair to observe ignoble behaviours independent of their context, and probably more useful to appreciate the creativity and adaptability of Belizeans at certain moments when less than noble behaviours are called for. In the case of Belize (and probably of any clientelistic environment) these circumstances develop from the society's history and cultural baggage as much as from the immediate situation that is encountered by the individuals.

The descriptions that follow may surprise some because they are mean and mirthless. Many people from industrialized nations hold romantic notions about poor people in the tropics. You meet so many smiling faces. Everybody seems so polite and friendly. People care for each other. Life is simpler; people aren't always in a rush the way they are back home. They still remember the old ways; they take the time to make things from scratch. And underneath it all, they've never lost their faith.

This is not entirely hogwash, although it's a bit of a caricature because it's incomplete. Much of the niceness of tropical populations, including those of Belize, is exactly what it appears to be—simple affection. These are good people who, at specific moments, have to use social networking to get to their survival resources or retain them have to use the same courtly manners and smiles more instrumentally. Smiles and friendliness can be very instrumental, after all. And when I say that the same people with whom they interact are "instrumental" to them, I mean that they're proving useful or helpful for their purposes—a means to the end they have in mind.

In the big cities of the North, good jobs may go to the most talented and to the ones who push themselves forward. A total stranger can secure a job interview and land a good position on the basis of merit and good recommendations even though the North is hardly a stranger to nepotism. To get a job on the basis of merit, a good interview and good references, one needs to be friendly, self-motivated, knowledgeable and principled. But, one does not have to be a friend of the interviewer to get the job, or appear available for improper favours. Affection for its own sake is an affordable luxury where a meritocracy operates. The person being interviewed and one of the interviewers may become fast friends over time, but making this friendship isn't necessary, for promotions and other opportunities are available irrespective. There can be broad smiles and open communication that have nothing to do with personal advancement. People can afford to be friends solely for the sake of affection.

The apparent warmth of tropical people who smile so much and act so nice under the palm trees may impress people who come from Northern cultures. What is innocently accepted as mere affection between tourists and residents of the tropics may actually reflect highly instrumental behaviour, a ploy used to benefit the local person. To a person who is fairly naïve when it comes to instrumentality, it may be surprising to see the lengths to which people need to go to hold their place in the line or progress in a context of low trust. It may also surprise them to realize how destructive that kind of action can be to others.

Belizeans have developed a number of set strategies or "ploys"to cope with some of the not-so-nice realities they encounter daily in their own Valley of Means. These ploys are the games Belizeans will play, although to those involved there is little that is playful about them. There's nothing entirely unique about the survival ploys used in Belize either. You can see variants of them in other countries, developed or otherwise, and in office settings around the world.[4]

We refer to an "organizational culture" when analyzing institutions and looking at behavioural patterns that are typical for that organization. For example, mean gossip is a norm for the employees in some offices but frowned upon in others. Belize has its own organizational culture that parallels that of the General Motors corporation—in some ways it is probably worse than in other places, and in others it is probably better. General Motors (GM) has been deliberately organized to generate shareholder earnings and a particular organizational culture has emerged as a result of the way it operates. At GM, if the office culture is seen to be counter-productive, efforts can be made to change it. Belize too was organized to benefit its investors. It was colonized to extract profit from labour (i.e. the hewing of logwood for royal purple dyes) in the coastal wetlands. Later, the hardwoods of the sub-tropical rainforests further inland were targeted. The extraction was deliberate on the part of the entrepreneurial loggers and the few land barons who hacked their way into ownership of the northern half of the territory. The British colonials have now gone but the Creole descendants of the British and the African slaves remain, as well as the descendants of the slaves and their liberated offspring, the Mayas, the Mestizos, and others. Historians can use hindsight to read patterns into what has transpired and evolved, but overall, I'd say the planning has probably been more haphazard than that of General Motors.

Belize continues to evolve and so does its organizational culture. Negative patterns have emerged, ones that may be identified and rationalized. Such patterns have been no more desired than negative organizational cultures at GM. The difference is that GM has had recourse to social engineers and has made deliberate attempts to adjust negative behaviours in order to protect the bottom line. Belize has not been so lucky.

GM has had recourse to more than social engineers. The importance of the work ethic, of national pride or citizenship, and of religiously grounded morality cannot be over-emphasized. Governments, businesses and industries can elicit these values as a mechanism for correction when the time is right only to the extent that they have evolved in a society and are present within the breasts of workers. These values may be as present in Belize as in any other place. Where there's a positive spiral of growth and improvement in the quality of life, these values may be present and may be used to contribute to perpetuating the upward spiral. However, where they are eroded—that is, where growth is not evident, where opportunities are limited, and where there is low permeability of social barriers—the work ethic, national pride and attachment to moral principles may be similarly weak, and despondency great. In that case, there is little to stop a population from playing the destructive games.

As we have seen, Belize (and similarly, the Caribbean and the colonized world in general) has been through precisely such a history and as a consequence Belizeans have developed a strategy of game-playing. In game-playing, improvisation holds the advantage of surprise, yet set ploys have emerged over time in Belize that help secure one's grasp on life and recourse to these set ploys is frequent. To some extent, Belizeans are quite aware of the game playing and some of the ploys have even been given names. The ploys are not necessarily unique to Belize and they exist elsewhere in the Caribbean under similar names. These ploys show up in different guises in other parts of the world too. I have invented names for ploys that reflect the frequent behaviours with survival benefits I have observed in Belize, a clientelistic system. There may be ploys that are used elsewhere and not in Belize. Ultimately, it is not the specific ploys discussed below that are important but the fact that such ploys can exist and be of survival value to local populations. It is also true that it is in the face of these behaviours that an effective community development strategy must operate.

Ploy No.1: Badmouthing

If somebody tells you negative things about a third person, she or he is seeking your agreement. This is an attempt to form an alliance between the two of you and to force a wedge between you and the third person. Giving people a bad name in this way is a method of holding them back and improving your own opportunities. Once a person has been stereotyped it is more difficult to judge that person by what the person is doing and saying at the present moment. Rather, that person is prejudged by his or her reputation and this becomes a good reason for being very cautious about becoming too intimate with others.

Examples of Bad Mouthing

MOCKING A COLLEAGUE

L is a Scout leader's assistant who has announced his intention to become a Scout leader himself someday. L coaches the cricket team of the Scout Troop. One Saturday afternoon, L's team loses badly against a solid team they had previously beaten because some of the better players from the Troop did not show up for the game. In front of other Scout leaders and members of the losing cricket team, L's

Troop leader announces, "What happened, L? I think you say you was a coach. You di one 'slow coach'! These li' bwai [little boys] can't play cricket at all!"

MUSLIM

There aren't many Muslims in Belize. There is one mosque, however. One of my former students is a Creole who was born in Belize and converted to Islam. He came to the first class wearing his caftan and prayer cap. Another student flashed his eyes in my direction as though to be sure I was paying attention and then said to the Muslim student, "Sell me one pound of pork." All the other students laughed.

FENCE QUARRELS AND MARIJUANA SALES

Ms. U is a churchgoing woman who regularly attends service on Sundays and hymn singing on Thursday nights. She and her neighbour once got into a quarrel over the boundary line between their properties when the neighbour started to build her fence on what Ms. U claimed was her side of the boundary. The fight got out of hand and a policeman had to come to quiet the row.

In the presence of the policeman, the neighbour announced, "Ms. U, you been selling marijuana to the li' bwai [teens in the neighbourhood]—an' it done!" The policeman then searched Ms. U's house and found a small cache of weed in a jar in the living room. Ms. U was jailed briefly, during which time the fence was quickly completed.

In the first scenario, the Scout leader attempts to undermine and discredit L in the eyes of the other leaders so that he can forge an alliance with them against L. The assumption is that if he can make the other leaders believe that L should not be raised to their level, then his own insecure position is solidified. The effect of the derision on the young team that has just lost a game either goes unnoticed, or is unimportant to his sense of self-preservation.

In the second scenario, the mocking student evidently knew the Muslim student. Before I had a chance to discover how intelligent the Muslim student was, his classmate portrayed him as a mere butcher. I don't know whether he was also aware that Muslims don't eat pork. The humiliation he endured before an authority figure might destabilize the Muslim student enough to reduce his performance and thus reduce my own assessment of him; perhaps the mocking student would be at less of a disadvantage. To achieve his end, the mocking student used the laughter of his allies against the hapless Muslim student.

Ms. U has been skirting the law and bending morality to make ends meet. In the heat of a personal feud, the neighbour breaks solidarity with Ms. U and forms an alliance with the authorities, who then eliminate her opposition long enough for her to advance her property line. While there is an immediate advantage to this ploy, the neighbour has jeopardized any further alliances with Ms. U.

Ploy No. 2: Blue Crab

The Blue Crab ploy is famous in Belize. You will hear people refer to others as Blue Crabs in a bucket. Elsewhere in the Caribbean the ploy goes by similar names. The anthropologist, Peter J. Wilson, wrote a book, *Crab Antics: The Social Anthropology of English-Speaking Negro Societies in the Caribbean*, about the way African-Caribbean people in Old Providence Island, Colombia strategically use the advantages of respectability (if they are "somebodies" who have resources and family connections) or reputation (if they are "nobodies" who only have their personal skill as fishermen, coconut tree climbers, dancers, singers, lovers, etc.) to recommend them. In the neighbouring Island of San Andrés, people say, "Black crab nevah get outta basket yet!"

In the frenzy to clamber out of the bucket to freedom, the blue (or black) crab will pull all the other crabs back into the container. The struggle to get out of the bucket becomes crueller and more strategic when humans engage in it. People know they are keeping others from progressing, yet they prefer to have other people at their own level rather than seeing them succeed. What is broadly enough believed eventually becomes a reality. If everybody thinks others deliberately attempt to hold them back, then holding other people back becomes a deliberate offensive and something to be done unto others first.

Belizeans explain that people behave like Blue Crabs because they are so "small," that is, so jealous, that they just can't stand seeing good things coming to others. Another explanation is that people like to keep others within their grasp. If you rise too high, others can't finger you (or squeeze, perhaps) for assistance. That provokes a kind of defensive reaction, as we'll see below. You have a need to free yourself from their clutches.

Examples of the Blue Crab Ploy

WIN AND LOOK GOOD

Nurse F is a great basketball fan who has retired. During her career, she was a woman of some prestige who represented Belize internationally on a number of occasions. For years, she has been Chair of the Women's Basketball

League of Belize (WBLB). However, by far the greatest part of her efforts are invested in her own basketball teams. She trains girls' teams in several age groups and the effort pays off, as Nurse F's teams generally win. At the worst, they make it to the playoffs. They have the sharpest uniforms too.

Nurse F is so anxious for her girls to look good that she'll use her influence in WBLB to rearrange game schedules to get her teams started against the weaker ones so as to build up confidence among her players and she'll play mind games with the other coaches to weaken the confidence of the opponents. She'll cite regulations to disqualify other teams, but uses the same tactics on behalf of her own teams. She even did these things to a girls' team fielded by the orphanage.

Nurse F admits that she puts more effort into her teams than into WBLB. She says that making the League great requires the co-operation of others; building up her teams is something she can manage herself. It's better, she tells people, to do something for a few girls if you can't help all.

SABOTAGE

An environmental NGO hired a secretary for the Dangriga office. When its outboard motor needed repairs, the contract went to the secretary's husband. Although he worked for one of the maritime companies in Belize as its machine maintenance man, he was contracted to fix the engine in his off-hours. For months, he was seen fishing in the NGO's boat, but he kept sending them messages that he was still waiting for parts to fix the outboard. One day, the Manager of the NGO phoned the maintenance man to announce that he was coming to retrieve the boat and outboard that very afternoon.

The engine worked badly on the short trip home and died just when reaching the NGO's dock. A later inspection revealed that sugar had been emptied into the gas tank, spoiling the engine. The maintenance man said he was surprised and that he had no idea how that had happened.

HIDING MONEY

Miss R is an honest, hardworking and dependable mother of eight children. She told me she has to hide her money from the children but that they often find it and take it anyway. I asked whether the children couldn't be trusted to improve if she talked to them about it.

"You don't know these children," she replied shaking her head and laughed.

LAND GRAB

Mr. J went to one of the business community development banks for a loan so that he could buy a 12-acre site along the highway for improvement and resale as house plots. He took the bank officer to see the site. His loan was rejected on the grounds that the site was ill-situated for housing and too costly for community development.

Mr. J told me it's lucky he's not a violent man. He's just learned that the same bank officer has taken a loan and purchased that site for housing development.

In the first example, Nurse F has high prestige by virtue of her status and her service to Belize. But she lacks the opportunity to take on the greater challenge of making an athletic league sustainable and building up the abilities and the confidence of girls from all the teams. Nurse F's contribution to the systemic community development of Belize has been stymied by her conviction that co-operation is futile. She is surely not the only frustrated Belizean with great talent and a willingness to contribute to the benefit of others.

The machinist in the second example exhibits Blue Crab behaviour because he has attempted to prevent the NGO from getting ahead because, without a fishing boat, he will be left behind. The machinist has been fishing to survive at the expense of the NGO. The effort to progress is not absent—only a way to do so without harm to others—or better still, that brings benefits to others.

Mama and her children are playing a game. Mama hides her resources from the children; they, in turn, attempt to take it for themselves. Rather than working together as a family unit, they all try to maximize benefit for themselves as individuals. Still, every child that manages to outsmart mama learns an important survival skill in this environment.

The bank officer blocked Mr. J's access to loan funds for land community development. In the meantime, he linked himself up to the opportunity from which he took pains to exclude Mr. I.

Ploy no. 3: End Run

The End Run is a common ploy in many cultures, including Belize. A person wants to improve him- or herself, but feels blockaded by a superior. The person then attempts to form an alliance with the superior's boss in order to channel opportunities around the blockade. This ploy is made easier if the person one notch above the end-runner also feels blockaded by his or her immediate inferior. Because of the disloyal underling immediately below him, the superior is motivated to look for loyalty further down. So the boss' boss is not all that inaccessible after all and it stands to reason that person will be open to an end run. Many Belizeans say they feel blockaded by their superiors and some attempt an end run if the opportunity presents itself. As a result, loyalty of immediate underlings is questionable and the dependability of superiors is doubtful. In the end, the end run only abrades the utility of ethical behaviour, dependability, and confidential relationships.

Example of the End Run

BECOMING THE BOSS

Rhonda proved herself as a capable worker in her position as the Deputy Director for a bank in Belize. She recently left the bank to become Director of another one, but had trouble with the Board of Directors in her new job and left within a year. She returned to the first bank and asked the Director to take her back, which he did. Shortly afterwards, the Chairperson of the Board came to the Director to warn him about Rhonda. Rhonda, it seems, had come to the Chairperson saying negative things about the bank Director and saying she was capable of doing the job herself.

Rhonda hopes to advance herself by making secret alliances with the Board to which her boss reports instead of through making solid contributions to her organization.

Ploy no. 4: In Your Face

This ploy is most closely associated with rebellious young black men, although it can be used by anybody cornered into adolescent rejection of authority and authority figures. It is the antithesis of the Uncle Tom ploy (Ploy no. 5).

Example of the In Your Face Ploy

INSULTING THE NATION

A young man has been arrested for rape and murder. As he is handcuffed and paraded to the police pick-up truck, he smiles broadly at the cameras and mouths the words, "F... you!" rather than bending over to conceal his face. Once he is seated in the back of the truck, he turns again to give a smile and the bird to the cameras, and is then driven off to judgement and possible hanging.

Black males in the New World have two strategic choices: they can capitulate or rebel. In a racist world, they encounter a playing field that is seldom level and taking it on and making the best of it means more than ignoring the ignominy and the slights. This can mean making a compromise with representatives whose behaviours perpetuate the inequalities, even when the representatives are not aware of what they are doing. For young black males, supporting such individuals or collaborating with them means profiting by perpetuating the inequality and breaking the solidarity alliance with "brothers" who are similarly oppressed by the system. Accepting the given terms of the compromise represents a loss of manhood: balls for glory.

The alternative is rebellion. On these terms, being a man means showing defiance to representatives of the status quo. Rebellion involves being rejected by this world and its institutions; or at least, attempting to wrest a victory from the representatives of the status quo through vocal and vociferous intimidation. Since it's not pleasant to be reminded of your own treachery by some smart-assed, angry failure, the representative of the status quo may be temporarily intimidated into making a few changes. If the mouthy rebel broadcasts all your defects and secrets, he doesn't make a very dependable ally and so whenever possible, members of the status quo attempt to exclude the In Your Face rebel. That, in the long term, usually helps to ensure the rebel's failure. For the In Your Face rebel, the hero is the stud who flashes his ass at authority and wins: he may be the successful thug record producer; or better, the producer-distributor who evaded the blockade of the white distributors and reached the market on his own. He may only be the local pimp or pusher and is not lionized for his morality or civility, but for his moxie and the reality of his success: he has the ride, the chains, the rings and the women to prove it. At the least, he is the penitentiary tough—enslaved and chained by the Man—but defiant yet, and unbroken: he holds high the torch of brotherhood and keeps the flame of revolution alive.

For the Rebel, losing is inevitable. The Man is powerful and ubiquitous. He is, after all, the representative of Authority. There is no escape back to Africa—Garvey was framed and the freedom movement was dismantled. Martin Luther King, Jr. was shot; so was Malcolm X. Even though you are excluded from the Man's world and blockaded from an ultimate victory, you do not need to go down like a boy. Rebellion may be adolescent: the adolescent does, after all, require—nay, depend—upon the Man and his evil Babylon. There has to be somebody to fight. And maybe, at the last, it takes less daring to die with one's face to the enemy than to free yourself from the self-destructive engagement and to attempt an independent alternative or a productive bond with one's brothers in a communal undertaking. The nature of subjugation is such that everyone is atomized. At last, there's nobody to trust. As a song from the sixties went, "Every Brother Ain't A Brother!" The majority of them play the Uncle Tom. One never knows a friend from a snitch until the police surround you and the cuffs go on.

What makes the In Your Face Belizean black male's crucifixion so exquisite is the realization that it is his offended fellow-Belizeans who enforce the standards and who ensure his rejection. He is then suspended between a need to prove himself worthy of the respect of his fellows and the reality of his failure. The greater the history of failure becomes, the greater his anger grows, as well as his need to prove his worth. And yet, the greater his anger, the more urgent Society's need to put him down and exclude him.

Ploy no. 5: Uncle Tom

Harriet Beecher Stowe immortalized Uncle Tom in her Abolitionist romance, Uncle Tom's Cabin. Set in the Old South, it is a sentimental antislavery novel in which the book's principal character, Uncle Tom, is a faithful slave who is killed by a cruel master. The story was soon brought to the stage, where Uncle Tom took on a life of his own. In the vaudeville era, whites playing slaves painted their faces black and showed extreme servility toward their masters, thus defining Uncle Tom's meaning for modern times. Uncle Tom has become associated with the fawning slave, a spineless soul who is a traitor to his own people and who curries favour with the oppressors to protect himself, and possibly advance his own position. His own group hates him because he breaks solidarity with them—in fact, betrays them to the victimizers they fear and hate most.

Example of Uncle Tom Ploy

SIGNING THE PETITION

Non-unionized employees of one of the privatized public services were attempting to protest pay and working conditions. They prepared a letter of complaint and were collecting signatures. One of the employees went to management to tell them what was happening. He even gave the names of the protest organizers, who were then promptly fired.

The Uncle Tom ploy has value. The very lack of unity among disadvantaged groups and the difficulty they have in creating and sustaining effective lobbies or alternative organizations provides evidence of the popularity of this ploy. It is frequently easier for the individual to acquiesce when confronted with the threat of ugly consequences than to rely on the support of a non-existent or nascent organization. The loss of a little pride and dignity can sometimes be assuaged with a small reward. Besides, survival—even with a bit less self-esteem—is still survival. Unless he becomes a martyr for those remain, a dead Indian is no good at all.

Women, Exploitation and Ploys: Hiding the Pill; Playing the Field

The Belize Family Health Surveys conducted in 1991 and 1999 report that injectable contraceptives are very popular among users of artificial birth control methods because its use is not readily detected. Contraceptive pills are also very popular, but some women report that they hide the fact that they use contraceptives from their partners because their partners will beat them if they're found out. The men object to birth control because they want children. Children are a sign of male potency—they are living proof that a man is a man.

Some women also have more than one partner—a fact they do not share with either partner. This arrangement allows them to live above their means. The average woman in Belize is economically very vulnerable, as a study by Irma McClaurin demonstrates.[6] McClaurin says that vulnerability engenders a sexual-economic dependency on men that creates what she calls the "culture of gender" and that is expressed through unions. These unions may be consensual unions, marriages or working relationships. Both sexes see marriage, for example, as "a highly economic proposition." But these unions leave the women trapped in an economic-sexual cycle.

For the man, the act of reproduction represents proof of a woman's commitment,[7] but the economic responsibilities of having children may be more than he can bear in an economy in which he is marginalized and reduced to subsistence. When the man walks away, the woman becomes economically vulnerable and open to exploitation by another man. By the time a woman has aged and inherited a larger family than she could have wanted, few men want her any longer, or want the economic obligations of her many children.

Hiding the pill therefore becomes a strategy that is used to snatch a victory from a stronger opponent. Women need financial assistance from the men. They get to enjoy sex without the burden and expense of additional children and, where the arrangement works, having more than one male partner increases a dependent woman's options.

The Necessity of Ploys

Clientelism forces difficult choices on people either to ensure their survival or to serve their best interests for advancement in an atmosphere of constraints. Where there is clientelism, there is gatekeeping. A few individuals have direct access to resources and opportunities; everybody else has to go through others to gain access to enough benefits to subsist and to progress—if one is both lucky and shrewd. Clients therefore develop their ability to work people as well as the environment. Social manipulation becomes an art form and a substitute for the manipulation of money and materiel.

You play the manipulative games because everybody else is already caught up in competition and others may quickly devour opportunities that have not yet been snared. Any advantages a person may hold are watched with greedy eyes. Hence, strategies must be developed and deployed to elbow out, restrict and destabilize competitors; to solidify and amplify connections to patrons; to build useful alliances that broaden the potential for benefiting from resources entering the community; and to outmanoeuvre competing factions. Flexibility is also necessary. An alliance that abets access to an opportunity at one moment may restrict it at another. People who are now members of your alliance may soon tax your resources too severely. Your current adversaries may become attractive allies.

Life in a clientelistic environment is complex. It requires perpetual vigilance and enormous amounts of energy to react quickly, forcefully and appropriately. You constantly live with the expectation that others will take advantage of you. Every option must be worked. High intelligence is an obvious advantage; so are personality and looks while youth lasts. Wealth and connections are invaluable. You have to be ready to take advantage of the potential for opening or terminating alliances based on gender, kinship, ethnicity, skin colour, religion, political affiliation, employment, geographical location, and any other commonality or distinction that can be discovered or invented. Even though developers advise people in Third World countries to the contrary, the inhabitants of these countries frequently retain these ploys. It would be madness to follow the advice of good-hearted developers if you are convinced that the people around you will immediately make you suffer for it. The ploys hold the line against aggressors or take ground whenever that's possible.

The Belizeans reported in the above examples were not opposed to progress nor entirely barred from change by traditionalism. They were not necessarily immoral or cowardly, egocentric or evil. They simply faced ugly situations with few resources and did what they thought necessary to make a go of it. There is neither a need to extol their wisdom and nobility—to make a religion out of "traditional practices"—nor to demonize their behaviours. But there is, I think, a need to recognize that people aren't going to abandon required behaviours in favour of ones of dubious value.

If you and a crazed gunman held pistols to each other's heads, you would not be tempted to lower yours first. If a referee stepped in and said that your behaviour was dangerous, unlawful and morally repugnant, it would still be unwise to put down your weapon. The referee's reproach would simply be irrelevant because in the given circumstances the gun in your hand and the one held to your head would take precedence in determining your decisions. For community developers, the key question therefore becomes: what would motivate you to put down your weapon?

The Value of Greed

In all five of the ploys described above, people use the minimaxing strategy to maximize their gains and to minimize their losses. I once knew a water-taxi driver in San Andrés Island, Colombia, who took tourists to the offshore cays. Humperdink was in his early twenties: big, black, muscular, heavily oiled and scented. He wore a single earring and an iridescent thong bathing suit that concealed not very much of an awful lot.

I did some calculations and figured out that neither he, nor any of the other similarly equipped boat operators got enough scheduled trips to the cays from their co-operative to cover operating costs. Humperdink explained that the difference was earned from a range of additional favours and services and powders that were rendered to male and female clients after hours in discos, bars, casinos and bedrooms in exchange for cash and free meals and drinks.

"Them come here fi explore we," Humperdink announced.

"Do you mean 'exploit' we?" I asked to clarify—I used to be a high school English teacher in town.

"No, Prof.," he replied, "explore we!"

I asked him what he would do if he had to choose between a beautiful tourist and a rich one.

He answered, "I would give up the least beauty to gain the most money."

That's a minimax strategy.

When two Belizeans meet and only one of them is a minimaxer, the minimaxing strategy would be an effective way to improve that person's situation in life. In reality, because minimaxers frequently encounter minimaxers in their transactions, the behaviour has the effect of simply maintaining the status quo.

In a context of plenty and where there is economic expansion, there is room for laxity. People who feel they are progressing may have less need to drive hard bargains. There can be occasions where one opens the purse and spends liberally, or can relate to others in an altruistic fashion. However, in a context of scarcity—even where scarcity is more perceived than real, or where the possession of resources is skewed in the population—many people who possess assets feel themselves compelled to guard them closely and to move aggressively on those who appear to have valuable resources.[8] That immediately changes the approach of most anybody intending to be generous towards others; the likelihood is great that such people sense a similar need to engage in minimaxing behaviour, simply because their assets are being targeted.

Intensive minimaxing causes wariness on the part of people. There is a heightened expectation that anybody who approaches you is attempting to take unfair advantage. Humperdink the water taxi driver once said to me, "White people like children." My ears pricked up, for that's what I used to hear white people say about black people. I asked Humperdink why and he pointed to a bevy of blonde and bikinied beauties on the beach and said, "You see them American woman over there? Anything you tell them, them a-believe!"

And after a time in San Andrés, there did seem to me to be a kind of blue-eyed innocence about the tourists from such a wealthy country. They were rich enough, at least, to come to San Andrés on vacation and were the products of families in which a steady supply of meals and clothes and transportation and education were never in doubt and never had to be extracted from anybody through trickery.

The fabled hero of the Caribbean is not Beauty whose kindliness converts The Beast, nor Prince Charming, whose manly and generous heroism saves Snow White. Rather, it is the West African folk character Anansi (Hanansi in Belize), the web-knitting spider trickster who is similar to another West African folk hero who reappears in Southern USA as Brer Rabbit. Anansi "play fool fu ketch wise" as they say in Creole and he always outsmarts his dangerous foe. Anansi does not get to deal with giggling, nearly naked young women eager to "explore."[9] Usually, Anansi faces dangerous opponents like Tiger or Brer Bear. Like Brer Rabbit, Anansi needs to lay low and not let it be known that he was born and bred in the briar patch. Where Beauty and Prince Charming are ideal-ists from the top of the European social pile who can afford their nobility, Brer

Rabbit and Bra Hanansi are pragmatic because they have to be.

The unfortunate effect of ubiquitous minimaxing—of laying low or concealing your hand, as it were—is reduced trust. The long term result of continual interactions that limit alliances and that attempt to hold people to their socio-economic position is one of conservatism and lack of economic dynamism. Therefore, poverty and skewed ownership of wealth will tie a population to poverty and skewed ownership. The price of poverty is poverty, and that implies indirect access to opportunities; in short, dependency and clientelism.

Greed and Moral Development

The unintended but almost inevitable side-effects of the five survival ploys we discussed include low trust as both an effect and a cause of the behaviours; reinforcement of a negative personal self-image that was originally inculcated by slavery and colonialism, but perpetuated by the ego-bashing actions of those all around; the formation of negative alliances aimed at outmanoeuvring competitive factions rather than creating societal improvements; solitary action in an environment that rewards co-operative initiatives with pain; atomization of community; and reinforcement of a negative image of one's society through the observations and opinions of those all around. These six side effects of clientelism are relevant to establishmentarian as well as anti-establishmentarian developers because they all serve to diminish the effectiveness of their efforts.

Here are some of the ways that community development efforts are distorted by clientelism:

Effects of Low Trust and Solitary Action

When minimaxing behaviours around an individual reduce that person's ability to depend upon others, the person is encouraged to resort to solitary action. The result of past efforts to co-operate has generally proven unrewarding or even punishing. The person's effort has not been met with equal endeavour on the part of others. What the individual has contributed has been used by others for their own benefit. Resources invested to generate surplus have been co-opted and sometimes the surplus gets co-opted as well.

To strengthen an institution, or to stop the injustice caused by the actions of an exploitative class requires a measure of trust and conjoint action on the part of a target population. It therefore becomes the responsibility of the developer to motivate members of a target group to engage in co-operative or conjoint action. However, the proven experience of members of that target population flies directly in the face of that kind of behaviour. The task of individuals within target groups is then to remain civil to well-meaning developers while evading co-operation. Evasion may take the form of missing meetings or arriving late, not fulfilling promises, taking action with little enthusiasm, leaving actions unfinished, or distorting actions to benefit the individual while denying benefits to others.

Effects of Low Self-Esteem

Clientelism demands subservience to patrons or their gatekeepers. There is an operative hierarchy with less prestige ascribed to clients and reduced opportunities for them to achieve. One of the by-products of clientelism is reduced self-esteem. In fact, for the perpetuation of a clientelistic system, reduced self-esteem among clients is of advantage because it restricts aspirations that undermine the mechanism. Clientelism is not able to prevent such ambition entirely, only to contribute to a person's limited belief that she or he is able to carry out the tasks associated with a higher rank. The desire to be seen as being important underlies desire for reputation among clients and for respectability among patrons.[10] If a person's status is elevated and she or he is appointed to a rank of any consequence because being in that position would be useful for another person's schemes, it is probable to see the newly-appointed person lording it over others as a way of actualizing his or her importance. This behaviour is also a means of fending off the aggression of former peers who tend to see the person as a usurper who has no more rights to privilege than they have.

Crab Antics are counter-productive for developers. The effort to hold back anybody who steps forward first effectively keeps people from doing so. Developers then assume the obligation of cajoling individuals into participating in projects. Individuals who do assume positions of responsibility discourage others from participating in community development action either by "bigging up" themselves, as they say in Belize (that is, making much of themselves), or by communicating disdain for others, or both.

Effects of Shifting Alliances

Clientelism necessitates the maintenance of fluid social relations as a method of accessing scarce survival resources, including jobs, goods or services. A political campaign, the arrival of a canoe full of fresh fish, the return of a relative from the US, or the sexual maturation of a young lady may be considered examples of opportunities that need to be maximized. These events may become available to you or to your current alliances. They may, however, become available to a member of a competing faction, in which case it would be to your advantage to become an ally of that person. As a result, clients must be adept at making and breaking alliances and to be instrumental about allegiances. Friendship may exist for the purpose of benefiting individuals.

Developers who bring project resources to a target group soon discover that people affiliating with their project are doing so for instrumental reasons. Local individuals may end up possessing new resources and the project objectives are not achieved. For example, a co-operative food shop may be built and stocked using project funds as well as members' share deposits. The shop may be located on land "donated" by one of the members. Once the shop is operational, members of the co-op may then be forced to make purchases for unaffiliated relatives who wish to take advantage of the low-cost privileges extended to members. The shopkeeper may be forced to extend loans to relatives, or to useful allies, which are not repaid. When—almost inevitably—the co-op shop goes out of business (either during the lifetime of the project, or not long after it finishes), the shop reverts to the landowner. Then the shop is operated as a private business. To avoid this eventuality, developers are required to call for restrictive legislation and punitive constraints—in other words, they have to resort to authoritarian measures to defend the shop. The target population has successfully converted developers into patrons.

Effects of the Idealization of Outsiders

Clientelism implies a power differentiation between patrons and clients. There is a love-hate relationship that exists between them because of mutual need and wariness. The foreign developer, whether from the industrialized North or from the big city within the developing country, is associated with the patron class. The developer possesses education and resources. Sometimes, there are ethnic and/or colour differences as well, with the developer looking more like the local patron class—frequently, individuals of a lighter colour and members of an historical oppressor class. While the developer's intent is to relate to the target population on an egalitarian basis, the expectation of the target group is that the usual status differences are to continue. They have no reason for expecting anything else. Furthermore, the survival tactics they employ are designed for unequal relationships. Equality puts them at a disadvantage: equals are equally unfortunate. The target population will attempt therefore to sustain an unequal relationship. While the developer is attempting to promote democratic intercourse and decision-making, the traditional client group is attempting to rely on both the traditional leaders and the new one for direction. Because their peers are attempting to absorb the new resources that have become available, they are also relying on the developer to catch and punish others and to grant favours to them. As a result, developers are required to engage in educating the target population to move away from the habits of dependency and into action that is based on the principles of democracy and confident self-worth.

It is no wonder then that those concerned with seeing the world improve should dislike clientelistic behaviours and decide they must be changed. Clientelistic survival mechanisms represent the very antithesis of what the developers believe must come to exist. Co-operation must replace low trust, low self-esteem, and self-hatred. Co-operation must replace competition and social unity has to replace atomization. The existing values only bring pain and retard improvement and people who make use of them are being backward and destructive. It is obvious that the opposite behaviours are intended to produce good for one and all. People with the wrong attitudes are also being stubborn since they are very unwilling to give up their practices.

The great contradiction is that developers and the survivors of clientelism are at cross purposes. The developers loathe greed because it undermines institutional community development. It also undermines the class solidarity that is necessary to destroy the mode of production that causes the poor to suffer. At the same time, the poor derive value from greed because it sustains them. The is a gap that exists between the current mechanisms that keep the relationships in the society going and the better way that might come to exist as a result of the developers' efforts. If the poor knew how to negotiate the gap, the poor might value the New Jerusalem of the developers. In fact, so might the current oppressors of the poor if they really saw how a new mode of production might bring with it a less anxious form of social relations with those who are poor at present and capable of turning on them.

The difficulty lies in this period of change, that is, in the lifetime of the project. Here, most developers have little to offer by way of enticing their target people to cross the divide. In these circumstances, preachers are at an advantage. If Heaven is the New Jerusalem, the target population is told that they don't have to worry about death anymore. Everybody has to die and we all fear death, but the preachers offer an incentive for going through the experience with a greater sense of calm. Developers have to worry about the period that falls between a rotten present and a better tomorrow. The interval offers few advantages to the poor and most certainly doesn't offer any to those who feed on their weakness. Furthermore, they can offer no guarantees of success and the experience of the target population is that previous attempts by developers to change the status quo have been painful failures.

In summary, then, where the practice of community development is based upon moral assumptions, an adversarial relationship necessarily evolves. The demonstrably destructive behaviour of rich and poor alike within developing nations makes it necessary for developers to motivate members of a target group to engage in co-operative or conjoint action when individualism is the preferred strategy; to cajole individuals into participating in projects when they resist doing so; to promote restrictive legislation and punitive constraints because project participants tend to take personal advantage of opportunities; and to educate the target population away from the habits of dependency because they demonstrate a preference for it.

We have already shown that there is a certain logic to the behaviours used by target populations in clientelistic systems and that in these circumstances it is illogical to heed developers. To the extent that moralizing chooses good over evil, anyone who proceeds upon such a moral premise may be said to be a friend of the poor and the oppressed. Yet, ironically, to the extent that moralizing opposes the poor and the oppressed, any person acting on that basis may be said to be their enemy.

Our objective, therefore, has to be to find a way of relating to Third World populations that is neither adversarial nor laissez-faire and that enables those populations to find ways of increasing their survival and community development alternatives. To do so, a rapid survey of the major theories and strategies underlying most community development work is in order. We will look particularly at the extent to which any of the theories contend with the adversarial relationship and the extent to which any employ local minimaxing strategies.

Structural Theories and Related Strategies

THEORIES ARE CONCEPTUAL frameworks. A conceptual framework gives us a way of looking at the world. A Zen Buddhist and a Southern Baptist can look at the same world and see it very differently because they have their own perspective on things. Community development theories offer explanations about society and social change. They organize change in the real world into a pattern and explain it. Among developers, debate about different community development theories relates to their utility and relative explanatory power. Which theory we prefer partly depends on our practical needs. Theories therefore aren't right or wrong so much as they are more or less useful to us.

Community development strategies differ from theories. A theory may be compared to tinted glasses. It affects the way we understand the world and how we see. A strategy is more like a recipe. It suggests a way to hasten desired change—what we're to do to achieve the best possible results. Strategies rest upon a particular theory, or a combination of theories. Our theoretical understanding of how the world functions naturally shapes the strategies we develop and the way we interact with the world. If, for example, I think my canoe is leaking (that is my theory), I may attempt to stop the leak with my big toe and then bail out the canoe with the cap of my sun blocker (that is my strategy). But if I think my canoe is burning (a different theory), then I will use the cap of my sun blocker to scoop up water with which to extinguish the flames (a separate action, intended to be relevant to what I think is occurring). The first theory allowed me to pursue a strategy that got rid of water; the second, to find water.

Belizeans live in an environment characterized by high rates of just about everything: high dropout rates from schools, high unemployment, high rates of teenage pregnancy and high death rates as a result of botched abortions. High single parenting, fairly high infant mortality rates, high rates of crime, violence and incarceration, high rates of HIV/AIDS...the list is seemingly endless. If we wished to interact effectively with one or more target populations within this environment, we would need an effective strategy. In order to develop effective strategies, we need at least a basic understanding of the theories of community development that allow these strategies to emerge. As we'll see, there's a poor fit between both the theories and the emergent strategies on one hand, and the reality of Belize on the other.

At this point, we have probably come to realize that Belizeans are hardly passive unfortunates in the Third World. They don't behave like despondent, hopeless wretches awaiting salvation through community development programs. The community development literature sometimes gives that impression about people from non-industrialized countries like Belize. And TV ads show bloated bellies, and flies on the faces of starving African children. Maybe that pathetic image attracts badly needed donations to community development organizations. It may also be a way of getting a comfortable and complacent audience to understand that conditions in the developing world— and this includes unprincipled capitalism—are killing people and destroying the environment. Although Belize is among the better off countries of the developing world, Third World conditions do have some application there too.

Developers often refer to the people with whom they work as the "targets" of community development. Now while the term is useful, it does make objects out of thinking people. Consequently, we may expect the developing world to be utterly lost without us, but Belizeans, among many peoples, are vital, energetic and full of humour notwithstanding the hardship and tragedy in their lives. In Belize, the "targets" of community development are certainly moving targets. When developers gallop out to the rainforest with their saddlebags laden with grants and technical assistance, they find Belizeans busily seeking survival and self-improvement on their own. Naturally, Belizeans have their own uses for what's galloping into the neighbourhood and have refined ways of securing it. The developers' objectives may be at variance with that of the local population and as a result, many community development programs go awry. In an analysis of a community-based watershed-management project in India, Meenakshi Ahluwalia notes that

> It is imperative that the "community" should not be considered as a set of passive recipients but should be acknowledged as comprised of people with diverse interests and resources who may actively shape the outcome of any intervention.[1]

Having glimpsed some of the actual opportunistic behaviours employed by Belizeans, a realistic scan of common community development theories and strategies may now show why so many community development projects have a negative impact on local ploys and isolate developers from their target populations. By seeing what's missing from these theories and strategies we will also gain ideas about what we require from an appropriate community development theory and begin exploring some ideas about how to build a more effective strategy. As we'll see in the following chapter, better theoretical approaches already exist—though they have not yet, to my knowledge, been much applied to community development.

Since we'll be relating the theories and strategies to the case of Belize just to keep things concrete, it is worth recalling that what is true for Belize cannot be universally generalized. As it happens, Belizeans often select pragmatic, self-serving action where certain other populations prefer idealistic action and value social community development over personal advantage, sometimes over their own survival. For example, the original Israeli settlers on the Kibbutz preferred idealistic action. We might say that suicide-bombers prefer idealistic action even over their own lives. Therefore, as we evaluate community development theories and strategies against what we encounter in Belize, we should ask whether the theories and strategies are flexible enough to apply to all variants of human behaviour and whether they are able to move community development beyond the constraints of moralization.

Four Development Theories

Kwong-Leung Tang groups theories into four categories: theories of Social Conscience, Modernization, Dependency and Diffusion. This division allows

Tang to offer a theoretical scan that is brief, clear, and well organized.[2] Let's take a quick look at each of these categories.

Social Conscience Theories

Emile Durkheim, the father of information-based sociology, compared society to a living structure. In a modern society, groups of people specialize to carry out important functions. He referred to a "division of labour" among the specialized working groups within society and compared these groups to organs that sustain a living body.[3] When healthy, all the organs carry out their distinct functions in a way that contributes to the continued survival of that organism as a whole and to each of its organs. To take a trivial example, any two individuals greeting each other in the morning can help maintain the social cohesion needed to keep the system running smoothly. Neither individual invented the concept of saying "Good morning!", smiling and talking about the weather, though both find themselves doing it. That is just normal behaviour in society, something people learn from society—a norm that preceded them and that (if they keep talking about the weather) will still be there after they're gone. Established norms such as greetings have the power to help maintain the social structure. In a sense, the power of social norms locks individuals into replicating or re-inventing their society. Norms, rules and mores are positive and conservative social bonds that interested Durkheim.

In contrast, fights represent a failure of individuals to sustain necessary cohesion. According to Durkheim, external change that is introduced into a society too abruptly (e.g. industrialization in the nineteenth century) threatens the ability of that society to function. Loss of social cohesion reduces the ability of specialized groups to make maximum contributions. Other "organs" that rely on such contributions will be negatively affected too and the society will begin to disintegrate. When there is disturbance of a society, individuals feel like they no longer fit because their accustomed relationship with society has changed. Durkheim called that feeling of discomfort we get when we expect "good morning" and are treated instead to a cold shoulder "anomie."

The example we used may be trivial, but when society fails badly, the negative impact on its population can be very significant. In his book, *Suicide*, Durkheim introduced the use of statistics into sociology to demonstrate an inverse relationship between suicide rates and the status of the Parisian stock market (or bourse).[4] Durkheim predicted that market fluctuations would more frequently affect unmarried, non-commissioned soldiers (that is, poor individuals with fewer ties to society, and therefore, more prone to anomie), than those with many social ties. Astoundingly, the statistics clearly showed that whenever the economy worsened, more bachelor soldiers killed themselves. The relationship was remarkable because most of the unmarried soldiers would have been too poor to be investing in the market. Thus, Durkheim was able to add credence to his argument that "society" was no mere abstraction. It generates and perpetuates powerful "norms" that shape a population's behaviour. It even has the power to kill.

Social Conscience theories make use of Durkheim's ideas about social norms to explain community development action taken by NGOs, nations and international organizations. It can be seen that societies will intervene when there's a fight between individuals. In most societies, including that of Belize, social norms are such that people tend to rush between combatants, trying to patch things up—apparently because the fights threaten everybody's stability. In Belize, a neighbour may do it. When there was ethnic war in the former Yugoslavia, the United Nations intervened. If the intervention is effective, the social order is preserved. Just as social niceties aren't so much invented as inherited, so is fence-mending. According to Social Conscience theorists, fence-mending is implicit within more evolved society.

Such theories accentuate positive and relatively altruistic action by individuals who bring disaffected parts of the social whole back into the fold to eliminate the obstacles to social evolution. In addition, Social Conscience Theorists argue that the social norm of breaking apart feuding individuals evidently evolves. More advanced societies try to end regional conflict among less advanced ones. We even see them develop pro-active strategies to preclude the need for conflicts to erupt in the first place. By extending credit to micro-entrepreneurs, for example, we are attempting to head off the need for the unemployed to become revolutionaries. That widening and deepening sense of social obligation, the Social Conscience theories suggest, is an example of very evolved norms from very evolved societies.

Kwong-Leung summarizes three of the major criticisms levelled against this explanation of community development. In the first place, we're dealing here with a kind of well-meaning ethnocentrism. Behind the effort to have the poor and miserable "Have-nots" join our more evolved middle-class paradise is the assumption that they want to do so. Furthermore, there is an assumption that their world is less evolved and innately inferior to ours.

Social Conscience theories critics also observe that there's no supporting evidence for altruistic community development. They say that everybody's in it for some personal benefit—even if it's the pleasure of having helped somebody else. The Social Conscience explanation of what's wrong ignores political process, economic development and class interests. After all, this theory is an outgrowth of Durkheim's structural functionalist perspective on the world. He was not asking why societies fail to endure, but what humans do to maintain social cohesion and solidarity. There is as much evidence for social cohesion as for social conflict, but Social Conscience theories really don't have a way of explaining class conflict.

The third criticism of the Social Conscience theories of the world is connected to the previous one: Social Conscience assumes that goodwill drives public policy. Now goodwill may drive altruistic community development organizations and charity organizations, but it's probably not the principal motivating factor behind Belize's Parliament, for example. A Parliament exists to negotiate resolutions to competing interests, not to sacrifice for others.

Belizean behaviour is inconsistent, as the examples of minimaxing strategies in the previous chapter showed. Belizeans are evidently adept at forming instrumental, co-operative alliances and are equally capable of engaging in competitive action against other factions. As individuals, Belizeans are able to leave their current alliances in pursuit of more promising alliances with competitive factions and are able to rejoin the old alliances at a later point. In 2002, when the bus company offered unacceptable service and raised fares, some riders demonstrated, even throwing rocks at the police. These volatile acts were committed by a population descended from people who seldom had slave rebellions and who are generally considered to be pacific to the point of complacency.

Social Conscience theory, which tries to understand why people try to patch things up, is an inadequate tool to deal with such behavioural subtlety. Social Conscience theories offer an explanation for the altruistic and healing tendencies in people—including developers and target populations. But they are ethnocentric theories and cannot account for calculating behaviours. They are not able to explain anti-social aggression or manipulative behaviour. And they certainly are not able to help us understand vacillation between pacific and rebellious behaviour within the same society.

Social Conscience theories also expect a constantly evolving and creative building of alliances within societies. Such an outlook suggests that community developers should promote strategies that pull contestants apart and even cajole them into activities that preclude the necessity for fights to erupt in the first instance. As moralistic theories, they—perhaps unwittingly—motivate developers into antagonistic relationships with their targets.

Modernization Theories

Modernization theories try to systematize or chart the process of national community development and so they look like valuable tools for those attempting to hasten the process. Patterns that are characterized as successful in one place may be deliberately replicated elsewhere. The modernization theorists that operated in the 1960s made two general observations. One was that social systems around the world have been influenced by western technological institutions. Some of what works in America, for example, has been adopted elsewhere, or adapted to local conditions. There is much evidence to suggest a propensity for this strategy since aping one another is an innately primate characteristic. It is one of our principal ways of learning and we do it as individuals. It should therefore not be surprising to see strategies replicated from one farm to another, among car manufacturers, or even from one part of the world to another.

Walter Rostow observed a process of linear economic growth that passed through five stages from "traditional" to "mass consumption" societies.[5] In defining his observation, Rostow said the process applied around the world and that barring exogenous factors (by which I mean factors originating from outside the process defined by Rostow, such as wars or years of drought) every nation would pass through the stages, one at a time, in the same sequence and direction. You can roughly pin countries to one of these stages and predict which one is to come next, or understand, given the exogenous factors, how its evolution was being delayed. For developers, the implication (generally based on an oversimplification of Rostow's schema[6]) is clear: it might enable us to help nations master the next stage more quickly, or possibly even help them bypass some stages altogether and leapfrog into modernity. Clearly, such an adaptation or distortion of Rostow's theories held great promise for development.

The optimism proved to be unwarranted and there are two principal concerns have been raised about Modernization theories. The first is that

Modernization theories are ethnocentric—exactly like Social Conscience theories. They assume that everybody wants to be a western capitalist and that everybody should want to be one. Generally speaking, there is a demonstrable tendency for populations and governments to emulate the trappings of western societies and economies. People living in the largest urban centres will patronize makers of blue jeans, KFC, American music and Marlborough cigarettes. Similarly, some of the economic and management models successfully practiced in the bigger economies are praised and promoted elsewhere and have been used as loan conditions by the World Bank and the IMF. However, beneath the western capitalist skin of developing countries, the minds and guts of the societies and systems remain quite true to regional and national histories, cultures and current events, as we have noticed in Belize. A society can look and move like a duck when it really isn't one at all.

A related criticism of Modernization theories is that by accentuating the similarities in the community development of industrialized countries, the differences among them are necessarily masked. By masking the unique blend of conflicting values and ideologies that are responsible for some of the differences, we only see part of the picture. Belize for example is much affected by its arcane land tenure legislation and historical tensions among the various regions of the country and ethnic groups. These factors are reflected in the operation and programs of the political parties. And that, in turn, affects the behaviour of Belizeans of different races, income levels and locations.

As a result, and notwithstanding the generalizations that can be cited to make development appear similar across nations, the development of specific nations will be unique. The closer we look at similarities, the more dissimilar they become. For developers, it is the differences that matter. Modernization theories limit us to studying the superficial appearance of similitude. They do not encourage us to examine the unique formative pressures. They also burden us with values. A hierarchy is established in which "primitive" nations are valued less than modern, industrialized ones. The function of community development is to move people up the hierarchy toward a fixed objective. That encourages the use of didactic strategies to stifle improper attitudes and behaviours and to impart improved methods.

Belizeans admire much about the United States and other modern economies, but not everything. They have the ability to take aspects of US culture and use them in original ways. In the US, blue jeans may be worn to project an image. The image is bound up with a cowboy past. It has something to do with being rugged, with being an outdoor sort of person. Jeans are form fitting. On the proper form, they may be attractive. We might surmise that, in the US, blue jeans are all about independent achievers—lively libertarians, if you will, pursuing happiness.

In Belize, blue jeans are worn because they're American. Americans are rich and powerful. Belizeans like being identified with power for their own reasons. Some Caribbean scholars identify a hunger for legitimacy, for respectability or for reputation among the people of the Caribbean.[7] Perhaps blue jeans, when worn by Belizeans, reflect a longing for legitimacy.

As a rule, Belizean minds are not focused upon moving a nation towards American modernity. Modernization may excite developers, but may be a bit of an irrelevancy for many Belizeans. Some parts of the world reject the American model altogether and may be pursuing Moslem fundamentalism and personal purity, for example. Modernization, let alone blue jeans, is an irrelevancy here too.[8]

The historian Robert Nisbet takes on theories like those of Marx or Rostow more directly.[9] Nisbet argues that community development and growth in the Third World are not, by necessity, immanent, cumulative, unidirectional or unilinear.[10] That expectation flies in the face of history and Nisbet cites numerous examples to make his case. For example, economies are tied. So economic growth or recession in major economies will have some kind of effect on dependent economies. Niches filled by some countries will blockade others. When the economy of Belize becomes attractive to Central American *campesinos* looking for jobs in the agro-industry and at the same time becomes economically untenable for urban Belizeans who seek opportunities in Houston, Los Angeles and New York, the socio-economic community development patterns in Belize will be uniquely affected.

The complexities of the weather and regional climactic patterns and the nutrition and health of the population can also vary enormously. History is so filled with examples of social change that is multilinear, that progresses and recedes and that does not become increasingly "civilized," that Rostow's presumption of historical "unfolding" appears to be an irrelevant and ethnocentric imposition of Western—especially American—historical oversimplification upon everybody. The progression of stages never can be confirmed except in those countries that Rostow used to establish his model in the first place. You also can't ever use the stages to make predictions. In the end, defending Rostow becomes counter-productive and Occam's razor cuts through the myth of stages: the simplest explanation is best.

Dependency Theories

By the late 1960s, neo-Marxist Dependency theories had become popular among Third World intellectuals as a challenge to the Modernization theories favoured by capitalist countries. In the manner of Conflict theorists, they divided the world into centre (or developed/metropole) and periphery (or underdeveloped/satellite) nations. Their perspective was that the success of the former group has created the unfortunate condition of the latter. For the countries on the periphery, access to modernization has been effectively and permanently blockaded by the developed nations. The extraction of their natural resources leaves nations at the periphery impoverished and impotent, and all their systems have become co-opted by the capitalist economies and are dependent upon them.

One of the problems with this pessimistic description of the total subjugation of everybody by a few is that it is then possible to offer only limited policy options, if any. The game has pretty much been lost already and isolation is one of few alternatives. South Yemen and Somalia have sometimes cited as examples of this isolationist strategy.

Another problem with the Dependency theoretical approach is that it doesn't always fit the facts. Some of the nations that were supposed to be highly underdeveloped have experienced rapid growth, as well as periods of dramatic economic shrinkage—Taiwan, Indonesia, Malaysia and the Philippines come to mind. The characterization of underdevelopment and the behaviours that are supposed to flow from it tend to be inaccurate or simplistic and the degree of independence and creativity of so-called underdeveloped nations is sometimes greater than the theorists have expected. In contrast, rapid growth has sometimes been easier when isolation is abandoned, as has been the case in China and perhaps even Vietnam.

The model of dependency and underdevelopment is both simplistic and deterministic. When nations evolve in unexpected ways, this points to important factors that affect them and that have not been included in the model. Dependency theorists seem to forget about factors like climate, geography, culture, class struggles or decision-making. Economic forces, which are automatic and impersonal, are the only ones thought to be affecting the interrelationship of nations. But, when closely examined, the interrelationships are highly varied.

Although is seems as if Modernization and the Dependency theories are polar opposites of each other, they do share one shortcoming in common. Both attempt to build development models by lumping whole nations into categories and then generalizing about them. The Modernization theorists look for a hierarchy of nations in community development; the Dependency theorists see an unbalanced conflict between nations that "have" and those that "have-not." Both theories fail to make very good predictions because they ignore the unique features of each country. In the end, these features that have to be left out of the model may prove to be as significant as the similarities.

Dependency theories are about the ownership and control of resources and the generation of wealth. There is no doubt that Belize is a peripheral nation. It exports raw materials and buys them back again from the manufacturing countries at the economic centre—such as the US and Britain. Ownership and control of resources and the limited ability to generate wealth are critical issues. But in Belize, regionalism, political clientelism and authoritarianism are important factors that shape that country's development. So are factors of cultural pluralism and Belize's geographical location between the Caribbean, Mexico and the Central American nations.

Strategies that emanate from the dependency perspective will focus on ways for Belizeans to regain power or, if that is deemed impossible, on better methods of making do with what is available. This implies a need to galvanize support to confront those who hold power and to regain it from them. Alternatively, it means that you have to find ways of getting them to resist temptation to regain power and instead making do. Meanwhile, local strategies in Belize often have to do with self-aggrandizement and immediate gratification. Therefore, developers may be pulled into ideological conflict with target populations.

Diffusion Theories

The final group of development theories summarized by Kwong-Leung are diffusion theories or theories of faulty development. You might call them "Bad Advice Theories." They postulate that, though the colonial rulers have left, they still exert powerful influence over the developing countries and remain the authority figures for the policymakers in the erstwhile colonies. The advice they proffer is faithfully adopted and the principal beneficiaries are those who are closest to systems and economic innovations instituted in the developing countries. But the advice is faulty because it ignores local realities and the policies that are adopted are inappropriate or incorrect. The national economy suffers as a result and so do most of the people. To correct the problem, the former colonial countries give out new advice.

Critics of this explanation observe an overemphasis of the importance of external factors such as imperialism, colonialism, and international organizations. In African nations for example, the colonial powers offered a model of how things were to be done and who was to be considered important. This didn't mean that local ways and local elites had entirely evaporated. The argument may be more valid in the New World, where orphan populations were introduced from many locations and sometimes deliberately mixed to reduce collusion and the threat of rebellion. However, anthropologists from Melville Herskovits[11] onward were able to demonstrate that much was actually retained even in the most culture-hostile situations. A recent paper on Belize suggests the same ability to retain or adapt cultural practices of the various non-European ancestors of modern day Belizeans.[12] External institutions may be important, but they aren't the only team in town.

Another criticism has been that the internal factors have been downplayed. These "internal factors" refer not just to the institutions, but also include the ongoing local processes such as class conflicts, labour movements, and political machinations and the panorama of survival ploys. They must not be ignored.

Diffusion theories also ignore local ability to devise original solutions. One cannot assume that Third World people are simple replications of the colonial masters, or that they only repeat behaviours recommended by authorities or by history. If people can learn from these examples, it follows they can also learn from the immediate conditions around them and that they have the ability to devise strategies that can benefit themselves, even if that's done at the expense of the rest of the population, the environment and the economy. Some may argue that the ploys described in the previous chapter relate to Belize alone, or at best, to the Caribbean population. I counter that their argument is probably untrue. The behaviours described may re-appear in culturally unrelated situations if the formative pressures are analogous. But, to the extent that the criticism is accurate, it serves as an acknowledgement of the local ability of Belizeans to devise original solutions and as recognition of the limitation of diffusion theories.

Since Diffusion theories decry the adoption of irrelevant advice from former controlling powers, we can expect that community development strategies that emanate from such a perspective will try to help former colonial nations strengthen resistance to foreign influences and develop indigenous programs and policies instead. This approach at least has the merit of trying to determine what is appropriate for national development. However, if policymakers in a developing country are pursuing personal benefits and undermining opposition initiatives, regardless of the validity of their sermons, developers will be preaching to the deaf. Furthermore, in a clientelistic system, the voters will already have been co-opted by the politicians and are unlikely to forsake current assistance from politicians for the purpose of attempting risky improvements to the national system unless there is some form of coercion.

Five Common Weaknesses

In addition to the particular problems associated with each of the theories summarized, there are weaknesses common to them all that limit their relevance and utility for community development.

A Focus on Structure Over Process

All of the theories presented above attempt to offer explanations of change in social structures that can be applied from one state to another. The people involved in social change are no more than objects acted upon by social forces.

Social Conscience theories assume deepening social obligation and increasing generosity as a by-product of progress. It is the state of progress (i.e. the structure) that matters to the theorists, not the categories of interactive behaviours (i.e. the processes) that are typical of specific states at various levels of progress.

Similarly, Modernization theorists are interested in the particular states of economic growth (again the social structures) and in the structural characteristics of nations that are thought to resemble each other more and more as they progress. The theoretical focus does not really consider the changing pressures on people or the ways in which people adapt their behaviours and interactions as a result of the changes.

The Dependency theorists study the clash of metropole and peripheral nations to see how the former underdevelop the latter. Then they tend to make faulty predictions by ignoring all the interactions in process that they consider unrelated to structures in conflict. The actual alliances and factions (i.e. the processes of survival) within either camp are not included. The same tendency is true of the Diffusionists. They will make categories of imperialist and colonial nations and of international organizations. They tend not to delve into people's class, labour or political alliances. They neither examine the conditions under which one sort of alliance is chosen over another, nor study the way in which local alliances actually devise original strategies. In addition, Diffusionists also do not trace the impact of their solutions on other groups.

However, in Belize, we observed people remaining isolated, organizing into alliances, or feuding with others. These processes of social interaction and the way they change the status quo have to be explained. Developers need to know the conditions under which people behave as they do so that they can determine appropriate roles and activities for themselves.

A helpful theory must also be able to order and interpret the volatile alliance and competition of political parties, labour unions, and groupings based on colour, religion, gender, ethnic groups and so forth over time. The pressures of economically powerful nations, former colonial powers and international agencies have to be encompassed by a relevant community development theory as well as by the varying pressures of local opportunities and threats. There also has to be a place for a range of values and ideologies within the alliances and factions within nations and across regions that contributes to the many ways that people interact and institutions operate.

Link Needed Between Environment and Behaviour

A second consistent gap in the four theoretical approaches is that they offer no way of connecting the behaviour of individuals to the structure of a society like Belize or to the changes it's undergoing or to the pressures that affect it. There's no way to connect societal changes to changes in an individual's behaviour. The Social Conscience theorists claim that more developed nations produce citizens whose sense of social obligation and depth of generosity is more profound than that of people in less developed nations. Assuming for the moment that this is true, one is still left confused: how does this occur? One can provide counts of dollars per citizen collected in the two types of nations and calculate the hours of voluntary service per capita. The higher income countries may score better on both accounts, but these figures don't tell us what a society does to make its people greedy or altruistic? How does this come about? How does rising income generate greater generosity? Or does income rise because the people in some countries are more generous than in others? If it takes altruistic people to have a developed country, then how does one make greedy people more generous?

Modernization theories define the community developmental stages through which nations pass as they come to be like the industrialized nations.

But what are people doing to cause this to happen? Within any stage of community development, nothing is said about the pressures that cause people to move their society to the next stage nor about the way in which they make it change.

Dependency theories examine the ways in which rich nations underdevelop the poor ones. There are effective blockades that prevent competition with the nations at the centre and there is often a destructive extraction of resources in the underdeveloped country. In a Third World country it should be in everybody's interest either to reduce personal risk by accepting the inequality, or to benefit from the relationship if possible. If this is the case, why has there been rapid and robust economic growth in some of them? The Dependency theorists are silent about the opportunities offered to some individuals within the satellite countries that allow them to develop strategies that move their countries to offer competition to the metropole nations.

Diffusion theories study the way colonial nations charm their former colonies into accepting bad advice and give examples of such influence. In the face of all the other choices pressuring the Third World decision-makers and of people who pressure them, we would benefit from knowing which choices are made and the bases for making them.

For developers, it is precisely the interaction between individuals and their environment (that is, pressures from social, cultural, economic, environmental and political quarters) that is part of what needs to be made clear. These are the factors that shape the choices made by the population. The decisions they take are the stuff of social change. For this reason, an ability to link individual and environment is part of what is required in an appropriate theory of community development.

Inability to Track Change

From the perspective of developers, a third theoretical shortcoming is the inability of any of these theories to track change. The various theories can only show us "freeze frames" of different societies or of the same society at different moments in history. Social Conscience theories can't demonstrate the process whereby generosity increases and Modernization theories have no way of demonstrating the passage of a society from one stage to another. Dependency theories cannot show under-development occurring and Diffusion theorists cannot track faulty policies flowing from bad advice.

None of the four approaches is designed to show us a society in the process of transition from one condition to another. We require a theory of social

125

change able to do that. For developers who are interested in supporting beneficial change, a theory of development needs to be a theory of change and should be capable of explaining how change occurs. Theories that explain the influence society has on individuals, as well as the effect individuals have on society cannot be linear because there is a dialectic between the environment and the individual.

Poor Ability to Predict and to Test Predictions

None of the four groups of theories can offer developers much help in making scientific predictions or in testing them. Yet the ability to just that should be a critical capability of a theory that attempts to explain social change because developers need to know if their efforts are having an effect. The conceptual frameworks presented focus on social structures and are therefore in a poor position to allow predictions about what populations will do. They describe depths of generosity, stages of growth, or increasing underdevelopment as universal inevitabilities, but do not explain the role of populations in achieving those changes. They are frequently wrong about the inevitabilities they forecast because the factors related to them are not included in the descriptions. When reality doesn't comply with their expectations, they need to fault "exogenous factors." Marx had to do that whenever he had to backfill on his predictions about the inevitability of state socialism that failed to emerge from the tottering British capitalism of the mid-nineteenth century. Marx's *Eighteenth Brumaire of Louis Bonaparte* was written to explain why France reverted to dictatorship instead of progressing, as he had predicted, to State Socialism.[13] To explain the unexpected turn of events, he was obligated to depart from class conflict and to define sub-categories of classes and the immediate forces affecting them—forces that were external to his theories.

In analogous fashion, the Modernization theorists would have to tell us that the Philippines would have reached "economic take-off" (one of Rostow's terms) except that exogenous religious/ethnic tensions in the south distracted that country from an otherwise inevitably bright economic future.

To this point, therefore, we still lack a community development theory that is capable of permitting hypothesis testing and that can allow us to learn lessons from failed predictions which can be incorporated in new predictions. Such an approach would gradually improve our predictive capacities.

Moral Limitation of the Theories

A final characteristic common to the four approaches is that each of them rests upon moral assumptions of right and wrong, rather than upon economic assumptions of more or less. As a result, strategies emerging from any of them are directed at getting what exists to change in the direction of what ought to exist. That in turn makes it necessary for local populations to change behaviours. Ultimately, therefore, getting them to do so becomes the responsibility of the developers and necessarily encourages them to make target populations do what they apparently would rather not be doing.

For example, the Social Conscience theories seek to explain why modern societies increasingly become involved in achieving global social justice. The assumption is that societies should be doing so. Where Third World populations, or classes within them, hesitate to promote social justice, or are responsible for denying human rights, moralistic community development behaviours would encourage developers to get local populations involved, or to stop making others suffer. A moral assumption underlying Modernization theories is that within the hierarchy of community development, higher stages are of greater value than lower ones. The purpose of moral community development work is therefore to ensure that nations achieve the higher levels more quickly. Consequently, some method of convincing them to do so seems like an acceptable thing to do. In a similar way, Dependency theory values the independence of peripheral nations over their subservience to those at the centre. The purpose of moral community development work is then to end the negative relationship. Diffusion theory places greater value on independent judgement and choice than on slavish implementation of the bad advice handed out by the more powerful nations. In these cases, the moral action of developers should be to get local people to think for themselves and to be bolder about taking independent action. Why not find some way of convincing them to do so?

Three Community Development Strategies

Louis A. Woods and John M. Perry have identified three major national economic community development options—or recipes for hastening change—that are available to Belize.[14] These options are dependency, autarky and regional interdependency and they are logical applications of one or more of the four theoretical groupings described by Kwong-Leung. While the particular circumstances Belize faces are unique, the strategic alternatives Woods and Perry describe are included here because they are broadly applicable to many, if not most, developing nations and encapsulate the development work that is actually attempted.

The alternatives Woods and Perry offer per se are not moralistic. That is, any one of them cannot be said to be better or more evil than any other. Yet they do raise some moral dilemmas, such as the issue of forced inducement. The moral problem doesn't lie in which course of action to choose, but in what you have to do to other people to make any of the choices work.

Dependency

Dependency is the non-strategy that flows from the dependency theory described above. The underdeveloped nations exist in a world of unequal exchanges with nations at the centre. At an earlier time, it was hoped the trading relationship with the more industrialized nations would allow earnings to flow down to the satellite nations. Careful harbouring of earnings and strategic reinvestment would yield economic growth and an ability to redirect surplus into poverty alleviation programs such as education, nutrition, health, shelter, water and sanitation, infrastructure, transportation and communication. Dependency theorists demonstrate increased polarization of wealth within and between developed and underdeveloped nations and classes. Also, they demonstrate the blockades and the mechanisms for wealth extraction that promote dependency and worsening poverty. Clearly, dependency relationships are destructive. However, continued dependency has not been the fate of all poor nations. Some, especially the "Asian Tigers" (Malaysia, Indonesia, Philippines), have demonstrated periods of remarkable growth. Because the descriptions are not quite accurate and because they are so lacking in recommendations for change, other strategies have been considered.

Autarky

Autarky, or self-sufficiency, was recommended as an alternative to dependency and reflects the influence of both dependency theory and modernization theory. Under autarky, the key to self-sufficiency is import substitution. In many developing countries, for example, you can buy locally made or imported breads—breads made from imported wheat. Import substitution meant cutting off the importation of foreign wheat and wheat products and substituting for them local products such as corn tortillas. Stiff importation tariffs or complete bans were imposed in some countries to give the nascent home industries a chance to develop.

For example, Belize produces delicious Spanish peanuts. Yet when somebody tried to produce peanut butter locally, the experiment failed: once the tariff wall went up against the international producer, Jiffy, so did the price of local peanut butter. Locally produced peanut butter cost more than Jiffy used to cost. And it tasted bitter. The reason for the bitter taste is simple: between the peanut halves at the tip you find a little "Santa Claus" that becomes the new shoot if the unroasted nut is planted. This tiny piece of the nut has to be removed to make the peanut butter taste right and the Belizean company didn't have the foreign capital to buy the extractor and may have lacked the technology to use and maintain the equipment if it did obtain an extractor. To buy that equipment and its replacement parts, you'd have to have access to hard currency. That comes from exporting goods and services and the bitter peanut butter wasn't yet good enough to export. An inevitable cycle develops: the more imports you substitute, the less hard currency you have to purchase the foreign goods you do need.

Beyond the basics of production, the peanut butter venture was doomed for other reasons too. The peanut butter jar and the label looked primitive. Belizeans had just come out of a demeaning colonial relationship with Britain and nobody wanted to tolerate a product that was both costly and primitive at that time—especially when they had been eating the savoury American stuff that made you feel modern. Even more so when that modern stuff was cheaper.

Who was to benefit from purchasing local peanut butter? The government and the manufacturer might say all Belizeans, from the farmers and factory workers to the consumers and the economy, would benefit. But first and foremost, the factory owner would benefit and why should the poor man suffer to benefit him?

The principal source of income for government was (and still is) from import and export tariffs. The local product wasn't yet good enough for export and Jiffy import tariffs were drying up. So altruism died fast in the face of economic reality.

And that, in a nutshell—if you will forgive the pun—is the challenge of autarky. That which is eventually good for the whole may not be desirable to the individual in the short term. To gain their support, Belizeans would have to be convinced that their short-term agenda needs to be sacrificed for the greater good. That's a lot to expect—especially when the target population is currently struggling.

Regional Interdependency

As a strategy, regional interdependency represents a more moderate, but also more complex approach to community development than import substitution. It also reflects the influence of Dependency and Modernization theories. Regional interdependency works on the premise that trading relationships with a set of countries within the region should be established. As it happens, Belize has two to choose from. One includes the CARICOM nations of the Caribbean (who are, unfortunately, hard to reach given problems of distance and poor transportation links). The other is the Spanish-speaking, Central American Common Market (CACM) countries that have better developed economies and historically have not achieved extensive economic relationships with English-speaking Belize, which is claimed as a province by Guatemala.

With reduced or non-tariff agreements in place to make regional products cheaper than those imported from the metropolitan countries, products and services that are not readily available in one or more of the other partner countries may then be traded within the trading block. There is much product duplication within a region, but there are some desirable trades too. This alternative is more moderate because it is still possible for participating countries to retain trading linkages with the metropolitan countries—it is just that the degree of dependence on the metropole is reduced as intra-regional trade increases.

There are some practical obstacles that challenge regional interdependence, including identifying product niches within the region, since many can be quite similar, given a degree of uniformity across member nations. Participant nations also have to arrange and maintain equitable and functional trade agreements that take note of pricing, legislative and other variations among the nations in the trading block and they have to enforce the regulations of the agreement. Given the degree of competition among importing and exporting countries, maintaining equitable and adequate intra-regional trade can be a challenge. The partners in the agreement also have to retain the support of participating governments in the face of reduced import/export tariffs, which is a principal income source to them. Finally, participants in a regional interdependency agreement have contend with paying high transportation costs, given equipment shortages, sub-standard roads, and slow border crossings.

Perhaps the toughest challenge for such an approach will stem from intra-regional trading relationships that include obstacles created by creditors, producers, packers, shippers, government trade/customs officials and vendors.

There will be problems of inefficiency, ineffectiveness, non-economic behaviours. Those problems will ultimately result from individual greed, sloth, dishonesty and other forms of irresponsibility.

The human obstacles can be attributed to the rational, survival-oriented behaviours of workers, bosses, owners, bureaucrats and politicians functioning within clientelistic environments.

The Interdependence of Process and Structure

So we have come full circle. The success of otherwise rational strategies is frustrated by the need of individuals to succeed. The strategies of autarky and, especially, of regional interdependency, clearly have merit—if they can be made to work. They are designed to resolve the socio-economic needs of nations and deliver benefits to economies and to the population in the mid- to long term. Their flaw is that they tend not to pay enough attention to current transactions, to what's occurring in the Valley of Means. It is the immediate needs of poor and rich alike that become a critical factor for developers—not just those concerned with social justice and community development, but also for those who concentrate on national economic issues.

Evidently, for community development to have impact, neither regional economics nor individual decisions made across populations can be accentuated or prioritized. Neither can systems in the one area be implemented independent of initiatives in the other. Macro- and micro-level socio-economic community development are of a single cloth and holistic methods of approach and implementation must be developed that allow community development initiatives and initiatives at national and even regional and local levels to become mutually beneficial.

As a result, we must build an appropriate community development strategy that makes use of a process-oriented community development theory that is capable of explaining the inter-relationship of individual interactions and socio-economic change at any level. All possible outcomes must be contemplated by the theory. We will now devise an approach that allows us to support local decision-makers' grasp for the ends they seek in the short-run. As developers, we will ensure that two additional results occur: first, the personal efforts of individual minimaxers must open new possibilities to other minimaxers; and second, the self-serving action of all minimaxers must change the socio-economic opportunity matrix. The original best option for individuals is competitive and necessarily destructive of others and of the environment. The evolving best choice for individuals must become increasingly co-operative and of mutual benefit to all minimaxers and to the natural environment.

The Development Potential of Process Theories

FROM OUR PREVIOUS discussions, we have been able to recognize that in places like Belize where there is clientelism, there is a frantic organization and re-organization of social alliances as individuals attempt to get a close as possible to those who are able to provide them with scarce and badly needed resources. If possible, they make direct alliances with patrons or their gate-keepers. If this is not possible, they ally themselves to others who have better access. They engage in competition with other factions to reserve coveted resources for themselves, but if the alternative faction appears sufficiently successful, they might choose to abandon their own alliance and associate with the competing faction. We saw that the result of all this animation is a kind of "dynamic stasis" where the overall structure of society—the interdependence of the classes of rich and poor—remains unchanged, notwithstanding the fevered scramble among survivors and some shifting of roles. The dependence on patrons and the competition with peers strengthened the position of the patrons and undermined the solidarity of the clients as a class. As a result, effective pressure groups that are able to exact or sustain change seldom come into being and community development stagnates. The paradox of underdevelopment is that everybody wants the situation to be different, but nobody can afford to go first.

For successful community development to occur, it is necessary that the survival strategies of a critical mass of people shift. Developers try to facilitate this process, but the structural theories and strategies they generally employ and which we have reviewed are not appropriate for their needs and put developers into opposition with their targets. In spite of the obvious differences between them, all the theoretical approaches focused on the social institutions and the related strategies focused on ways to make them change. Human activity was largely ignored in favour of society and its by-products. Human activity serves as an impediment to the success of the corrective strategies. What matters—or rather, ought to matter—to developers is that behaviours affect structures and consequently we need to examine how they do so.

Group Behaviours May Shift Over Time

In 1971, two University of Wisconsin anthropologists, Sidney Greenfield and Arnold Strickon, introduced a theory of social change that they called "Populational Decision-Making."[1] They knew that social characteristics such as passivity and aggression distinguished populations, but described them poorly. In the Caribbean, for example, Jamaicans are known for their aggressive nature and history, while Belizeans are characterized by their placid nature and peaceful history. Yet Belize has experienced slave rebellions and violent labour action, just as Jamaica has. Like Jamaica, Belize also has maroon communities comprised of the descendents of escaped rebel slaves (Gale's Point Manatee and Sittee River). Neither the Jamaican nor the Belizean characterization is particularly accurate and neither characterization explains the inconsistencies in the society. How can a society be both pacific and violent? We have seen that structural theories either deal well with conflict, or with social continuity, but not with both.

Greenfield and Strickon realized that none of the existing theories could explain the inconsistencies and they therefore attempted to set out a theory that could make sense of the apparent paradox. They called their theory Populational Decision-Making and their quasi-Darwinian metaphor of adaptation concerns itself with populations of individual, goal-directed organisms in an environment.[2] In an unpublished paper, Greenfield and Strickon subsequently elaborated on their theory and its origins and likened social change to the Darwinian theory of natural selection and adaptation[3] :

> By analogy we maintain that some of the varying behaviours performed by
> some of the members of a human community will enable them to obtain more
> resources—more of their goals—than will the behaviours performed by oth-
> ers. These behaviours in the environmental setting could be viewed as being
> more adaptive than behaviours that obtain fewer resources for those who per-
> form them. Extending the analogy then, it would follow that as in the
> biological model where successful variants have more offspring, so in the
> social world those behaviours that result in the acquisition of relatively larger
> amounts of available resources for those who perform them may be consid-
> ered more adaptive. The more successful variants of behaviour then could be
> expected to be found in increased frequency at later periods of time. The result
> would be a process comparable to Darwin's theory of natural selection. But
> whereas in biological evolution the effects of natural selection are transmitted
> by genetic means, in the model of social reality, we are proposing the effects
> are transmitted by means of learning.[4]

Individuals are goal-directed. The goals for which they strive may be more
complex than food, water or shelter. Greenfield and Strickon argued that people make decisions within "social contexts in which they are interacting with 1)
material and biological things in the environment, 2) other members of their
communities and, 3) the symbolic abstractions and definitions they have come
to share with specific others."[5] Recent research findings by C.P. Fong and R.S.
Wyer support Greenfield and Strickon's 1977 model: individuals' decisions are
dependent on situational factors, which include the expected utility of the outcome—which can be measured not only in financial terms but also in units of
affect and the perception of risk associated with the expected outcome.[6] Both of
these factors are affected by gauging others' decisions. The relative weight
assigned to the importance of others' decisions can vary according to national
culture. Risk perception varies with national culture.

The way people go about achieving their goals is therefore intimately
bound to the situation they encounter. The situation is variable and therefore so
is the behaviour that emanates from the situation. Some situations evoke a
placid response and others an aggressive one. Behaviour makes sense when the
contexts (historical and current, natural and social) are known. Individuals
within a particular group go through the process of allocating the resources
available to them. Strickon and Greenfield say their focus on process is additional to descriptions of social structure. They do not imply that

decision-makers operate in a vacuum independent of their environment. Roles, statuses and the expectations that accompany the behaviour of individuals exist prior to their decision-making. Existing formal and informal institutions and the people who have roles within them can provide individuals with access to desired resources. Strickon and Greenfield consider the ways individuals actually manipulate the resources they control within the constraints of their circumstances. The economic assumptions that are inherent in their decision-making approach are made explicit by Samuel Popkin, a political scientist who used data from Vietnam to support his assertions with regard to used cost and benefit. Popkin expects "that peasants are continuously striving not merely to protect but also to raise their subsistence level through long- and short-term investments, both public and private."[7]

A strategy is a problem-solving behaviour. Decision-makers may be more or less aware of the strategy they use. To be an effective and established strategy, it is enough that a choice be made that may be of some advantage to a person, and that the choice be repeated. A person may also make a lateral transfer of the strategy across a set of similar situations, a mental process psychologists call "generalizability." For example, a person might tear up stems and leaves to get to the carrot they're after. The person may try the same action to open a box of Cheerios for the first time. Repeatedly tearing up things to access a reward represents patterned behaviour. Personality represents a complex of patterned behaviours. Just as we develop patterned ways of getting at carrots and Cheerios, so we also develop patterned ways of dealing with our neighbours. A person develops an established way of interacting with others through trial and error over time.

The Greenfield and Strickon theory of Populational Decision-Making departs from those investigated in the previous chapter in a number of ways. For them, the focus of attention is not on the way in which society affects individuals—as it is with the structural theorists. Populational Decision-Making reverses the perspective by observing individuals within a context of opportunities and constraints to detect the impact they have on societies. Viewed as decision-makers, individuals appear to be less the pawns of circumstance than they are when viewed from the opposite perspective. Their behaviours are demystified. The structural functionalist perspectives show us isolated soldiers who kill themselves when the market fails, but when these soldiers are observed as individuals, we can see the results of their decision and their interaction with material and biological objects, with other people, and with shared concepts and meanings, as a way of gaining something they value, or to avoid the loss of something they cherish. Even suicide is a choice.

Durkheim talked about "mechanical" solidarity as compared to "organic" solidarity. Mechanical solidarity accentuates the sameness of segmented labour groups in "primitive" societies. People tend to live parallel lives. If one woman pounds grain with mortar and pestle, so do all. If one youth hunts, so do the rest. Unity, or "mechanical solidarity" comes from shared behaviours and beliefs.

By contrast, some women in a modern society (an organic one) may assemble watches while others may calculate solid fuel needs for rockets. There is a more elaborated division of labour. Durkheim's "organic solidarity" comes not from the sameness of the lives of women, but from their economic interdependence. Rocket scientists depend on bread makers who depend on farmers, who depend on weather satellite rocket scientists.

Using the structural-functionalist perspective, we can either see patterns of social continuity which stem from a unity of vision—the by-product of mechanical or parallel existences—or from economic interdependence which comes from effective organic solidarity. What we cannot see are exceptional behaviours beyond the patterns. The structural approaches encourage us to talk about what most people do. In a particular African village, as an example, let us say that most women pound millet for two hours, starting at dawn. In process terms most women are therefore located at the centre of a distribution curve of a population of village women. The dawn millet pounders are the majority of women. They represent the mean point; they are the average village woman, the ones behaving "norm-ally."

In contrast, process theorists like Greenfield and Strickon think in terms of behavioural distributions instead of behavioural norms. In addition to identifying the average behaviour of village women, the process viewpoint shows us a distribution curve, a behavioural range among the village women regarding millet pounding. Not everybody does the same thing, Greenfield and Strickon remind us, and Durkheim was only typifying a range of behaviours. Unfortunately, the useful typification he engages in masks exceptions. If you studied the African village women well, you'd see that their behaviours vary. Some women might pound millet in the evening while most pounded at dawn. A very few might pound at midday, and some may pound at various times of day. Some women might delegate all millet pounding to their daughters-in-law and a few might have worked out a barter relationship with a neighbour, exchanging fowl for readied dough.

A little later, we will see that this range of strategies is as important for community development as is the description of the average or typical behaviour. It is the exceptions that account for social change. In this case, the women bartering pounded millet for butchered fowl may be on the cutting edge of change in their community, if the pun can be forgiven.

The accompanying diagrams represent evolutionary social change and are based on a theoretical scenario that helps us to clarify the Greenfield/Strickon theory. Their model of social change is complex and specifically includes cultural, environmental and social considerations in the decision-making of individuals. For the purposes of the example, however, I rely only on straight financial transactions in order to make the mechanics of the Greenfield and Strickon model as clear as possible. Without keeping the breadth and complexity of individual choice in mind, it is possible to dismiss populational decision-making as "mere financial choice," yet what I am attempting to introduce is a paradigm for less judgmental assessment of Third World dynamics than what we often encounter, and less manipulative development responses to them.

For many people who find themselves in situations where income is lim-

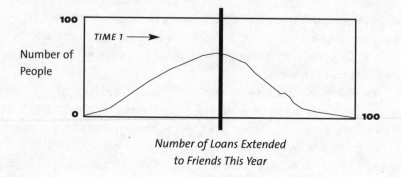

Figure 6.1
Loan Decisions: Time 1

ited, the need to borrow is great. So too is the need to lend. People who lend today are in a strong position to borrow tomorrow. Figure 6.1 represents graphically the imaginary lending behaviours of Belizean people over the period that we can call "Time 1" (T1) . While most of the people did extend loans, a few tried extending no loans (left end of curve). However, the typical Belizean extended a moderate number of loans (represented by the mean point in the middle of the curve) and fewer extended a large number of loans to friends (right end of curve). To the left and right of the mean line, different individuals are trying a range of strategies. Those on the left of the mean line resist giving loans. We can call these "stingy strategies." The fewer loans people offered, the further to the left they appear on the diagram. As we move further and further left, fewer people use this more extreme strategy. In contrast, the further people are located to the right of the mean behaviour, the more loans they are giving. But as we look to the right of the diagram, we see that fewer and fewer of them are attempting this "generous strategy."

The space outside the curve represents the Belizean environment within which loaning occurs. The diagram reminds us that the inter-relationship between the Belizean behaviours and the environment is critical. Belizeans generally engage in a minimax strategy—they tend to limit giving and to maximize

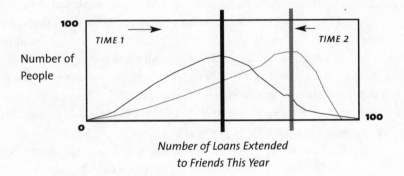

Figure 6.2

Loan Decisions: Time 1 cf. Time 2

getting. This graph shows that how much is given can be typified. But also, how much is given can vary.

Figure 6.2 adds a second curve to the first one. It also shows the distribution of Belizeans who extended loans. This second distribution happens at some later time we'll call "Time 2" (T2). Now we can see that the situation has shifted towards the "generous strategies." The new curve is skewed to the right, indicating that the average Belizean has now increased the number of loans extended. We can see that there are still some people extending no loans, but there are fewer of them.

The second graph shows an interesting development. If minimaxers hold back on their giving, why are some Belizeans lending more than others? And why would the average loan increase from T1 to T2? We know that humans are decision-makers. They have the ability to choose a strategy, more or less consciously, as a result of traditions, memories and current realities. Some combination of these three factors has been at work between T1 and T2. There has been social change as a result of decisions made within a specific population; hence, the theory is called Populational-Decision Making.

To explain social change over time, Greenfield and Strickon have introduced a Darwinian metaphor of selection that is based upon choice rather than genetic factors. At any moment in time within the distribution of behaviours that are attempted within the community, there are a few people whose strategy will later appear to have been avant garde; a better adaptation to changing circumstances than that of the average person located at the mean point of the curve of behaviours. Greenfield and Strickon call these people who later turn out to have been ahead of their time "entrepreneurs" because, as Joseph Schumpeter explained, they have been experimenting with new combinations of factors even as conditions have been shifting, and because they are discovering a relatively more rewarding innovation.[8]

For our purposes, we use the term "entrepreneur" in the broadest, most generic sense to refer to people who make new combinations. In the past, "entrepreneur" has been associated with people who cause other people to suffer. But that is no reason to shy away from the term—especially if it's part of a powerful paradigm for community development. Somebody who starts as a business is of course an entrepreneur. Scrooge in A Christmas Carol is also an entrepreneur—and for most of the story, not a not very admirable one. But the campesino I knew in the steep hills above Medellín, Colombia was an entrepreneur, too. He rented a landowner's farm on the mountainside and right at the top, he proceeded to install a pond full of Tilapia fish that he sold at the local market. Using rocks from the farmland down the steep mountainside, he built anti-erosion terraces which he filled with flowers and vegetables that he could tend standing upright. He walled the terraces with grass and used the run-off from the pond to irrigate the terraces. He chopped and mulched the grass that grew from between the rocks on the terrace walls to use as fertilizer in the flower and vegetable beds and then sold the organic flowers and vegetables in the Medellín market in the valley.

In the lend-to-friends example, there is an entire distribution of behavioural combinations that are being attempted. Some people decided not to lend to anybody. However, by T2 it turns out that the stingy strategies were less rewarding and so most of the people abandoned this strategy. The ones who engaged in more loan-giving in T1 were the entrepreneurs. But had the shift in strategy rewarded the stingy lenders more than all others, and had Belizeans swung towards that alternative, they, and not the liberal lenders, would have been seen to be the successful entrepreneurs.[9]

The majority of people shifted strategies between T1 and T2 for some reason and are lending to a larger number of friends. Evidently, the "generous" strategies employed by only a few entrepreneurs at T1 have proved to be more effective behaviour, given the current conditions. Perhaps the unemployment rate among poor Belizeans has increased, making it prudent to obligate many borrowers. Perhaps there is another explanation. But the fascinating thing about observing human decision-making is that we now find ourselves making predictions (hypotheses) about how the interactions of people might change if certain adjustments to the environment should continue to occur. And it is important for us as developers to be asking these questions because when enough people adopt new behaviours, social change also begins to occur. When the changes are beneficial, we are almost witnessing community development. That is, some of the conditions of community development are being met. These have been examples of unplanned social change. We have yet to venture into planned change.

While the concept of populational decision-making offers a real breakthrough to developers, we still need to try to explain how people go about making choices. This is an intricate and difficult issue that doesn't have any answers that are entirely satisfactory. Clark and Marshall review the problems with a number of the decision-making models which have been proposed, specifying the shortcomings of each.[10] Ultimately, they are most comfortable with a blended approach which says that to decide, people first satisfice (i.e. choose the first solution that complies with their minimal criteria—not necessarily the best solution) and then engage in utility maximization (i.e. finding the equilibrium point which provides the most benefit at the least cost—getting the most guns by giving up the least butter). By this, Clark and Marshall mean to say that people decide by finding an acceptable solution and then making the most of the choice at the least cost to themselves.

Their conclusion reminds one of the minimaxing observed among Belizeans and of Greenfield and Strickon's observation about Populational Decision-Making: the population's behavioural mean will swing in the direction of the most successful known survival strategy.

In a population, the decisions that are made and the modal behaviour can both be determined. Given some environmental forecasting, it is possible to predict which of the entrepreneurial behaviours will prove most rewarding in the near future. It is also possible to verify the prediction. If the prediction is off, the factors needed to improve predictions can also be investigated. As a result, developers have one of the important screws they need for improved success. When environmental conditions shift, target populations respond. So it isn't necessary to change the minds of grown-ups. Regardless of their mindset, they're quite capable of adjusting their behaviours when motivated to do so. And when enough of them do so, the social reality changes too.

Several screws are still missing. The target groups of primary interest to developers are the people locked into demeaning and impoverishing dependence. The greater that hopeless dependence, the greater the likelihood of their social atomization. Every individual in a dependency relationship seeks the patron's support, competing against the others in the process. There is little willingness to trust other clients and little desire to abandon the patron. Yet, paradoxically, when there is a spontaneous strike, riot or rebellion, collective action can also occur. Community development will depend on the operation of effective and sustainable collective action and on the decision of dependent individuals to participate in it. So we need to know more about it to define useful principles governing collective action.

Transactions Unite Individuals

In Figures 6.1 and 6.2, we were still looking at the decisions that are made by individuals in isolation. Figures 6.1 and 6.2 didn't actually show us change in

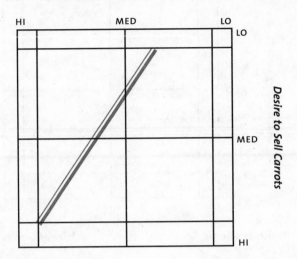

Price of Carrots   **Seller's Logic**

Figure 6.3
Carrot Seller's Logic (Sell Dear)

progress either. To this point, we have only been reviewing snapshots that froze behaviours at two moments in time. In our imaginary example, change in the borrowing and lending behaviour of many individuals occurred in Belize sometime between the first and second snapshots.

The next example (Figure 6.3) looks at a transaction between two individuals, a carrot buyer and a carrot seller in the fruit and vegetable market of Belize City. This is not yet an example of social action, but it is moving us in the right direction. Figure 6.3 shows the logic of the carrot seller. There are consequences for the buyer and seller if they complete the transaction, as well as if they fail to complete it. Completing it means a financial gain for the seller. A second criterion in her decision-making would be the loss of carrots that might bring her greater income if she had only waited a bit.

The seller has to decide whether she's better off selling now or waiting. At the same time, the buyer needs to choose between having the carrots and giving up the money, or doing without carrots and having the money, or waiting to buy later in order to have the carrots and a bit of money left over. In this example,

143

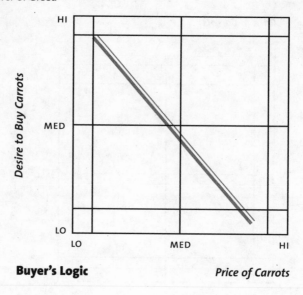

Figure 6.4
Carrot Buyer's Logic (Buy Cheap)

both individuals are attempting to optimize their situation and dealing with multiple criteria.

It is generally accepted that multi-criterion optimization in its present sense originated towards the end of the nineteenth century when Vilfredo Pareto (1848–1923) presented a qualitative definition for the concept while dealing with economic problems that featured several competing criteria. The ultimate aim of any transaction is to attain maximum optimality—that is, the level of enjoyment that a person (here the buyer and the seller of carrots) will derive from a transaction.

Figure 6.3 represents the situation for the carrot seller. In this example, the seller considers the price of carrots against her desire to sell the carrots.[12] If the price for carrots is high, then the seller's desire to sell carrots will also be high. As soon as the price drops below a medium price, her desire to sell the carrots is low. Similarly, if the price is medium, the desire to sell is about half way between low and high.

Figure 6.4 plots the strategy of the carrot buyer. The desire to buy carrots is high if the price is low and when the price is high, it is low. Now if Figure 6.3 is superimposed over Figure 6.4, we can see exactly where a transaction will take

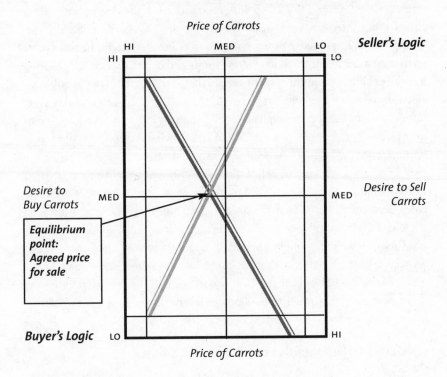

Figure 6.5
Comparison—Logic of Carrot Buyer and Carrot Seller

place (Figure 6.5). The point at which the transaction takes place is called the "point of equilibrium" and in the case of this example represents the price at which carrots must be selling to induce both the seller and the buyer to enter into a deal. The situation is said to be "Pareto Optimal" because "you can't improve anything at all without making the situation worse in some important respect." This is the point where the price and the desire to hand over carrots intersect for both the buyer and seller.

In the case of the carrot buyer and seller, we are witnessing a transaction at the moment it is occurring, as well as the conditions that give rise to it. As with Greenfield and Strickon, we are still able to predict. In fact, we can predict with some accuracy. Should any of the factors influencing the Pareto Optimal change and consequently affect the desire to buy or sell and/or the price asked or offered, we can project the new point of transaction. If the buyer's and seller's curves don't intersect, no transaction will occur. Though illuminating, this example still represents an oversimplification of life—especially because we're restricting ourselves to economic transactions and because we're still ignoring issues of culture, environment and social relations. The purchaser is only considering one purchase, whereas in real life he may need to decide about using his money for a number of purchases. The seller may also have a range of issues to consider. For example, this may be her last bunch of carrots, this buyer may be a stranger, and the person who walked up just after this buyer may be the mother of her son's wife. In Belize City, with only 49,000 inhabitants, that's a real possibility and it does begin to introduce realistic social complexities that enter decision-making. That consideration changes the calculus a lot. One could elaborate formulae to handle such complexities, but for our purposes, it is the logic of weighing options and of finding a point of equilibrium that concerns us. This example shows that we can at least make predictions about what will occur on the basis of the reality of two individuals. By extension, it follows that we can also make predictions about the interaction of groups, or of a group and an individual who are involved in transaction.

Relating Social Interaction to Behavioural Change

Greenfield and Strickon's major ideas about Populational Decision-Making are, first, that individuals need to be observed (in addition to societies) within a context of opportunities and constraints so that we can detect the impact they have on societies and, second, that individual observations are more useful when viewed as behaviour distributions than as ideal types. The process viewpoint reflects a distribution curve that represents a behavioural range of decisions across populations. Third, when enough people adopt new behaviours, social change also begins to occur and over a period of time, these social changes may be viewed as changed behavioural distributions.

What my second example—the one about the carrot transaction—adds to the discussion of social change is the realization made by Greenfield and Strickon that there can be a range of social transactions occurring around any issue at any given time. For the people buying and selling carrots, conditions will affect the price of carrots, or conditions will affect the desire to buy or to sell carrots and so the volume of carrots, or the expenditure on, or earnings from carrot dealings will change. It is the range of exchanges (money, carrots, greetings, ideas, cannon balls) that occur between people that ultimately tie individuals together—into friendly alliances, into competitive relationships, or into warring factions.

We can now take my carrot transaction example and extrapolate from it some elements that may be applicable to interactions that occur within a given population. The idea of a Pareto Optimal (not ideal) transaction point that permits an alliance between two individuals may be applicable to—and may explain—the alliance of an individual with a group seeking a collective good, or the alliance of two or more groups. It may also explain competitive or even hostile exchanges between individuals, individuals and a group, or between groups. At the level of two individuals, or an individual and a group, or of two groups, we can predict the formation of an alliance, a competitive relationship or a factional dispute. We can also predict the nature of the interaction.

All this language about "points of equilibrium" and transactions should not be confused with reaching a fair deal. A Pareto Optimization is simply a solution that, when applied, can't be improved without leaving somebody worse off. A used car salesman can walk away from an unfair deal as the value-for-money winner. The deal was still reached because the buyer wouldn't agree to spend more, just as the salesman wouldn't agree to receive less. We're looking at the mechanism of transactions here, whether they are fair or not.

The term "entrepreneur" is being used in the broadest, most generic sense to refer to people making new combinations. Somebody starting a business, is of course, an entrepreneur. The *campesino* represents the sort of entrepreneur who is important for those of us interested in community development. He was a poor and dependent individual who increased his income. When his lease expired, he also convinced a judge to force the landlord to pay for the valuable improvements or let him keep renting at the same rate. The *campesino* won. When I last visited him, he and his sons were frantically making more terraces as a way of holding onto the land and of increasing their income from it. The *campesinos* around him on the mountainside had already begun to adopt that fellow's farming and litigious practices. This entrepreneur strengthened his own position and that of his family by creating new combinations. His cutting-edge re-combinations evolved into a tiny social movement. The mean point on that mountain side was shifting and change was occurring spontaneously in the face of clientelism and dynamic stasis. The relationship between the Medellín *campesinos* and the landowners was still not fair, but what was happening between peasants and landowners on the vertical farmlands above Medellín at least made a more level playing field a possibility.

The word "entrepreneur" has in the past been associated with people who cause other people to suffer. But that is no reason to shy away from the term—especially if it's part of a powerful paradigm for community development.

The Logic of Collective Action

As we have just seen, appropriate conditions can induce a mutually beneficial transaction between two individuals and the same logic may apply to a collective shift in behaviour. By extension, it follows that conditions can shape interactions between collectives, or between them and individuals. But under what conditions will such collective action occur?

Mancur Olson reversed a popular assumption of social scientists—that people instinctively act on common interests and that inaction needs to be explained—in a book called The Logic of Collective Action.[13] Olson argued that, rather, it is collective action that is hard to explain[14] because self-interest will prevent individuals from participating in collective action—notwithstanding objective evidence to the contrary.[15] If, for example, a coastal town wanted to collect funds to build a lighthouse, the principles of self-interest suggest that there shouldn't be many contributions coming in. Anybody withholding assistance would still be able to make use of the completed lighthouse. This is called the "free rider" problem. It's a problem because, notwithstanding the obvious logic of withholding assistance, people will contribute anyway. What is their motivation?

Olson argued that larger groups tend to discourage individual participation because they reduce benefits to any one member. That is because overhead costs for large groups increase and thus raise the cost of the service to be offered, and because non-participation in the group (and use of the benefit) has no social cost—nobody knows who you are so you can't be censured or targeted for retaliation. In small groups, an uncooperative individual risks both.

How then, Olson asks, do collective action organizations overcome the free rider syndrome? He stresses the role of selective incentives, that is, special opportunities that are available to an individual beyond those offered by achieving the collective good. Membership, in other words, must have its privileges, but ironically, privileges may prove costly if too many are offered. This in turn can reduce returns to members and discourage others from joining.

Besides, selective incentives also involve some costs and paying for them also involves a collective action.[16] Furthermore, empirical evidence suggests that private incentives have a smaller effect than is indicated by the theory.[17] Olson's argument "does not take into account the existence of interactions between the actors"[18] and as Elinor Ostrom observed, "substantial evidence from experiments suggests that cooperation levels for most one-shot or finitely repeated social dilemmas far exceed the predicted levels and are systematically affected by variables that play no theoretical role in affecting outcomes."[19]

There are some people, such as Daniel Klein, who have tackled this inconsistency.[20] He examined the largely unprofitable turnpike companies of early America (roughly 1795–1840) that conferred vast benefits to the communities they served. Broadly based stock subscription solicited from both the rich and the not so rich citizens in isolated communities paid for the roads, but paid poor returns on their investments. Benefits derived from new turnpikes would be equally available to stock subscribers and free riders alike. Why then were turnpikes so broadly financed? Klein concluded that in isolated, cohesive and effectively managed towns where concepts of community independence and self-reliance ran high, it was possible for leaders to induce broad participation by using social pressure tactics among their friends.[21] Klein also noted that

> The ability of voluntary association to provide infrastructure, education, security, and poor relief depends on the exercise and spontaneous community development of certain institutions, activities, and sentiments. Since governmental bodies dominate these services it is no surprise that our faculties of sodality remain degenerate.[22]

The observation may be of comfort to "less government" conservatives, but is not quoted here in defence of their agenda.[23] It also has relevance to the issue of individual responsibility-taking and the ability of clientelistic nations to develop. Klein has isolated a relationship between intrusive government and the vigour of citizen self-reliance. We have already identified clientelism (that is, dependence of the citizenry on political patrons for problem resolution) as a predominant mode of governance in many developing nations and so Klein helps us to explain why clientelism is such an obstacle to socio-economic community development. Intrusive patrons devitalize citizen self-reliance.

Factors Promoting Collective Action

The concept of Populational Decision-Making says that when the environment is changing, the mean behaviour of a population will gradually shift until it resembles the most effective strategy worked out by some entrepreneurial individuals because the population generally employs a minimax strategy—the least investment of what they value, for the greatest return of what they desire. Work done on collective action and reported in the previous section suggests that negative incentives (e.g. fear of censure, punishment) also encourage decision-makers to participate in social movements bent on obtaining a common good.

Collective action is assumed to occur where communities are closed and homogeneous, where progressive leadership is vociferous, where the spirit of local self-sufficiency is buoyant, and also where there is little intrusion by government. According to Daniel Klein, this at least was the case in the isolated towns across Colonial America. Such conditions hardly apply to clientelistic communities where atomized individuals drift from one alliance to another and where dependency is high and leadership is cautious but highly integral to the decisions made by the population.

But even where the fear of censure and punishment is reduced, there are examples of enthusiastic participation in collective actions, such as the spontaneous bus boycott in Birmingham that followed Rosa Park's refusal to move from her seat. A Lithuanian acquaintance provided me with another example that occurred during the 1988 "Singing Revolution" and the collapse of Soviet domination by 1991. She remembered country relatives crowding into their tiny Vilnius apartment. They were among the thousands who had appeared to replace exhausted citizens who had been putting their bodies between Soviet might and the radio station and other vital installations. The sustained rebellion was spontaneous and it contributed to the defeat of the Soviet Union:

> The Baltic Nations, Estonia, Latvia, and Lithuania, emerged on the world news scene in 1989 as if from nowhere. For 50 years they had literally disappeared from the map, subsumed into the monochromatic zone of the USSR. On August 23, 1989 people in the Baltics formed a human chain stretching 430 miles through all three Baltic nations. This massive demonstration, called the "Baltic Way" human chain, told the world that they existed as nations yearning to be masters of their own destiny. Independence was finally obtained in 1991.[24]

Ironically, she added that the ensuing years of corruption and unemployment had caused Lithuanians to observe that if the call went out today for heroes, nobody would appear. Neither the intimacy of a community, nor the vociferous behaviour of its leaders applies to the altruism of Lithuanians. So the lack of leaders would not explain their subsequent egoism. If leadership and intimacy are not the primary motivators, what are? Gerald Marwell and Pamela Oliver offer a helpful observation:

> For most people, however, the most prominent and convincing evidence of a group's efficacy is probably the group's size and command over resources.... In this simple fashion, the decision of individuals who come into contact with a group or its organizer is clearly interdependent of the decision of others.[25]

At about the same moment, enough Lithuanians realized that the Soviet Union no longer had the strength to resist a civil action. At a given moment, the euphoria of invincibility and the conviction of certain victory swept a nation, enough individuals took action to make the prophecy fulfil itself. Lithuanians joined the demonstration because other Lithuanians were also doing so; the movement appeared unstoppable to everybody. Later, pervasive corruption and greed convinced Lithuanians of the futility of involvement in collective action.

We can now identify three factors that effectively motivate individuals to take collective action: 1) Availability of selective incentives desired by members of the target group; 2) Fear of censure and punishment for non-participation, diminishing the attractiveness of alternative opportunities; and/or, 3) Belief in the adequacy of a group's power (i.e. size, resources, tactical shrewdness). Otherwise, as Olson and the Lithuanians have observed, it is self-interest that will motivate the individual.

* * *

Approaches to community development work that are grounded in process theories contain a number of ideas useful for defining community development strategies based on economic thinking. Such approaches offer insights into the principles that shape the choices people make in a context of scarcity and dependence. They relate individual choices to behavioural shifts in a group or society in response to environmental flux. They explain the formation of alliances of individuals or groups with other individuals or groups and they offer us ideas about the incentives that stimulate alliance formation and induce a preference for collective action over solitary and competitive strategies.

Individual, self-serving action, as well as more collective behaviour, are both extensions of the same impulse—action taken on the basis of a personal decision to minimize loss and maximize gain of whatever is valued by the decision-maker. Collective action is a kind of conjoint and concurrent positive greed.

Our ideas about social change, the formation of alliances and reliance on collective action have been taken from unobtrusive observation of populations and environments. Community development, in contrast, is intended to increase people's opportunities through deliberate interventions. It would be interesting to see how the lessons learned above can be organized into a deliberate strategy for dismantling clientelism and for replacing it with a more co-operative basis for survival—which is exactly what we're going to attempt in the next chapter.

Greed Can Dismantle Clientelism

Supply-Led Development Projects—Shortcomings

A MORE EQUITABLE SURVIVAL strategy requires deliberate intervention and the construction of a demand-led project that can replace clientelism. But before we can begin to discuss such projects, we need to determine exactly what is lacking in other approaches, including supply-led projects. Although real projects do exist, I have chosen for the purpose of illustration to develop a hypothetical project that will help us understand clearly the shortcomings of a supply-led approach to development. I have drawn on my observations from several such projects and amalgamated the shortcomings within them into a single scenario that, I confess, deliberately exaggerates the weaknesses of a supply-led approach. I'm hoping this provides a useful way of concentrating the shortcomings for discussion.

The hypothetical construction project developed here has been kept as simple as possible for the sake of clarity—in reality, such projects are not nearly this innocent. Let's assume a certain Canadian NGO has already been involved in several house-building projects—in fact, let's assume this has become their specialty in developing countries. From the statistics available to them, they can see that, among other problems, a housing shortage is most problematic in the cities—especially in the capitals of countries where they do most of their work, perhaps in Anglophone West Africa. The project officer in the NGO's Toronto office has joined their field officer in the capital city of the target country in question and has visited the slum recommended by the field officer. They have had a tour of the neighbourhood, met some people and agreed that the houses were in terrible condition because of the mud, the poor drainage, the scarcity of public water spigots, the lack of sewerage, and adequate lighting. Also, the neighbourhood lacked other public services such as shops, schools and health clinics.

At a community meeting after the tour, they have asked the local residents what they felt they most needed. Up in third place—after "jobs" and "an elementary school" came "better houses." Based on the statistics and what they saw and commented on during their brief neighbourhood tour, the Toronto and local officers of the NGO were hardly surprised. Because this NGO specializes in house building projects, they decided it was appropriate to proceed since then at least people would get houses, something that was pretty high on their wish list and obviously needed. In their initial report, they did comment that "jobs" and "an elementary school" were important needs, and that it was a shame that the local government wasn't doing more about this. They noted that the committee should get their government to do more and that they should look for other grants to respond to these and other needs mentioned in discussions and in the report.

At the community meeting, the NGO officers had a good discussion about the size of houses. While it was clear that needs varied according to family size, it was agreed that, given the limited funding available to the NGO, a two-bedroom, one bathroom house for each of the 20 families would permit a fair start for all. As things were, many large families shared one-room shacks and in some cases there weren't even curtains to separate adults and children. The two-bedroom house would permit such a separation and the living/dining/kitchen area would be large enough that some children could sleep there at night. Besides, the community assured the NGO officers that it was easily possible to add a room or two in the future. The model they have built before has been designed to accommodate such expansion.

The kind of community enthusiasm they have encountered at this meeting has encouraged the NGO to hope that the lessons in self-help and co-operation that would be learned through this project will, in turn, encourage community residents to continue helping each other build houses and carry out a range of community activities. With co-operation, anything becomes possible, they say to each other reassuringly.

The NGO's house-building project was designed to work as follows: the neighbourhood committee, under the direction of the elected chair, was asked to draw up a list of the twenty neediest families—ones that had lived in the neighbourhood for at least at year and whose houses were in the worst condition. The NGO provided the funding for materials; the community provided the labour. A cost analysis showed that the labour was equivalent to the cost of materials or even higher, so there was about a 50/50 split between the NGO and the beneficiary group. The slum dwellers could hardly be expected to pay for materials: if they could, they obviously would not have been living in the condition seen by the NGO officers. It was clear that poor housing conditions were related to poor health—especially for children—so poverty could not be seen to be an adequate impediment to such an important developmental activity. Families that appeared on the list but who wouldn't help build the houses got no building assistance and another family was substituted in their place. Thanks to the Canadian International Development Agency (CIDA) program (funded by the Canadian taxpayer and monitored by the auditor-general), each dollar raised in Canada by the NGO was matched with a three-dollar grant from CIDA. CIDA was supportive of the work of this NGO because (based on CIDA's own research), responding to the housing shortage in Africa was a current priority for them and because the NGO had a good track record of getting the targeted number of houses built as well as a proven ability to control their administrative costs relative to their program costs.

When the project was ready, Canadian volunteers with plenty of house-building experience were flown to the tropical project site as part of the project cost. Their enthusiasm was high because helping people who really need help is wonderfully rewarding, because the local folks they met were so genuinely grateful, gracious and generous, and because it was February. The slum dwellers had practically nothing and yet they found ways to offer the Canadian volunteers snacks and modest, but very clever, handmade gifts—from little wire models of bicycles to beautiful shirts and blouses—and certainly had spent more than they should have. Some lifetime friendships were born during this visit, with many Canadians remembering their African friends at christenings, birthdays and holidays. The other reason for satisfaction was that by teaching carpentry and other skills, the Canadians hoped the employment opportunities for the slum dwellers would increase.

A project like this one is generally designed to last from 12 to 18 months, though one weakness of this NGO (from CIDA's perspective) has been that the projects tend to take 6 to 12 months longer than predicted. CIDA has spoken to the NGO about this; the NGO has promised to improve. To ensure that funds were not misspent, the NGO forwarded money to their bank account in the capital city. After the costing for the materials for each house was completed, the NGO field officer delivered a cheque to the local neighbourhood committee for sufficient funds to build the first house. When expenditures were accounted for (original receipts are required by the NGO field officer), the NGO field officer made an inspection of the completed house, congratulated the lucky occupants and the neighbourhood committee and then released funds to cover the construction of the second house. Occasionally, local communities were able to take on two or even three houses at a time and the NGO field officer, once she had a sense of the honesty of the local committee, was willing to release enough funds to allow this to happen.

By the time the project ended (12 months beyond the projected completion date), 19 of the 20 houses had been built and occupied. CIDA was not pleased about the delay, but they and the NGO agreed that the project had succeeded for the most part: planned activities were completed, almost all of the goals were achieved and funds were responsibly accounted for.

Why would I not consider this project successful and an example of good development work? As I see it, there are several problems. For one thing, this is a project that is completely supply-led. The NGO's research and field tour have made it evident that simple houses are in desperately short supply in this African country and in this neighbourhood. The evidence is quite objective and easy to defend. The people made it abundantly clear that they were willing to provide the labour and the NGO's past experience has shown that all the houses eventually get completed, though the last few are slow to finish. That's what happened this time too.

That slow finish may be a function of the project design. While enthusiasm for the project is initially high, what repeatedly happens in projects like this is that those who have already received a free new home seem less willing to help other attain theirs. They gain nothing by putting out the labour and they lose nothing (save censure and disrespect) for refusing to help. With fewer people available to help as the project finishes, the final houses take longer and longer to complete. In this project, nobody took on construction of the last house. The costs and benefits of ensuring sustained community participation have simply not been considered by the NGO.

A project like this one depends entirely on what is supplied through foreign financing. All risk is assumed by CIDA and the NGO. Should local residents not deliver labour as promised, the local residents who are willing to help build their own houses are no further behind than they were before the project was conceived. Usually, when the flow of project funds ceases, so does the house-building and the community co-operation initiatives. Frequently, the NGO moves on to a new project in another neighbourhood and is not aware of what goes on in the old neighbourhood. The report evaluated house-building activities and results; it did not assess changes within the organization of the target community, nor changes in the level of community self-sufficiency.

By working in this way, the NGO is able to accumulate an excellent record of families with new and better homes. Yet no additional houses or community initiatives are possible because nothing has accrued to the community beyond construction skills. While such skills are needed in this African capital, it is political gatekeepers and patrons who control the provision of jobs. Patronage works on the basis of what would-be workers can offer a patron, not on the level of skill they have. If the would-be workers are already in the politician's pocket, they have nothing new to offer—their votes are already promised. If they are not supporters of the politician, they can hope for no assistance. There was no assessment of the bonds of clientelism operating within the target community nor of they way they affect the social relations of production (i.e. decision-making) nor access to the means of production.

In any case, the development momentum begun by the NGO and the good-hearted volunteers soon evaporates in the target community. A few charitable links with the Canadian volunteers and 19 solid houses is what remains of the project. There is no community organization—beyond the local neighbourhood committee—that is able to define local priorities, to galvanize community members into united action for change or to martial the needed financial and technical resources for new projects independent of the existing patrons and gate keepers.

The NGO had made the mistake of working through the local neighbourhood committee without putting adequate checks and balances in place. The likelihood was great that at the very least, their chairperson had the support of the local politician. If true, it means that awarding the 20 houses to the families had become a highly political affair that related at least as much to patronage as to the poverty of those who were ultimately granted houses. The development process would have been hijacked by the political one and the Canadian NGO and CIDA may have remained unaware of this. The process for portioning out houses would not have been transparent in such a case. The real basis for deciding who got a house would not have been made known. Those who badly need better housing but who lacked the political leverage surely would have suspected that an injustice had been done to them and would have resented what happened. And the 19 lucky families have been made grateful, which is to say, dependent.

Finally, the NGO has lost a potential development opportunity in this neighbourhood by asking the wrong questions and by focusing on the housing it had wanted to supply from the outset. A housing project cannot be sustainable where people cannot afford to pay for houses, depending instead on politicians for their sustenance. Ask any impoverished community what they want: better housing will be near the top of their wish list because there is a desperate need for housing. For an NGO with house-building experience, it was easy to supply housing to this community. It was also easy for the housing NGO to convince itself that house-building was necessary after observing the bad condition of houses on the tour that preceded their community meeting and hearing it mentioned by the people.

Projects that supply housing materials have not left anything resembling an effective and sustainable collective action organization behind. There is no mechanism that, once initiated, may feed continuously off local demands instead of depending on short-term, externally supplied grants. It is the establishment of a functional demand mechanism which is the route to obtaining housing for the other families of this community for which they themselves can pay.

But ask members of that same community what they wish to achieve for themselves as individuals and how they hope to achieve it. Or ask them how much co-operation they're used to getting from their neighbours, for what purposes and under what conditions—and then a very different understanding of the "community" and of local objectives emerges. Questions like this, asked by community developers who have spent adequate time in the neighbourhood and established trust, will begin to reveal the underlying presence of factions, competing patrons, gatekeepers and issues of low trust. As seen in this invented project, such factors diminished the achievement of meaningful, durable changes. The information thus revealed, however, also gives developers the facts about the social, political and economic systems at work in the community they need. This is the information needed to construct a truly demand-led project—one whose opportunities elicit the kind of action from community members which create opportunities for other residents.

When people ask development officers for jobs, schools and housing they are saying what they say to the patrons: these are the things they badly need and hope to see supplied. And they are, as the NGO officers were able to see for themselves, quite accurate in their assessment. These are among a long list of essentials for a longer life of better quality. But as I've tried to suggest in this example, neither longer life nor life of better quality will flow to the communities in this way. Nineteen families may do marginally better in new, adequate houses. But their lives remain just as constrained because of the debt of obligation they probably owe to the patron and his or her gate keeper for the opportunity.

I want to clarify another point. Many NGOs will indicate that they are not so innocent as to supply housing materials and volunteers and nothing more. I am sure this is correct. The critical issue, however, is whether the NGO's projects remain essential supply-led. This project was supply-led because it nurtured an existing supply-led environment instead of helping dismantle it. Too many development projects are never designed with an understanding of dependency environment nor fashioned with strategies to give birth to sustainable alternatives.

* * *

Not all development work is supply-led and doomed to failure. Where there are successes, we need to look within them for embedded principles that can help us develop a demand-led strategy. The five successful co-operatives discussed below are not presented to promote the co-operative model. Co-operatives have problems, too, but it is the demand-led aspects of the five projects that interest me. I believe that these demand-led factors are what has contributed to their success. If we can extract them, we can apply the same principles to collective action organizations other than co-operatives.

How exactly we define "success" is relative, so let's attempt brief definition to guide us through the description of the five co-operative projects. Once we have looked at all the projects, we can return to the task of extracting a definition of success from what we saw in the examples. The examples relate to experienced producers of goods or services at micro- and meso-levels, all of whom are successfully involved with producer co-operatives. Not everybody in the developing world is that lucky and there is not there always a profit to be made on all development needs in developing countries. Immunization, education and road paving are examples of needs that do not provide an immediately visible profit, but we will get back to discussing these issues in the next chapter.

Co-operatives are businesses that are owned by the clientele that requires their services. The clientele come to own the business by buying shares. Having shares entitles them to a vote, but while surplus that is not needed to sustain the project is paid to each shareholder, any shareholder is entitled to only one vote. Dairy co-operatives exist to process milk for dairy farmers and to sell the products on their behalf for a fee. The dairy farmers own the processor as a co-operative. Fishing co-operatives work the same way. Service co-ops do too: a taxi co-op, for example, organizes dispatching, thereby reducing cut-throat competition among the drivers. It may make bulk purchases of fuel and car parts for all of them at reduced cost and it may also repair their vehicles. A credit union is a co-operative that deals in financial services. It offers its members savings, loans and other services. If a co-operative earns more than it spends, it's in a position to share a portion of the surplus with the member-owners. [1]

Successful producer co-operatives must sustain a mechanism that enables three-way interdependence based on demand (see Figure 7.1). In the figure, the market cannot be accessed by a dairy farmer (A) unless a plant pasteurizes the milk. So, the individual farmer must depend on a co-operative processing plant (C).

But an individual farmer cannot maintain a processing plant alone. It takes the milk from a sufficient number of milk producers to make the plant viable. So, the farmer and other dairy farmers (B) are necessarily interdependent; they cannot sustain the dairy processor without each other.

The plant survives by selling milk and value-added milk products (e.g. cheeses, creams, yoghurt, butter). It competes by expanding or improving infrastructure and equipment. To stay in business, the plant must pay an adequate percentage of its income to the farmers so that it can attract the quantity of raw milk it needs and enough share investments to use as collateral for business expansion loans. The plant first holds back some of the gross take from its sales for needed reserves and operating costs. Then the net surplus is divided among the shareholder dairy farmers, based on the number of shares they have

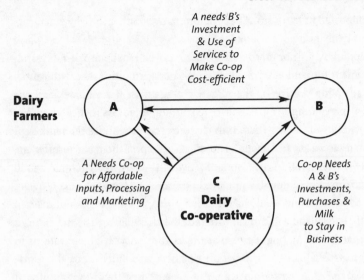

Dairy Farmers

A needs B's Investment & Use of Services to Make Co-op Cost-efficient

A

B

A Needs Co-op for Affordable Inputs, Processing and Marketing

C

Dairy Co-operative

Co-op Needs A & B's Investments, Purchases & Milk to Stay in Business

Figure 7.1
Three-Way Dependency for Sustainable Collective Action
(Dairy Co-operative)

purchased. The co-operative business therefore depends on the farmers and cannot stay in business without their shares and provision of goods or services.

The five co-operatives described below have all managed to establish this rewarding three-way interdependence in a clientelistic context where individuals are customarily bound to their patrons. Additionally, each co-operative represents an innovative strategy that distinguishes the behaviour these formerly dependent people from the modal behaviour of their peers. As an indirect result, a modal shift is evolving in the survival strategy used by the people who become owner-beneficiaries by joining the co-operatives. They are moving themselves from dependency and competition with peers to co-operation and separation from patrons, and it is worth examining how this happened.

Self-Targeting Mechanisms: Demand-Led Choices

Seibel and Parhusip observed the successful micro-finance work of the private bank, Shinta Daya, in Indonesia.[2] Although the authors don't offer much discussion on this point, it would appear that the bank's micro-finance strategy succeeded by letting low-income clients select the economically sustainable tools that appealed to them from a set of alternatives rather than by encouraging the poor to abandon old strategies for new.

Whether knowingly or inadvertently, the bank had made use of a demand-led development model because it had created opportunities that its research suggested were supportive of the clientele's agendas. This model had the advantage of preventing the bank from assuming an adversarial relationship with its clientele—of talking them into changing those realities the bank supposed the clients ought to change. The onus was upon the bank to offer the right services. Had Shinta Daya done otherwise, the targeted clientele would have ignored them. In that way, Bank Shinta Daya would have been made aware of their costly mistake and would have needed to drop their program, or to learn from the mistake and adjust it to the liking of the clientele.

In essence, the bank put one of Greenfield and Strickon's observations to work: there is a distribution of behaviours that occurs within the target population. Some of these are entrepreneurial in the sense that they are examples of new combinations that bring a better return to a few members of the target group. Bank Shinta Daya attempted to offer the opportunities that allowed more members of the group to benefit from the entrepreneurial strategy. As it

Figure 7.2

Demand-led Development Model: Doing Good By Doing Well

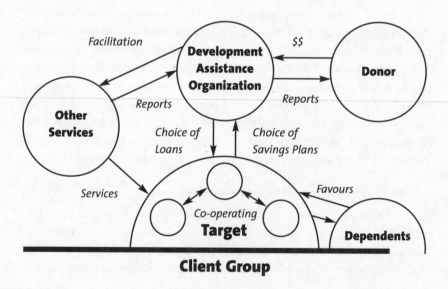

happened, Shinta Daya came up with a win-win strategy: it offered benefits to the clientele; it also brought more clients to the bank.

Following the Bank's logic, we can see that a three-way winning situation is possible—a situation that responds to the clients' demands, that benefits the bank and that brings about societal improvements. For example, if the Shinta Daya clients were attracted to micro-credit loans to start micro-industries and if these tiny manufacturing initiatives were increasing employment opportunities in neighbourhoods where few work, then a single initiative would be attaining triple benefits.

In Figure 10, Bank Shinta Daya is the development assistance organization that channels donor funds into the community (i.e. Target Client Group). Individuals within that group may choose to make use of the savings and loans opportunities of the bank and may select the savings and loan plans that suit their needs best. The project is designed to become sustainable. Interest paid by borrowing members of the target group increase the fund's size. Competitive interest rates on loans allow the bank to pay an attractive rate to savers from the same target group (or the general population using the Bank). Their deposits also help the fund to grow. Borrowers are not particularly interested in savers; nor for that matter, are savers much interested in borrowers. Each maximizes his/her own objectives. But in so doing, each assists the other. By making use of the development mechanism common to all (i.e. the Bank) each is able to do good by doing well.

Guhan's examination of viable social security programs for developing nations also makes a demand-led recommendation—or at least includes demand-led elements in its formula.[3] Because so many people in developing countries are in need and can be scattered widely, Guhan proposes mixing true, costly and geographically-focused social security measures with self-targeting employment schemes. To Guhan, "self-targeting" means "self-selecting" mechanisms—demand-led development methods as we call them here—that do not preach, cajole or dictate, but that are attractive because of their relevance to user needs. In Guhan's case, specific incentives and sustainable mechanisms are more called for than specified.

Guhan's self-selecting mechanisms should not be equated with the some-times punitive welfare-to-work schemes mentioned in the previous paragraph that force needy people off the welfare rolls. The approach Guhan recommends and the one used by Bank Shinta Daya are incentives-based approaches that attract users by offering better alternatives. That is, they respond to client demands. Disincentives, if included, are used to increase the relative desirability of the proffered incentive compared to competitive incentives. This may be done by making the alternative costlier to accept. Guhan does not force income-generation in cases where the costs to participants outweigh the benefits. It will be seen that demand-led development methods are used in all the projects described below.

Five Examples Of Demand-Led Choice—Co-Operatives Within Clientelism
Example 1: Tomato Sales—Bogotá, Colombia

A credit union in Bogotá, the capital of Colombia, initiated a savings and credit project with low-income micro-entrepreneurs in the city. They invited tomato vendors to enter the program. The tomato vendors were women who stacked nine tomatoes in the mud just outside the entrance to the covered city market daily. They had no money for a booth inside and hardly anything to sell. For a couple of centavos, they could join a class to learn how to qualify for a tiny business loan. The payments defrayed the cost of the person training the women and of visiting them at the market during the week to offer guidance and support. At first, the bulk of the trainer's salary came from a grant from the Canadian Co-operative Association—CCA (matched by funds provided by CIDA—the Canadian International Development Agency). But by the end of the project, there were so many groups paying to attend so many classes and paying interest on so many loans that foreign grant money was no longer needed for the instructor's salary. That formula had been worked out before the project was approved.[4]

In the class, the tomato vendors divided into groups of four women called solidarity groups. Each group was to receive a single loan and divide it evenly. The money was enough that each of them could buy a couple more tomatoes to sell and also some plastic bags to make the tomatoes more attractive. After a week, the women were required to repay the loans with interest. Any woman who was unable to repay her share was to be covered by the other three women and they became responsible for collecting their contribution from the fourth woman. Nobody defaulted, of course.[5] Any group that repaid the loan plus interest was then able to continue to pay to come to class—and to qualify for the next (and larger) group loan. By the time the program ended, each of the ladies had built her own raised, covered platform with a selling counter, and each had purchased a scale. Each of them was now selling enough varied produce and because of the increased sales, was able to save enough to open up the option of becoming a member of the credit union that had run the program—either as an individual, or as part of a solidarity group. Most of them chose to stick with their groups when they became bona fide members of the credit union. Evidently, the women had become confident of each other.

When the groups received their first loans, something unexpected happened. En masse, a set of the solidarity groups marched up to the manager of the city market and successfully demanded the same access to the locked ladies' room as that provided to the women inside. That kind of political action never had anything to do with the credit union program. The solidarity group women independently maximized a micro-entrepreneurship opportunity. It became a chance to improve their social status. They evidently felt important enough to challenge the status quo.

The lending program was focused exclusively on recuperation of micro-credit given to micro-entrepreneurs and on the expansion of the micro-credit fund to perpetuate the program and to expand it to other participants. The women's attitudes were not at issue. By offering a single loan to a solidarity group of four women, social pressure ensured recovery of the loan—with interest. On the other side, the same social pressure ensured productive investment of the loan, expansion of income, and re-investment of at least part of the surplus generated by each woman into her tomato vending business.

As a result of participation in the micro-finance program,[6] the tomato vendors became part of a program that involved income-expansion and decision-makers within a group. A new self-image and a new level of self-esteem were the unintended by-products of their new objective conditions. It was not necessary to go about changing any of the women's level of consciousness to change their actions. The opposite proved to be true: attitudes apparently evolve to match people's changing reality. Responsible and self-reliant behaviours were the unintended consequences of self-preservation.

The tomato growers' solidarity groups evoked a successful—albeit minuscule—collective political action: totally disenfranchised women gained access to a government-controlled washroom. Independently, each of the women had employed a minimax strategy. However, because of the opportunity for collective action what was of benefit to one of them contributed to their benefit as a group. The existence of a collective permitted action to be taken in concert. Consequently, the demand coming as it did from the combined solidarity groups had greater impact than several individual demands.

The behaviour was not new to the women. Minimaxing is standard fare in a clientelistic environment. But the conditions had been changed. Prior to association with the collective, the cost of demanding the washroom key was greater to a solitary woman than the potential benefit. It was easy for the market manager to reject a lone, ragged, muddy nobody, but potentially embarrassing to reject an organized association of vendors.

When the weighting of costs and benefits changed, each woman retained the minimax strategy but now employed a collective method in lieu of a solitary one. The community development program delivered increased credit for more tomatoes to sell, but it had also quite unwittingly facilitated an alteration in the operating style and in the status of the women.

Since behavioural patterns tend to become habitual, one can suppose a certain level of comfort would increase with reliance upon conjoint action and economic interdependence to complete each cycle of borrowing and repayment. The preference for joining the credit union in solidarity groups instead of individually suggests this is right.

The micro-lending project established pre-set rules for the micro-entrepreneurs/borrowers. Not all features of the project were run on a participatory basis with the tomato vendors. The formula was figured in advance. The bottom line had to be fixed, but the interdependent elements of the calculus could be adjusted. Those numbers could be discussed with participants and variations could be worked out to their liking.

One of the biggest successes of this particular project was that the credit union operating the project devised a scheme that made itself self-sufficient and even allowed it to expand once it was running properly.

The pre-set rules that governed participation in the opportunity were such that the borrowers' self-interest was piqued. What developed was a win-win situation for the proto-association of borrowers in which the minimaxing behaviours of the participants provided personal rewards and also ensured the perpetuation of the fund itself, for each greedy participant, and a win-win-win strategy.

The credit union limited the use of donated funds for the purpose of initiating the mechanism. Technical assistance from the foreign funder could also have been made available through this program, but it wasn't required. Eventually, the credit union in Bogotá and a number of other organizations offering similar programs in other countries of the region did work with a foundation in Canada on related technical issues.

From the outset, the credit union made the vendors who participated in the project pay for everything they got. Given the initial degree of poverty among the women, only pennies could be charged. Still, admittance to class required a fee and loans that did not relate to poverty were calculated against the profitability of expected sales and the cost of loan monies. Even with a principal-plus-interest payment in hand, the women participating still had to come with a fee for the additional classes that were to lead to the second and larger round of loans. The entire project was built around transactions between the women and the credit union.

The credit union did a thorough cost-analysis of the strategy. It knew how much had to be earned from the project to pay the salary of a trainer/on-site coach for the entrepreneurship participants. It also knew that repayments from solidarity groups were highest when there were no more than four or five women per group. On this basis, it could calculate the number of solidarity groups needed per evening and the number of evenings it needed to run training sessions. Part of the calculus included the amount each woman had to pay to attend each session, the size of the loans to solidarity groups, the length of time the loans were to be held, and the interest to be included in the repayment. The credit union balanced all these factors to devise a viable formula—high enough to cover program costs on a continuing basis, but low enough to make participation attractive.

The political action taken by the vendors was not the primary objective of the Bogotá credit union program. In fact, it was never any kind of objective. Empowerment just happened; it was therefore not a result of deliberate consciousness-raising, but of something that happened spontaneously after the women were affiliated to an established credit union, after they had learned about business development and after they had united into small solidarity groups and taken a first loan from the credit union. If they were asked to choose a political action for these women, the credit union employees would in all likelihood not have selected toilet privileges as the first campaign objective. Dignity through bodily functions may be critical, but as a cause it is hardly noble. But the women themselves chose what they thought was important and—even more significant—what they thought was achievable.

At such a rudimentary level of organization, it is hard to imagine that the vendors would have taken on any other political causes through social action. I lost touch with the project after learning about this lavatory triumph and I doubt that they attempted further revolutions. But spontaneous rebellion, while rare, is not unusual. Larger scale examples appear in the larger initiatives reported below.

We should be careful not to assume that merely introducing credit opportunities to women will automatically produce totally positive results for them as individuals and as collective action groups. In a different instance, Grameen Bank in Bangladesh offered micro-credit services to women, but the initiative had a number of negative effects despite the bank's intention of contributing to their empowerment:[7]

> My anthropological research on the micro-credit program of the Grameen Bank shows that bank workers are expected to increase disbursement of loans among their members and press for high recovery rates to earn profit necessary for economic viability of the institution. To ensure timely repayment in the loan centres bank workers and borrowing peers inflict an intense pressure on women clients. In the study community many borrowers maintain their regular repayment schedules through a process of loan recycling that considerably increases the debt-liability on the individual households, increases tension and frustration among household members, produces new forms of dominance over women and increases violence in society.

Rahman's report underscores the importance of careful targeting and of assessing the impact of projects on intended direct and indirect beneficiaries, as well as on the sustainability of innovative development initiatives.

Example 2: Voting Cards, San Andrés Island, Colombia

About 30 fishermen organized a co-operative in an English-Creole population living on small group of Colombian islands (San Andrés Isles) located off the south-west Caribbean coast of Nicaragua. Each of the fishermen owned a dugout canoe and most of them had fitted their canoes with outboard engines. They would spend up to two nights and three days in their canoes to bring home up to 500 lbs of fish. Originally, after selling most of the fish from the canoes at the shore, they had to load the remainder into homemade wheelbarrows they called "boxcars" and peddle the fish through town. Only then could they rest. Their other choice was to sell to taxi drivers who doubled as fish peddlers, or housewives at the shore. Fish prices fluctuated with supply and number of buyers because there was no way of evening out prices by storing a glut of fish for times when fish were scarce.

So, when the idea was hatched, fishermen were more than happy to buy shares in the co-operative each week—and this happened notwithstanding the common wisdom that fishermen—Creole Islanders to boot—are notoriously unable to co-operate with anybody, and certainly not with one another. The cost of shares was painlessly low and the potential benefit was great, as one of them observed.[9] They took some of the money they saved through share purchases and built a shed near the place they beached their dugouts. They took the rest of it and bought a big new freezer. Then they hired a man to sell fish from the freezer. The co-operative took the fish off their hands right at the shore. There was no more need to deal with buyers and no need to push the boxcars through town.

Other benefits flowed from the co-operative idea. Taxi driver friends, porters from the airport nearby, and tourists on the beach were already purchasing fish fried in coconut oil from the fishermen. That became the beginnings of a bona fide fish restaurant. Things kept developing. When I last visited the co-operative, it was manually packaging fish, freezing them, and selling them in mainland Colombia.

But one event from the early days of that co-operative captured my imagination more than all the other successes. Originally the fishermen—like most of the other poor people in that location—were clients of the politicians. The politicians had the unsavoury custom of demanding the cedulas (citizenship cards) from the fishermen as a way of ensuring votes. On Election Day, a car would retrieve fishermen from their homes and ferry them to the voting booths. They would get their cedulas back then and be given a printed list with the slate of politicians for whom they were to vote.

One day, however, the co-operative Executive made a suggestion to the membership that reversed the situation. Instead of surrendering their cedulas, the co-operative decided to invite each of the candidates to a co-operative meeting. At that meeting, each was asked to tell the members what he would offer them and their co-operative in exchange for their votes. Then the members, in a separate meeting, decided which politician was the best friend of the fishermen and he was awarded a bloc of votes.

The strategy worked. The former manipulators were being manipulated. They used to divide to conquer. A few pesos, a bottle of liquor, the promise of a load of sand to help a poor man build his house had been enough to gain a vote. The individual sought out the politician to get what he could. Now, by bringing the competitors to face a bloc of votes, the politicians fell over themselves to please a significant interest group—one comprised of low-income fishermen.

The preferred politician was elected and made good on his promise to find a government grant to rebuild and enlarge the co-operative's restaurant on the main beach. The fishermen then had a second source of income.

Again, the collective political action was a by-product of a mechanism whose original attraction was short-term and personal: cash for weary fishermen instead of pushing the boxcar. The work of the community development organization was entirely confined to technical assistance related to the establishment of a sustainable business.

The project offered demand-led development education. Initially, the fishermen cared only about a freezer to get rid of their catch. Nothing else was relevant and nothing else was dealt with until it became relevant. Then when it did, it was possible to go back and develop strategies to resolve problems. For example, when drunken members disrupted meetings, or when meetings degenerated into aimless quarrels, regulations and procedural skills became desirable. Then members eagerly attended a workshop to develop the improvements they desired. The changes were subsequently applied because they were broadly valued. The order of teaching skills needed to operate and sustain a co-operative business was certainly less logical than a curriculum on how to make a co-operative, but did respond to the logic of necessity.

The collective action also indirectly benefited fishermen without dugouts. As consumers realized that they had access to a more dependable fish supplier, the demand rose. This in turn resulted in steadier work opportunities on the dugouts for those fishermen without their own canoes. However, fishermen without fishing equipment such as boats, outboard engines and nets did not join the fishing co-operative because the incentives were not appropriate for them. What appeared to be a "community" of fishermen turns out, on closer examination, to be sub-divided along many lines such as kinship and the ownership of enough land to purchase a dugout and present enough collateral to apply for a loan for an outboard. As Meenakshi Ahluwalia reminds us in his study of the social impact of watershed management initiatives in Rajasthan, India, "community" does not automatically imply generalized participation and harmony; it consists of diverse interests. There are differential abilities to overcome transaction costs to invest in institutions and environmental management in ways unexpected by a community development project.[10]

Example 3: Untouchable Female Mayors, Amul Dairy, Gujarat, India

Anand is a moderately sized city in Gujarat in northwest India that has a large campus that is owned by the National Dairy Development Board (NDDB), an offshoot of the Amul Co-operative Dairy. Officers of the NDDB told me about an unexpected victory they have witnessed as a result of their creation of village-level dairies across ten states of northern India. In all, nearly 30,000,000 people are members of these co-operatives. Many of them are poor. In fact, many of them are women, landless, poor and Untouchables. Traditionally, such people have survived by keeping a water buffalo. They are allowed to let their animal graze on the ridges of land that separate one wet-rice paddy from another. The relationship with paddy owners is symbiotic: the animals find their fodder and their owners find a way to survive. The owners of the paddies benefit because the social status quo is maintained and the muddy margins of their paddies are kept free of weeds and grass, and the water buffalo manure fertilizes the paddies.

When NDDB organizes a village dairy co-operative, it is the water-buffalo owners who are among the most eager to join: they need a sure market for the cup or two of buffalo milk they may have to sell. It is rich in butterfat and excellent for making ghee, the clarified butter popular in Indian dishes. The landless, poor, Untouchable women begin earning steady payments for a cup or two of milk delivered to the co-operative table in the village every morning and every evening. In the evening, they receive money for the morning delivery; the evening's delivery is paid for the next morning. The woman who sits at the table and receives and measures the milk, the one beside her recording the transaction and the other one paying out the money to the milk suppliers are all co-operative members trained by NDDB. They are now literate and carry out business functions in plain sight of all the villagers. These women may well be Untouchables, but they are doing serious business and are becoming trusted and respected individuals in the village. In more than one village, one of the co-operative women has become Mayor.

A reduction in social exclusion on the basis of caste was inadvertently achieved because of training for leadership functions within their own collective enterprise. Cross-caste alliances can emerge in the face of cultural barriers, and may co-exist with them for indefinite periods (notwithstanding Marx' expectation that contradictions get resolved). The economic formula for this project was pre-costed; the incentives and constraints that affect potential members are effective and affordable means of achieving co-operation and member interdependence. The Untouchable women who became village mayors did not come to the campaigns empty-handed. They offered voters what everybody wanted and needed and what nobody else could offer: appropriate social and financial management skills and demonstrated successes. They also arrived with a bloc of votes.

Example 4: Philippine Serfs and Landlord Renegotiate Relationship

The "co-operatives" in this case aren't quite bona fide, registered co-operatives, but operate much like them. Luzon is the northern big island of the Philippines—home to Manila and to Mount Pinatubó, the volcano that exploded in the 1990s. There's a lush valley on the island that is pretty much owned by a single aristocratic family. They left for Manila in the 1950s because rural investments had poorer returns than urban investments. The peasants were left on their tiny parcels and in the midst of their poverty and ignorance, essentially abandoned and leaderless.

The well-educated and socially conscious son of this particular family gained good experience in community organizing at utopian rural social experiments that were being tried elsewhere in the country. Then he approached his father for a favour. "Since you no longer reap benefit from your ownership of the valley," he told me he had said, "why not give it to a foundation I wish to create as a socio-economic community development experiment?"

His father agreed. Much of the land was then sold by the foundation to the government to be distributed to peasants as part of a land reform program. That brought operating capital to the foundation. The young man then began organizing the peasants in the different villages of the valley. This was not difficult: he was the heir and object of some deference. He created quasi-production co-operatives among them: those peasants with ducks were made members of the duck collective; others became members of hog and chicken collectives. Some belonged to several of these organizations. A cross-collective council was established for co-ordination and technical assistance was provided by the foundation.

The duck producers needed feed for their ducks, as did the pork and chicken producers. They got rice from the rice producers' group. They didn't have to pay much because the rice producers were in need of fertilizer and the council established a set of barter relationships. What money was required was borrowed from the foundation and collected from sales the council effected outside the valley. A portion of the earnings was deposited into a loan fund that the council eventually began to operate. Again, the federation provided the technical assistance.

The foundation also taught the producers how to co-ordinate the marketing of rice, ducks and other products outside of the valley. The foundation did two other things: it taught the duck, rice and other collective members how to elect leaders and it taught them how to manage their groups. The central and paternalistic role of the foundation was gradually replaced by the representative council. The credit union could assume the credit functions without paternalism, given that the collective representatives owned the credit union.

Rice production and the demand for animal feed eventually exceeded the manual milling capacity of the valley's homesteads. The valley needed a mill, but the cost of constructing one was too great for the rice producers' council. The foundation could have shouldered the loan, but it tried another strategy. Instead, the valley council approached the father of the project co-ordinator (the previous landowner) to co-invest in the mill with the foundation and the council. He agreed, saying that it was the first time in a quarter of a century that he saw an opportunity to make a profit out of the valley.

Individual peasants entered into collective action with the incentive of better income. By design, the success between the collective and the farmers, and among the farmers, was interdependent.

Example 5: Central American Consortium: Production/Export Co-operatives

In Canada, the Canadian Co-operative Association (CCA) has provided financial and technical assistance to producer co-operatives in several Central American countries. Initially, assistance was offered to a few individual co-operatives for the purpose of increasing productivity, reducing costs, and increasing the participation of women as producers, members, administrators and members of the Boards of Directors.

Project partnerships with the co-operatives were developed slowly and cautiously. Small grants for restricted activities with clear objectives came first. And at that, they only happened after an exhaustive review of the co-operatives' books and operating methods, and on the basis of personal knowledge of the administrators and Board members. CCA's staff knew what weaknesses existed in the co-operative institutions, what games were being played, and by whom. From the first, CCA's relationship was business-like: friendly and results-oriented. There are two categories of results in co-operatives and they are organically intertwined: the financial bottom line, and the transparent and democratic functioning of the co-operative.

For the initial projects, capacity development of the co-operatives was restricted. Simple and measurable goals were identified, such as more product that was in better condition and quicker field-to-market times. The tougher goals were tackled later as trust and confidence grew. Both sides smelled a better life for members, many of whom are micro- and small-scale producers. Because of the situation the co-operative members found themselves in, sustaining the effective relationship with CCA became of increasing value. That gave CCA its opening: it became easier to escalate demands. Acceptable business practices were required for transparency and objectivity. There were even times when CCA insisted on changed management practices that resulted in Board decisions in the co-operatives to change managers.

Within a decade, what emerged from a set of individual producer co-operatives in several countries has grown to a consortium of producers and marketers and providers of credit that operates nationally, regionally, and now—on a still sporadic basis—intra-regionally. But the consortium is no longer loose and informal. As a result of a number of successful intra- and inter-regional transactions (totalling just over $1 million US in sales by 1998), the system is becoming formalized and the Central American co-operative producers and vendors—and the small- and medium-sized farmers who own them—are becoming integrated into a globalized economy.

The Guatemalan members of this production/export consortium have as one of their members a federation of co-operatives who produce and export snow peas—at the time, to markets along the east coast of the USA. Co-op Atlantic is a federation of about 200 supermarket co-operatives in the four provinces of Maritime Canada. They sent some of their top brass to Guatemala to negotiate a shipment of snow peas. In the exuberant style of the Central Americans, the mini-delegation was received and toured through fields and offices and packing plants and then brought to the bargaining table before being treated to a royal lunch. Before lunch, the representative of the Central American snow pea farmers asked about the size of the order they could expect from the Canadians. They were considering a quarter container of snow peas. The Central American representative explained that they didn't accept orders below three containers. The Canadians had to admit that amount was well beyond their annual demand for snow peas. As a result, the Central Americans politely excused themselves from lunch because they had been holding off a delegation of Japanese with a need for five containers of snow peas. This goes to show only that the collective action mechanism can become large enough to impact an entire sector of the population of a region (e.g. small agricultural producers in Central America) and that the larger the mechanism becomes, the social and environmental agendas of the "little man" become more negotiable.[11]

Seven Mechanisms That Make Development Happen

In each of the five examples described above, co-operatives succeeded in changing the social relations of production that existed between people on the social, economic and political margins of society and those dominating the means of production (patrons), or controlling access to them (gate-keepers). In each case, the change was effected as a result of the efficient operation of a producer collective that—at least partially—moved productive consumers away from immediate dependence on the patrons and gate-keepers. The distribution function became the purview of the collective. But the collective also permitted independent access to the means of production. Poor people either found another route to the raw materials they required, or new things to do with different raw materials. And of course, if the collective in question was a co-operative, the collective was owned and democratically controlled by them. In effect, each project above allowed participants to take responsibility for their own lives because the design of the project was responsive to demands being made by those choosing to participate. Additionally, each project was designed to better the lives of others—for doing good by doing well. All of the projects were successful by integrating the productive capacity of individuals into a sustainable mechanism which, in turn, extended improved opportunities to others.

The following list extracts the common demand-development model characteristics of the five projects. If they are deliberately integrated into project designs, these seven elements will, I believe, improve the effectiveness of community development projects and programs. They include 1) creative response to greed, 2) pre-costed entrepreneurial strategy, 3) effective collectives, 4) the ability to convert private greed into collective benefits, 5) the opportunity to straddle multiple strategies, 6) the ability to evolve from benign dictatorship to democracy, and 7) the potential for cross-class business alliances.

Creative Response to Greed

Opportunism is a mindset that values the location of needed or desired resources and the ability to siphon them for personal use. Dependency is commonly the relationship that is established in patron/client environments between those with resources and those who desire access to them. Minimaxing is the strategy used to increase an individual's ability to seize resources while at the same time reducing to a minimum the losses exacted by the patron or gate-keeper in exchange. **We can summarize opportunism, dependency and minimaxing in a single word: greed.** It is a phenomenon common to policy makers, bureaucrats and to the poor.

Each of the community development projects we have discussed responds to the demands of greedy project beneficiaries. Each of them offered opportunities to maximize income under conditions that did not exact unreasonable counter-demands. The tomato vendors were greedy for loans to increase their incomes and each repayment was rewarded with the opportunity to borrow more. The fishermen demanded reduced working hours. Purchasing shares in the co-operative was considered low-cost and spread over a number of weeks, while providing the requisite reduction in work-hours. The members of the co-operative themselves observed that if the share money was stolen, it was no huge loss to them. The Indian milk producers wanted additional cash. They were lured into the program with a morning payment for a cup or two of milk they had delivered the previous evening. It required trust to accept the overnight delay, but the experiment was not very costly for them. The Filipino farmers also demanded cash. In their case, the altruism of the foundation established by their patron's son ensured rewards. For the dairy producers, a first reward preceded the purchase of shares as share purchases were deducted from milk payments. Fishermen purchased their shares so that a freezer and shop could be organized. For both groups, co-operative education was introduced only after members became involved in share purchases. The already successful and business-like Central American federation of producer co-operatives wanted additional international markets. Prior technical assistance for capacity development and the community development of efficient purchasing had been provided by the Canadian Co-operative Association (CCA). The request for technical assistance from the CCA was made spontaneously by the emerging marketing consortium as a business decision. By this stage of their community development, there was an improved ability to trust and delay gratification—in the same way the fishermen were able to invest first and be rewarded later.

Perhaps the lesser challenge is to attract members of the target population into opportunities that allow them to do good for others by way of doing better for themselves. The greater challenge will be to find relevant attractors for the policy makers and bureaucrats.

Pre-Costed Entrepreneurial Strategy

All five successes resulted from the community development projects aimed at creating surplus-generating collective action organizations. Surplus generation cannot be said to be sine qua non for diminishing the dependent relationship between patrons and clients. Any strategy that enlarges the survival opportunities of a population and reduces patron dependency can be considered a success—as long as it is sustainable.

A second feature of the entrepreneurial mechanism made available to clients in all five projects was that they were pre-costed for sustainability. Local populations might opt for maximum gain and minimum sacrifice. The provision of a sustainable option—one that if adopted by a minimaxer will have positive consequences for the entire group—is a critical necessity, however. Patrons and gate-keepers offer tough choices. So must developers. The patrons' choice benefits patrons at the expense of the clients the environment-economic, social, political and natural. The developers' strategy must benefit clients, their collective action organization, and the rest of their environment as well. This requires strategic planning and implementation.

Some people, such as Dichter and Brown, question the push for sustainability by donors involved in financial services (FS) projects as this may restrict loans to those who can repay and may narrow NGO action to FS services only.[12] I recommend that we avoid such problems because clearly the elimination of insufficiently productive community members is self-defeating. For this reason, we should not be targeting the sustainability of narrow, albeit important, service delivery mechanisms such as those providing financial services, but the sustainability of the target community itself. Ultimately, we need to involve ourselves in capacity development.[13] An holistic assessment is required to determine what services are needed to ensure sustainability and to determine how Peter is to pay Paul so that the community can thrive. Furthermore, reliance on multiple donors can help reduce the dangers of ideological dictatorship by donors.[14]

In all the examples, the entrepreneurial mechanism was made available to entrepreneurs. The number of classes offered to tomato vendors, the number of participants in each class, the cost of class attendance, and loan interest were all factored into a formula that paid for the cost of the trainer. Growing success among tomato vendors was necessary for the program to remain viable. Share purchases and fish sales to the fishermen's co-operative enabled their collective action organization to grow as an institution and to benefit the fishermen. The

Untouchable women who entered the Amul Dairy Co-operative were those willing to risk the theft of a single cup of milk by the co-operative. The amount paid for a cup of milk was enough to keep the women in the program, to allow the village co-operative to grow, and low enough to allow Amul Dairy to compete with milk and milk products in the marketplace. The amount paid to Filipino farmers for their livestock and crops was high enough to keep them involved, and low enough to allow their federation and co-operatives to hold back a fee to keep both of them viable. The margin between earnings of the national co-operative marketing federation in Central America and the regional consortium sale prices was sufficient to cover attractive payments to local co-operatives and local member/producers.

Effective Collectives

The collective that attracts participants has several qualities. It gives the appearance of sufficient power and legitimacy to achieve its stated objectives. Its performance is apparently effective enough too. It extends selective incentives as an additional attraction to each individual who will join. And it has a convincing ability to censure those who fail to join or who join and do not co-operate. The implied threat is valuable in overcoming the reticence of the undecided, but also helps convince them that troublemakers will be dealt with properly.

The credit union that approached the tomato vendors was already a successful, middle-class savings and loans institution boasting a modern bank-like facility. There would be few doubts about its power, or effectiveness.

The fishermen's co-operative was promoted by a non-Colombian who worked for a local ecumenical community development NGO. The Directors were known clergymen and the developer was a North American who had been a teacher in the local high school. The NGO and its extension agent had enough credibility and perceived skill to assist the fishermen with obtaining a freezer.

The Amul Dairy Co-operative has 30 million members—about the population of Canada. It's Executive Director and Board Chair are high profile individuals. When Amul comes to add another village dairy co-operative to its system, there is little doubt of its power or ability to succeed.

The Foundation that approached the valley of Filipino farmers was entirely new. It's driving force, however, was the son of the landlord who owned the valley who certainly represented political and economic clout and the ability to exact compliance from non-compliant peasants.

The Central American federations had successfully tested an intra-regional trade pilot project already. The inter-regional trade initiative implied low risk and was built on a foundation of legal agreements and prior successful dealings.

The collectives examined were effective in another way: they were financially sustainable. They were either able to generate enough surplus to remain in existence on the basis of marketing opportunities to minimaxing user-owners, or they maintained a long-term financing relationship with some other entity.

Ability to Convert Private Greed into Collective Benefits

Greed within clientelism generally yields pain and reduced trust and a consequent bridling of community progress. The collective action mechanisms reversed the usual effect of minimaxing. Each of the five projects described allowed entrepreneurial individuals trapped within clientelism the opportunity to make personal advances. Individual opportunistic risk-takers were enticed, as it were, into realizing personal rewards through a collective mechanism. Individual greed depended upon the greed of others. They were locked into a supportive alliance, the by-product of which was the perpetuation of the mechanism that attracted them in the first place. Its size and efficacy increases its allure to other minimaxers.

The contributions extracted from tomato vendors eager to expand their businesses and to access larger loans, as well as the interest paid on loans, covered the cost of instruction and expanded loans for all.

The purchase of shares for a fish freezer and the sale of fish to the co-operative to avoid the pain of selling fish increased the ability of the co-operative to purchase additional freezers and to purchase the catch from new co-operative members, as well as the additional catch that resulted from the improved equipment the richer fishermen were able to purchase for themselves.

The desire for nearly immediate cash for milk sales allowed the Indian dairy co-operative to purchase milk from more, richer members with additional water buffaloes, as well as from new members.

The desire to market subsistence crops brought new capacity to members of the Philippine producers co-operative and allowed new members to join. It also enabled the co-operatives to earn the funds needed to enter into business transactions that stretched across the boundaries of a single co-operative—such as the purchase of feed for animals and the sale of animal fertilizer to growers.

Opportunity to Straddle Multiple Strategies

Each of the examples allowed members to retain dependency linkages to patrons while extending independent income-generating opportunities. In all cases, the co-operative business opportunities were departures from the traditional patron ties. For example, the tomato growers were not forced to abandon tomato purchases from their suppliers, but were able to increase them and to diversify their purchases. Similarly, as part of the credit solidarity groups, they were better positioned to make bulk purchases and to investigate purchases from other suppliers. The demand for access to the women's toilet was, at worst, a threat to a patron who had never offered them any services. In fact, it was an opportunity to open a business relationship with vendors who were obviously becoming viable.

The fishermen had been dependent on taxi drivers and the managers of hotels and restaurants for the sale of fish and for the prices offered. The competition among fishermen kept prices low. All these buyers remained eager to purchase fish. By selling to their co-operative, they only succeeded in increasing the value of fish. Confrontation with the politicians was not risky. The politicians were simply outmanoeuvred by the organized fishermen.

The Untouchable milk producers were dependent on landholders to graze water buffalo, but the milk was used for the family. The cash income from milk sales to the co-operative allowed frugal participants to purchase extra animals. The village population benefited from the availability of milk and milk products and from the new skills gained by the women in the co-operatives (e.g. literacy, numeracy, record-keeping, group action skills).

The Filipino producers entered the co-operatives to gain access to a cheaper marketing strategy and a surer return on their products. They stayed with the co-operatives for the increasing benefits they offered and for the opportunity to increase their level of productivity and income. Traditional middlemen could be retained, if desired, and the co-operative could be used to vend a portion of their product. But gradually, the middlemen could be excluded if desired. In the meantime, the increased economic power of the co-operatives and the federation of co-operatives allowed the producers to reduce their dependence on the foundation established to initiate the production system.

Finally, the Central American co-operative export consortium attracted federations, producer co-operatives and their producer/members because of the opportunity to expand sales, income and productive capacity. The co-operative members of this system were largely free of clientelistic dependencies by the time this project was undertaken.

Ability to Evolve From Benign Dictatorship to Democracy

There was an element of paternalism at the outset of most of these projects, but because of the increasing financial investments of the participants in the collective action mechanism, control in the projects inclined increasingly towards the co-operative members and their co-operatives. The tomato vendors would not have been freed from their cycle of impoverishment had it not been for the largesse of their credit union benefactors. However, from the first the design of the project strategy was such that the business-like relationship within the credit union and the ones established among borrowers in the solidarity groups resulted in the economic empowerment of the women. It also left them free to opt into the program and to join the credit union as individual members or as members of the solidarity group. And it inadvertently positioned the organized women entrepreneurs so they could challenge the authority of the market manager.

The fishermen's co-operative was begun as a charitable act by the organizer. But the nature of the co-operative was such that fishermen turned to their directors for leadership within the first two years of operation. As described, political bonds of dependency were shattered in that way.

The water buffalo milk producers were assisted by the Amul Dairy of Anand, Gujarat. Initially, the relationship was a charitable act. But like the fishermen's project in San Andrés Island, Colombia, they were integrated into a business that required a payment for their product and they were trained to manage their own village co-operative.

Filipino producers benefited because of the charitable decision of the patron's son to establish a foundation. The foundation designed its interventions in such a way that producers were involved in organizations able to assume the management and business transactions originally handled by the foundation.

The Central American export consortium of co-operatives had benefited from the charitable technical assistance functions offered by the Canadian Cooperative Association (CCA) for the purpose of capacity development. However, the services were offered in such a way that the federations sold services to affiliated co-operatives and the co-operatives charged for input and marketing services provided to individual producer members. The experience and increased income earned by the system allowed it to move away from dependency upon CCA for grants and to purchase technical assistance as required.

Potential for Cross-Class Business Alliances

Perhaps the most intriguing phenomenon that can be observed in the projects is the unintended emergence of egalitarian transactions between the co-operatives (on behalf of their members) and former patrons. Where clients lack alternatives, it can be said that transactions between them and their patrons are constrained and destructive. However, where former clients choose to participate in business transactions with former patrons over other good alternatives, the dependent bonds of patronage have been broken. This happened in the successful confrontation between the tomato vendors and the market manager and in the successful reversal of positions between the fishermen and the politicians. There was an elevation of Untouchable women milk producers to the position of village mayor and the Filipino serfs were eventually able to attract an investment in their rice mill by their former patron. The Central American exporters were able to reject an export deal with Canadian co-operative buyers in favour of Japanese private sector buyers. Ironically, the Canadians were part of the CCA system that had enabled the Central Americans to develop their consortium in the first place!

★ ★ ★

Having observed the potential that exists for using an approach that initially builds change on the basis of grants and investments of the target population and works towards the eventual emergence of mutually beneficial cross-class economic alliances, it is perhaps worth considering whether a liberal market-based solution is being proposed. After all, haven't the rich and powerful disadvantaged the poor? Why should they not be made to contribute to the eradication of unequal human rights and socio-economic injustice? To make such an argument is to return to the original morality-based dichotomy between establishmentarian and anti-establishmentarian approaches to development and to locate the approach recommended in this book squarely—maybe even disapprovingly—within the first camp.

I suggest that the liberal shoe fits poorly. In the first place, to observe that mutually beneficial cross-class alliances can occur spontaneously—indeed, do so with some frequency—is not to support the Liberal solution that, according to some, is intended to maintain the status quo through strategies which buy off the oppressed.

In the second place, even to make a deliberate effort to devise cross-class alliances does not, I believe, equate the proposed approach with that of the liberal market-oriented school. The liberal intent, we are told, is to prevent a shift in the mode of production, to retain inequitable social relations of production based on exploitation of one class over another. But a cross-class alliance of co-investors represents a fundamental shift and opens tremendous possibilities for change. The have-nots have repositioned themselves and are in possession of enough of the means of production and in control of enough of the mode of production that they can attract the participation of those who formerly commanded both. The co-investment represents a kind of proto-egalitarianism. It would be naïve to pretend that it represents equity, but it does open the door to increasingly equitable relations between former patrons and clients, increasing choices to former dependent populations, and reduced need to cling solely to former patrons. As patron control of clients diminishes, former patrons increasingly need to look for additional co-investment opportunities to supplement the loss of a dependent clientele. Thus, one can conceptualize—and deliberately work towards—an evolution out of a class dependent marketplace. The onus, I think, is upon the Community Developers to have enough creativity and mental flexibility to discover how to support client populations' efforts to achieve such change.

Thirdly, for the anti-establishmentarian agenda to work, we would have to resort to measures that are intended to induce guilt among the exploiters and among the falsely conscious supporters of the status quo. We'd have to achieve class alliances and the destruction of capitalism. That approach has not worked well to date.

Finally, suppose the recommended approach worked, and former class antagonists co-invested productively. This would not exactly shatter the current mode of production, but if it fundamentally altered the social relations of production, how much should we care?

The Development Project as a Creative Response to Greed

THE SEVEN MECHANISMS for doing good by doing well through community development projects can be put to work among productive people with relative ease because such people are pre-positioned to maximize an economic opportunity. Sometimes, some of the mechanisms spontaneously emerge owing to a fortuitous presence of formative circumstances, including some degree of independence of patrons. However, this is seldom the case. More often individuals lack sufficient economic and political latitude or the necessary management skills to organize alternative strategies for survival through co-ordinated activities with peers. Patrons may claim their allegiance in exchange for cash payments, jobs or other favours. Counter-culture entrepreneurs can offer them attractive, anti-social alternatives (e.g. drug sales, burglary, prostitution). Alternatively, some beg. A demand model must compete against these alternatives by offering incentives that may not be intuitively obvious to developers or that may be considered ignoble. In this chapter, we are set to find out how an effective demand-based community development model is to be defined.

Before we can develop a sustainable demand-led development model, we need to recognize those categories of social service that are not suited to the demand approach and to be aware of a range of studies that provide project developers with important caveats. We also need to recognize the limitations that micro-finance and employment-generating programs—the backbone of sustainable self-development approaches—impose on us. Finally, we need to look at the way in which demand-led development might approach issues of gender equity and environmental enhancement.

Demand-Led Development And Non-Productivity

We should eliminate protection services for widows, orphans, the elderly, and those who are physically, mentally or emotionally beyond self-help from a demand approach to community development. Such people require welfare assistance—not community development—to ensure their protection. Welfare is not the same as community development because it is not a deliberate action to achieve sustainable change through participatory methods. However, we should (as S. Guhan recommends[1]) remain sensitive to the possibility of integrating population protection initiatives with sustainability promotion and poverty prevention. A blended approach to community development extends non-welfare services towards populations on the fringe of the protected group and an integrated approach may reduce costs and expand coverage geographically.

Other more legitimate community developmental services that require full or partial subsidization don't fit perfectly either. Public education and public health are examples, as are some categories of technical assistance and training. These are critical services for socio-economic change on a participatory basis and they are therefore genuinely developmental, but their cost is too great to be borne by the users alone. Also, the benefits they provide often extend beyond the user group. Improved education, for example, yields socio-economic benefits at the national level. Improved maternal health and education also have measurable and positive effects on both the family and the community. Technical assistance and training can have a positive effect on productivity and health too, or it can reduce the costs of incarceration if it is targeted at youth who are at risk of anti-social rebellion. So, even from a cost and benefit perspective, primary health care, effective education and some types of technical assistance and training should not be denied to the poorest citizens; some societal cost sharing is justified.

Such services have to be financed either by governments or voluntary organizations. Guhan somewhat vaguely suggests that funds can be found when there is a will to find them,[2] and De Soto identifies a fortune for development in unregistered properties, rendered inaccessible because of their informal nature.[3] Better provision depends on greater productivity and transparency, on modernized legislation, improved efficiency of the state, and on increased transparency. In clientelistic economies, the tax base is neither broad nor deep: not enough is contributed by too few. The very poor depend on the largesse of patrons. The very rich arrange loopholes and evade tax payments. Industry is either insufficiently productive, or organized to realize profits elsewhere. Often, the public service is more responsive to the patrons who grant access to government jobs and benefits than to the citizens who stand at the service windows, awaiting attention. Additionally, national cultural and political factors can fashion irrelevant educational content and stultifying teaching methods. Hence, it is not simply the need for social security service, nor the theoretical existence of ways to pay for it that need to be identified. There is also a need to figure out how to ignite enthusiasm for undertaking the political, programmatic and administrative changes. Clientelism and the resultant lack of demand for improvements—except at moments of destructive rebellion—certainly is one of the obstacles.

Foreign donor assistance may usefully fill the gap where governments are unable or unwilling to ensure the provision of local services though many experienced scholars prefer to phase out the need for a continual grant.[4] Poor target groups are sometimes able to cover part of the cost of their developmental service needs through the creation of sustainable collective action mechanisms. Whether there should be such beneficiary contributions might depend on whether such contributions make a demonstrable, positive contribution to the ability of target group members to continue increasing personal opportunities. Another consideration is whether such mechanisms represent the development of a more independent political constituency that can come to function as a tax-paying force, pressuring for greater accountability in government, and therefore, for the provision of further responsive services.

Some limited protection services can be offered in places where productivity is increased through collective action. For example, in Xinjiang, north-western China, a project of the Canadian Co-operative Association successfully provided micro-loans to female producers of sheep and wool carpets until this role was absorbed by the government. The co-operative was profitable enough to cover the cost of a physical check-up, including reproductive system examinations and pap smears, for all women in the organization. The program could not afford to cover follow-up services in the few cases where problems were identified. The women had to turn to state health services. But provision of screening service was a positive first step beyond savings, credit and micro-production services.

Self-Sustainable Approach to Development: Limitations

Just as it is important to recognize the limitations of demand-led development for all cases of poverty and social injustice, so we must face the impediments to a self-sustaining approach to community development initiated by the poor themselves. Reliance on micro-finance and MSE (i.e. micro- and small-enterprise development) activities would represent the backbone of such an approach, along with training and technical assistance. If it could work, the poor could move out of their conditions on their own.

Unfortunately, when it comes to micro-finance the poor prove to be stronger borrowers than depositors.[5] They add little growth to banks in the short term. They are in command of too few of the productive resources to make the financial institutions they use sufficiently powerful to free them from dependence on the rich. Although they generally investigate matters from the opposite perspective, academic case studies such as those conducted by Shahid Khandker bear me out on this. Khandker offers a succinct summary of his findings on the limited impact of micro-credit on the poor:

> Results confirm the earlier findings that programs make a difference to poor participants by raising per capita income and consumption as well as household net worth, thereby increasing the probability that the program participants lift themselves out of poverty. The welfare impact of micro-finance is also positive for participating and non-participating households, indicating that micro-finance programs help the poor beyond income redistribution and income growth. The programs have spill over effects on the local economy, but the impacts are very small....
>
> We must admit that micro-finance is only an instrument among a large number of poverty reduction strategies that policymakers must pursue to reduce poverty. Certainly growth is a significant factor in reducing poverty. Investment in human capital and other means to empower the poor are also important tools for reducing poverty. Similarly, micro-finance intervention reduces poverty for a small percentage of the poor, and certainly provides an institutional credit and savings facility to a large percentage of the poor, especially women. The role of micro-finance must be evaluated from such perspectives.[6]

In a different study, Verónica González Aguilar came to a similar conclusion about the relative benefits of micro-financing:

> Most poor people have benefited from micro-finance programs but...narrow targeting is not necessarily a condition for reaching the poorest. Some large-scale non-targeted schemes have proven to reach the poorest.
>
> More poor people can be reached through building competitive, sustainable financial systems which provide a wide range of small-scale financial transactions than through narrow targeted programs.
>
> Increasing numbers of practitioners are stressing the importance of offering a range of quality and flexible financial services in response to the wide variety of the needs of the poor.
>
> Micro-finance has its limitations. It should not be seen as the only solution to poverty alleviation. In certain circumstances other interventions sometimes could be more effective than micro-finance. For example, in the case of natural disaster situations, micro-finance needs other complementary interventions, like subsidies for responding to the needs of those clients who have lost their capital and personal belongings and do not have any liquidity to pay their current debts.
>
> Micro-finance is not appropriate for all poor people. In some cases micro-enterprises owned by the poor are not ready for or do not need financial products. In other cases, micro-entrepreneurs are not creditworthy.[7]

Self-sustainable development through micro-finance activities is hampered by the limited ability of the poor to save and by the partial applicability of micro-finance opportunities for some of the poor. Self-sustainable development is also hampered by the policies that restrict income-generation and knowledge among the poor. However, it is clear that micro-finance is a critical element for achieving strategies of development that allow the poor to do good by doing well. It is also clear that allowing this to occur places the poor in a position where they can negotiate for greater access to opportunities that are controlled at meso- and at macro-levels.

Despite their potential, income-generating initiatives face discouraging complications. First of all, there is the effect of minimaxing. The effect of minimaxing is clearly illustrated in a study of an Employment Guarantee Scheme (EGS) in Maharashtra, India, that was conducted by Martin Ravillion.[8] Here, the EGS effectively absorbed excess labour until State politicians doubled minimum wages in order to gain popularity (so Ravillion surmises). The landlords ignored the costly increase and the landless labour flocked to the EGS for better income. As a result, EGS bureaucrats protected their program (and their jobs, I surmise) by changing program regulations and refusing to expand job supply by insisting that current job creation projects be completed before new ones were initiated. What seems to have happened is that the minimaxing behaviours of politicians, landlords, landless rural labour and EGS bureaucrats alike appeared to be rational to the members of each group. As a result, what was best for each proved to be counterproductive for Maharashtra villages as a whole.

There is another problem, which is related to reliance on micro- and small-enterprise development for employment generation. A cause for optimism lies in the evidence that in many developing countries, the fastest growing employment sector is among micro-entrepreneurs and businesses:

> Micro and small enterprises (MSEs) constitute a large, vibrant, and growing part of the economies of many developing countries.[9] MSEs employ approximately one quarter of the labour force in developing countries, and are an especially significant employment source in sub-Saharan Africa. According to Mead (1994), MSEs were responsible for 40% of new employment in Botswana, Kenya, Malawi, Swaziland, and Zimbabwe during 1981–90. In Uganda, roughly 90% of all non-farm, private sector workers are employed by MSEs (Republic of Uganda, 1998). [10]

We can therefore see that MSE development activities certainly do have an important role to play in economic development as do micro-finance activities. Furthermore, the apparent willingness of the poor to work towards their own development—where the incentives are attractive to them and where governments and more advantaged groups lack the will—underscore the value of MSE activities. But the same study reports that employment growth comes not from existing micro-enterprises but from the creation of new ones.[11] Hence, development assistance must be provided for measures that support the expansion of existing micro-enterprises if the obstacles are merely technical. MSE development does not proceed automatically. If MSEs cannot be helped to expand, new ones must constantly be initiated. Either way, the poor must continually rely on external assistance.

P. Wickramasekara provides devastating evidence against the self-sustainable community development approach.[13] He conducted a careful estimation of the potential employment and output capacity of two small Sri Lankan villages in order to gain some idea of how such potential could be realised. He did not consider innovative modes of income generation, but only the full use of available natural and human resources in traditional ways. Some of his findings are very encouraging. He says: "The analysis shows that per capita income could be raised about 31% in both villages if these activities [i.e. locally sustainable agriculture, manufacturing, carpentry, masonry, trade, commerce and other services, capital construction and irrigation activities] were undertaken."[13] He further concludes that the related costs of training, technical assistance and start-up financing are not prohibitive. So, in theory, it is neither economic growth nor the local economy's absorptive capacity for labour that are the major hurdles to successful development.

Sadly, the source of the obstacles lie at meso- and macro-levels, not within communities themselves, as Wickramasekara's conclusion about the obstacles to village development indicates:

> The existing formal and informal institutional framework has not been evolved for ensuring either effective resource mobilisation or egalitarian growth.... It is also unrealistic to expect informal associations such as the "Credit Co-operative" or "Labour pool Societies"...or Milk Producers' Co-operative...to contribute significantly to bring about a change. What is basically required is an institutional framework which would ensure effective participation and satisfaction of basic needs of the poorer strata in the two villages....
>
> [The study] **highlights the difficulties of following a path of self-reliant development by smaller units since most possibilities are linked to national-level policies.** Despite the differing background of the villages, the factors causing poverty and low level of development have much in common...: the achievement of development possibilities consistent with an egalitarian pattern may not be possible without certain basic changes in the institutional framework. Mere injection of capital would have limited impact.... The on-going district integrated rural development projects cannot be expected to have any substantial impact on the rural poor who have been identified as the target group...the overall distributional pattern would remain largely unchanged given the existing land-ownership pattern. [14]

The immediate village-level solutions, in other words, are too puny to spring villages into sustainable development, increased jobs and higher levels of income given the constraints the villagers face at meso- and macro-levels. The principal constraints to self-reliance are external in origin and include limited access to land and to fixed and working capital. Sometimes, there are demand constraints on products as well in the market place beyond the village.

If the situation described is generally true, only in rare situations could we expect to see the wretched of the earth throwing off their chains without also seeing policies change.

Policy makers may lack the political will to make fundamental changes needed for development to proceed, given their obligations to those whose best interests are served by maintaining the status quo. The lack of political will perpetuates the poverty of people at the grassroots as well as their dependence on national and local elites and on the limitations imposed by the globalized economy. But the dependency and atomization of the poor limits their ability to insist upon fundamental change, and they seldom do.

Adjusting the Sustainable Self-Development Model

It seems as if we are unable to break free from the constraints of atomization induced by universal minimaxing, or from poverty that is the result of skewed patterns of land tenure that favour the rich, or the inaccessibility of productive credit related to non-formalization of land tenure, or the low skills related to institutional management and market-oriented production.

So how are we to overcome the factors constraining the growth of micro-enterprises? Perhaps the anti-establishmentarians are correct: we have to destroy the mode of production and overthrow the exploiters who stifle fundamental change. Only, we have already seen that it is seldom in the best interests of the exploited to act on behalf of their class interests, since doing so flies in the face of their personal interests. We are calling for irrational behaviour if we expect that consciousness-raising tactics will overcome survival tactics. Maybe the workers of the world should unite. But, for reasons described already, they probably won't. [15]

Even so, I think we have already identified sufficient useful information to start moving towards sustainable development and away from dependency. We may do so, I believe, not by thinking in terms of a single leap from chains to freedom, but rather through an iterative process of strengthening the collective hand of actors. In fact, we have seen curious examples of collective action organizations that have achieved enough self-sufficiency (even within the contexts of clientelism) to re-negotiate a piece of the economic pie that was badly divided between themselves and former patrons upon whom they had been completely dependent. In some cases, each slice gained brought with it the possibility of additional and larger gains in self-sufficiency as well as opportunities for additional re-negotiation with patrons. In these precious examples, and through a relentless cycle of growth and re-negotiation, participants positioned to do good by doing well have eroded the constraints and reconstituted the local mode and social relations of production.

In the face of the constraints that prevent the poor from realizing the full productive and employment capacities of their environments, the three-way demand formula of interdependence (cf. Figure 7.1) that was needed to generate collective action organizations that were healthy enough to begin negotiating productively with oppressors has been at work, though nobody may have been particularly aware of what was occurring. We need only find incentives interesting enough to the very poor and/or the very insecure to attract them into a profitable mutual assistance mechanism. These incentives should be able to offer larger productive and learning opportunities at each iteration to help position the poor at a point where they can renegotiate constraining relationships. As seen in the cases presented, when collective action organizations become productive, they can offer attractive co-investment incentives to those currently functioning as impediments.

Caveats for the Design of Demand-Led Projects

Up to this point, we have seen only that the three-way demand-led development phenomenon can serve individuals with enough independent control over resources to select another alternative over clientelistic dependence. Sufficiently seductive conditions might be arranged for people with less independence, less control over assets of survival value in the social marketplace, and/or less confidence in their abilities. Meenakshi Ahluwalia says:

> An analysis of social differences existing behind any image of community may allow projects to take seriously the claims of the socially excluded and actively negotiate outcomes and alternative livelihood sources for certain social groups. [16]

Much research testifies to the precision with which development assistance to intended recipients must be targeted and the care needed to ensure that development assistance is used by recipients for intended purposes. [17]

T. Kepe examined the factors that affect co-management discussions between villagers and nature reserve managers in the Eastern Cape Province of South Africa. [18] A range of local and macro-level variables affected the way individuals relate to each other and to their environment. In Kepe's study, these variables included the type of activity (e.g. hunting or grass/thatch gathering), health, gender, kinship, role in social networks, membership in neighbour-hood groupings, mutual aid norms, reliance of villagers on work parties or mutual aid, status and closeness to the wardens, and opportunities/obstacles created by state reserve-use policies.

Kepe's work underscores the importance of not holding overly romantic notions about the target community in the Third World. The community is not a monolith and Kepe notes that "while these policies [i.e. ones giving commu-nities responsibilities to decide on the directions to take] have good intentions, the assumptions on which they are based—such as those that suggest commu-nity coherence and harmonious interaction between rural communities and the environment—have become subject to increasing critique." [19]

It is therefore necessary to take account of a dynamic and shifting set of sub-groups within any community and to be prepared to see them engaging co-operatively or competitively, depending on the resource and the issue at hand. I have called such sub-groups "alliances" and the sub-groups with whom they compete "factions."

The same dynamism and variance in roles and functions may apply to col-lective action organizations that intend to function on behalf of target groups. Norman Uphoff defines three social sectors (i.e. the public sector, the private sector and the voluntary or collective action sector) and elaborates on the char-acteristics, unique advantages and development utility of each. [20] He concludes that the voluntary sector—which includes non-governmental organizations (NGOs) and grassroots organizations (GROs) should not be dismissed as "residual" and should be more deliberately included in development as a part-ner by donors and the State engaged in development work.

L.D. Brown and D. Ashman are able to confirm distinct roles for the NGOs and GROs. [21] Their analysis of 13 African and Asian projects involving inter-sec-toral co-operation among public agencies revealed distinct, critical and consistent roles for GRO-centred and NGO-mediated projects. According to them, long-term success tends to be associated with higher degrees of partici-pation and influence by grassroots partners and NGOs:

> the implementation of grassroots-based programs may be marked by conflict and turbulence as well as cooperation, but the programs are also likely to cat-alyze further development initiatives by grassroots groups....
>
> [NGOs, as key bridging organizations,] require less grassroots participa-tion in decision making and less management of inter-organizational conflict projects that respond directly to the concerns of grassroots organizations.

They are also less likely to generate independent grassroots initiatives on other matters.[23]

Leach, Mearns and Scoones also remind us not to assume a one-to-one correspondence between community organizations and communities. Both terms mask complex and dynamic realities, and the inter-relationship of community and organization is complex as well:

> Such formal, community-level organisations may be a very poor reflection of the real institutional matrix within which resources are locally used, managed and contested....
>
> Multiple institutions are involved in resource management [and] amid this multiplicity of institutional forms, different people rely on different institutions to support their claims to environmental goods or services...it is frequently combinations of institutions, acting at particular historical moments, which shape particular trajectories of environmental change.... Many of these institutions are informal. They are also dynamic, changing over time as social actors alter their behaviour to suit new social, political or ecological circumstances.... These [local institutional] roles are not independent of the relations of power and authority which shape such organisations... [and] the assumption that "indigenous" organisations make decisions according to consensus, or to principles of democratic and equity-oriented decision-making, is frequently badly misplaced. The fact that women may be represented on watershed management committees in Rajasthan, as Meenakshi Ahluwalia shows, is no guarantee that their priorities for watershed development are heard or implemented.[23]

Therefore, in the process of designing demand-led projects targeted at the grassroots, it is necessary for donor agencies and local NGOs to work in a participatory manner with a range of target community members to identify the current set of alliances operating in the community, the incentives attracting individuals to them, the types and volumes of on-going exchanges, the factions with whom they compete, and the relevant patrons and gatekeepers upon whom they depend.

By plotting, sizing and costing current transactions, the NGO and donor agencies will understand the dimensions, the scope and the complexity of the processes now at work. Out of such an understanding, and with the continued assistance of community representatives from various parts of the tangle of interacting sub-groups, it will be possible to design effective demand-led projects, to test their effectiveness, and to adjust them accordingly.

Elite Capture—Resource Misappropriation and Leader-Disciplining

European democracy emerged, it has been suggested, when absolute monarchs were forced to negotiate with their own populations for the resources needed to protect their states from hostile neighbours.[24] Jean-Phillipe Platteau and Frederic Gaspart observe that donors inadvertently undermine this kind of democratizing process and strengthen clientelism whenever they channel assistance to client communities inappropriately, that is, through a local patron.[25]

A local patron who relies on donors for financing may offer very little of the resources received from the donors to his constituents and may pocket the remainder. Under these circumstances, the clients must be grateful for anything provided and may even extol their patron's generosity. In truth, they have done marginally better because of his intervention with the donors. Worse, donors may even insist that patrons first organize distribution with recipients before they will forward assistance. Thus a patron is positioned to make a take-it-or-leave-it proposition to the clients (what the game theorists call "the ultimatum game").

Platteau and Gaspart offer a Leader-Disciplining Mechanism (or LDM) that donors can use to enhance the negotiating power of the clientele who are faced with a situation where the elite capture resources that were not intended for them. Where a patron controls access to the community action organization, payments should be made in at least two installments—of which the second should be larger than the first. The amount to be received by collective action organization members from each installment must be negotiated by the patron and the clients before funding by the donor begins and the donor agency must have adequate fraud detection technology at community level to verify that conditions of the first installment have been met before releasing the second.

The authors observe that a "social norm of intertemporal fairness" will operate between the first and second installments and will cause the clients to restrict the patron's ability to share less of the benefits with the clientele in the second instance than they had negotiated in the first.[26] Another explanation is that "[the grassroots clients] are keen to defend their future interests because they anticipate that other games are going to be played later."[27]

Platteau and Gaspart observe that the LDM can be more effective where an alternate local leadership is waiting in the wings to replace the current patron if fraud is detected. It can also be weakened if there is severe competition among donors, as this allows patrons to turn to a less careful donor if possible.

A Word about Gender Equity and the Environment

Gender equity, or any sort of equity situation, is frequently promoted as a social justice issue: unequal treatment of people whether female, black or Jewish is wrong and unfair, and therefore shouldn't be tolerated. The Social Justice approach finds the behaviour wanting because it is morally wrong. Moral developers may then turn to guilt in an attempt to change destructive behaviours towards minorities and the poor.

Similarly, a moral approach relies on scare tactics and guilt to encourage protection and enhancement of the natural environment: the planet is dying; it's either your fault or the fault of international capitalism; and it's up to you to stop it. It may be true that you're "either part of the solution or part of the problem." However, the truth doesn't often stop the despoilers and profit takers—they continue to profit and cope with their guilt.

Moralization and the division of populations into problem solvers and problem aggravators is counter-productive to the extent that it increases hostilities and hopes for sufficient class-based solidarity to defeat antagonists. More effective solutions may lie within strategies that make gender equity and environmental protection/enhancement profitable for both sides, with the understanding that profit means whatever attracts both sides and whatever achieves equity and environmental objectives in the process.

There may certainly be some "Jerusalem" situations in the world, akin to the seemingly insoluble Middle Eastern division between Palestinians and Israelis over control of Jerusalem. Yet, even in that case an effective agreement was nearly reached in the Camp David accord by Begin and Sadat during the Carter administration, and may yet be found. Certainly, we should not fail to achieve profitable equity and environmental sustainability for want of trying.

A recent issue of *Insight* contains a brief article by Errol Alexis, who suggests that three factors motivating anti-equity men in sexual relations with women in the Caribbean are power, trust and pleasure.[28] In a different study, Errol Miller observed that the many Caribbean men who dominate women are themselves dominated by a few men.[29] Such analytical approaches are helpful, I think, because they connect issues of gender equity to the larger contextual frameworks (in this case, abusive male agendas and the pressures nurturing them) within which abusive anti-feminist acts are conducted. They are also valuable because they help us think about strategies and incentives that may permit gender behaviours to shift towards equity by working supportively and creatively with anti-feminist men, rather than defining them as the problem and ensuring their alienation.

Project Design: Lessons For Effective Demand-Led Development

The project design lessons provided by the development scholars cited in this chapter and the previous one can be summarized into the following caveats. When designing community development projects, we need to devise incentives and constraints able to deal with:

Dynamic Alliances, including multiple alliances, competitive factions, the dynamic context within which individuals switch allegiances among the factions to minimax effectively;

Socio-Environmental Interdependencies, local and mutual impact of populations upon the environment, and the environment upon populations;

Project Capacity Limitations and Interlocking Needs, the importance of linking multiple project initiatives to respond to sets of critical, interlocking needs;

Long-term Impact Strategy, design factors which ready populations for renewed and broadened, post-project initiatives, including alliances with former patrons and objectively verifiable indicators of progress towards the desired impact;

Exit Strategy, to avoid prolonged interdependencies of donor and recipients and to achieve the sustainability of mutual assistance mechanisms and of the beneficiaries who control the mechanisms;

Leader-Disciplining Mechanism, incentives and constraints in the project design which undermine the ability of traditional elites to capture and absorb resources intended for collective action organizations; and,

Gender/Minority Equity and Environmental Enhancement Mechanisms, incentives and constraints in the project design which enhance the negotiating capacity of women and other dependent social sub-categories, and which enhance the vigour and sustainability of the natural environment.

The bottom line for the Community Developer is that both formal (i.e. objectively verifiable data for hypothesis testing) and participatory (i.e. hypothesis generating, autochthonous, spontaneous and sub-group specific) data collection and analysis techniques should be put to use in order to develop a good understanding of the dynamic interaction of key community alliances and factions, of the incentives and constraints motivating individuals to join some alliances, compete against others, and to understand the conditions under which community members are likely to move from one alliance to another.[30] An understanding is also needed of the positive and negative effects that the alliances have upon one another. The model that is ultimately developed has to be simple enough to be manageable, yet good enough to help Community Developers devise an intervention strategy which facilitates a reduction in dependency of one or more target groups upon their patrons. The model also has to assist Community Developers devise project strategies which enhance the opportunity for target groups to achieve co-investment with former patrons, either during the planned project, or at some point after that.[31]

Five Scenarios of Demand-Led Projects

WE HAVE ALREADY DISCUSSED some theories of development and we drew seven principles from the core of Populational Decision-making and Collective Action theories. Using these principles and the seven lessons for demand-led projects we extracted at the end of the previous chapter, we can now sketch out five demand-led development projects that are targeted at dependent populations currently in the thrall of patrons and their gate-keepers. The five projects are designed to eat away at clientelistic dependencies.

The first two examples are adaptations of actual projects that have enormous potential. The first of these is quite effective locally, but it is limited in its impact and is not financially sustainable. The second is already effective and financially sustainable, but could do more to shift the social relations of production between the project targets and those who make their lives difficult. I tamper with these two actual projects (at least on paper) because they already embody many of the elements of the demand-led model. By suggesting adjustments, I can highlight the value added by the demand-led approach.

In contrast to the first two project examples, the other three projects are invented scenarios, albeit inspired by familiarity with a range of valuable elements in many projects that I have studied over the years, or that I have been involved in. This is a bit unfair because the real world is the trial by fire to which they have not been subjected. If they are implemented, these three scenarios would need much more adjustment in their detail and design—based on very careful assessment of the target population and their environment. My intent, however, is not to present the invented scenarios as something superior to the first two examples—especially since I have attempted to strengthen them. But the three scenarios may be valuable in demonstrating what I think good demand-led development projects ought to look like. Also, they are intended to serve as practical project responses to existing challenges faced by Belize. Before offering these proposed demand-led solutions, I suggest what I expect the supply-led "solution" to each challenge would be. In this way, the reader has an opportunity to see whether the demand-led alternative might be more effective and whether it is practical enough actually to be of interest to funders and implementers.

The first example we look at is Nigerian Villagers' Unsustainable Productive Credit Fund. We have to ask ourselves as developers what we can do to make a micro-credit program that already charges interest become financially sustainable and a significant voice for entry into credit and political spheres that are presently closed to them.

The second is Street Kids Incorporated—SKI Courier Bike Service. With the assistance of a Canadian employed by UNICEF, Street Children from the Dinka and Nuer population of war-torn southern Sudan successfully organize and operate a bicycle messenger service in Khartoum, a mostly Arab metropolis where Dinka and Nuers are treated with fear, suspicion and hostility. However, the participants remain politically tangential and therefore face limited growth potential. Are there ways to build on their astounding success?

The first of our invented scenarios involves the Creole street-corner youth in Belize City who are unemployed and dependent upon the richer Belizeans and donor agencies. These funders filter their resources to the youth in the form of assistance and control mechanisms through local politicians and their gatekeepers, the police and social workers. The youth organize a multi-purpose collective action association called CAT$. Their atomization is their weakness; yet they mistrust one another too much to unite. Can they challenge the economic and political barriers that perpetuate their weakness?

Mayan Forest poachers in villages beside a Belizean ecological reserve face the same barriers mentioned as the Creole street youth, in addition to which they also sustain a destructive relationship with the natural environment. Is there opportunity to convert their apparent weakness into meaningful strength?

University lecturers are both under-utilized and unresponsive to local Belizean development needs. Their university system is 80 per cent dependent upon government financing. Lecturers are responsive to the priorities of the university administration who, in turn, are bound both to the local government and to Central American and US academic accrediting agencies. As a result, the quality of instruction and applied research in a developing nation like Belize suffer. We have to determine whether there is a demand-led project option that can generate a win-win-win situation for students, the university (including administration and faculty alike) and for the nation.

In the five projects objectively verifiable changes have to occur in the modal behaviour of the target groups. Changes in objectively verifiable indicators (to be defined before activities begin) would enable us to determine whether reduced patron dependency has occurred and whether there is movement towards greater egalitarian interaction between project targets and the political economy that has excluded or controlled them in the past. These indicators would also be employed to gauge progress towards the sustainability of the facilitating mechanism used by the project participants in the course of assisting themselves. I believe that the verifiable indicators can be selected easily enough; however, they are not the point of this exercise and therefore I do not discuss them any further below.

Project 1: Unsustainable Productive Credit Fund—Nigeria

In their discussion of donors and sustainability in the provision of financial services, N. McNamara and S. Morse describe a micro-lending program that has been provided in Igalaland, Nigeria, since 1970 by the Diocesan Development Services (DDS)—a member of the Catholic Secretariat of Nigeria. The DDS makes use of Farmers' Councils (FCs) that have been patterned after the traditional Oja or mutual-aid societies.[1] The latter body meets weekly and receives standard weekly contributions from attendees. Collections, less entertainment and refreshments, are given to one attendee each week. The FCs, in contrast, save weekly contributions and distribute them to members at the start of the growing season. Soon after introducing a savings scheme, the FC needed to accept a grant to increase the size of the loan fund. They then started charging interest on their loans (12 per cent per annum) and they allowed loans of up to double the amount of savings a person had. Further loans were available only upon repayment prior to the next growing season. The fund was sustainable before the FCs accepted a loan to meet growing demand from borrowers.

Over the years, FC members demanded additional services beyond loans, including health and organization training. These, too, were provided by the diocese. These services could not be covered by savings and for this reason, the diocese sought foreign funding—a step that, unfortunately, created a problem. Rather than using the foreign funding to initiate self-sustaining solutions to local problems, it was used to cover the cost of such solutions and continued foreign funding was sought.

In the mid-1970s, World Bank financing was introduced. By the mid-1990s, loans were extended for agriculture and for off-farm activities (e.g. milling, food processing) that were aimed primarily at women. In the mid- to late-1980s, the donor changed its approach: "The FC project...[was] to become entirely self-sustaining, and this change was expected to be achieved almost instantaneously (within a year or two)."[2]

The tight economic times that resulted from Nigeria's Structural Adjustment Program (SAP), in addition to the need to achieve sustainability quickly meant that DDS would have been forced to raise its loan interest rates substantially and to pull away from the delivery of badly-needed additional services to farmer-members and their families. Ultimately, DDS was able to preserve low interest rates and ancillary services by diversifying its lines of credit and relying on several donors beyond the World Bank.

Interestingly, the lesson that the authors of the article drew from this from this experience was not that project designs needed to be adapted to keep community services self-sustaining. Rather, they concluded that donors should be careful not to micro-manage projects and not to place too much emphasis on loan fund sustainability:

> In all this discussion the central question is that irrespective of the rights and wrongs of specific pressure imposed by donors, do they have the right to decide what is best for a field-based ngo while they reside many thousands of miles away and far removed from the local context within which the field partner is operating?... A line must be drawn between "participation" and "control."[3]

From the perspective of sustainability, I think that a more relevant central question has to do with the ability of the Igala population to move away from dependency on the DDS and to be able to contribute to, and benefit from, the development of Nigeria. This perspective removes us from the defensive/offensive position taken by the authors:

> Although never fully sustainable, DDS did make great strides in that direction, and the problem was never with the desirability of the ultimate goal per se, but in the time scale and other operational conditions that the donor wished to impose.... DDS always felt that it was doing the best it could under the prevailing circumstances, while helping to tackle poverty alleviation. [4]
>
> There was simply no scope for discussion or compromise [regarding rapid achievement of FC—fund sustainability].... What dynamic produced this abrupt change in direction was never entirely clear.... [5]

The World Council of Credit Unions (WOCCU), for example, has for many years recommended a move away from an annual cap of 12 per cent on loans to borrowers. Credit Unions—especially those in developing contexts—require more income to cover costs. They need to increase interest payments to borrowers as a way of attracting greater savings, and they can't do that without increasing the cost of borrowing. Borrowers will not save if inflation is greater than interest paid on deposits. The authors admit that from the outset external financing was required to increase the size of the loan fund. And they note that the SAP and the need to achieve rapid sustainability threatened DDS' ability to offer other needed services. Notwithstanding DDS' intention to help farmers achieve sustainability, the marginal economic design of the FC program was exposed by changing conditions.

But DDS was opposed to higher interest rates for borrowers. Their reason was the poverty of their borrowers, which was a result of their limited ability to produce. The suggestion was that the obstacle facing the producers was not the cost of loans, but the size of loans, and the availability of more profitable investment projects. Had larger loans been extended for more profitable investment, the poverty of the borrowers would no longer have been relevant. Better return on their investment would have made repayment of higher interest quite painless.

Inadvertently, the DDS had created the problem themselves by reducing the target groups to objects of pity (the "potification" or "poor-thing-i-fication" of the borrowers as people in Belize might say). [6] What McNamara and the other researcher had done was to critique the donors instead of assessing the project design with which the donors were concerned.

Once we realize the design flaw (i.e. micro-loans for essentially subsistence level agriculture keeping borrowers dependent on DDS) it becomes possible to define the project strategy—and the project details—necessary to allow the DDS clientele to break out of cyclical dependency on DDS and traditional patrons. Within the distribution of survival behaviours among the DDS clients, the majority of individuals are attempting to improve their situation. For all of its concern and hard work to extend micro-credit to this clientele, DDS appears not to have provided the set of opportunities that allows its constituency to achieve the change they desire. DDS' welfare approach to lending has inadvertently worked against DDS' farmer clientele.

If it hasn't happened already, representatives of the FCs need to sit on the Board of Directors of DDS so that negotiations between DDS' needs and the producers' needs can yield win-win compromises that can be made into policies. FC representatives, of course, can reflect the positions of traditional leaders who are not influenced by the producers and who, instead of pushing for important changes, may seek policies that perpetuate their advantage over disempowered producers. The problem and effective counter-measures have been discussed above and do not require further consideration here.[7] We will assume that DDS has been able to bring voices to the table who truly reflect the smaller producers' interests and ambitions and who are willing to articulate them and to vote for policy changes.

In the second place, investment opportunities for the small producers will need to be investigated that can generate enough surplus for borrowers to increase savings potential and still cover the higher cost of larger loans. Opportunities need to be tailored to suit the interest of borrowers on the basis of gender (e.g. men farm; women invest in off-farm milling and food processing). Other researchers remind us that there may be other important sub-groups of borrowers whose opportunities need to be specially designed.[8] The investment strategy that will allow each sub-group to break free of dependency can also be designed with a view to intensifying the robustness of the natural environment—if the borrowers will be making use of it.

Additional short- and longer-term technical assistance (TA) and training will be required to support borrowers' efforts to increase and adjust the skills they need to turn healthier profits. Some of the services may have to be available permanently; these will have to become sustainable. To do so, the producers may have to pay for some of them out of their increased income. The Catholic Secretariat of Nigeria and/or DDS may also want to consider co-investment in a surplus-generating company to sell some of the affordable services to the producers. Alternatively, district or national levels of government may have to absorb provision of some of these services.

Governments, especially those chronically short of cash, are not eager to absorb additional costs. But producers who pay more taxes will want better service in return. This implies a need for the development of negotiation and advocacy skills, and hence, the inclusion of appropriate training and TA. Furthermore, the power of negotiation and advocacy are linked to the unity and power of the constituency represented by the negotiators and advocates. But the creation of such a constituency would be inherent within the development of a surplus-generating collective action organization. That may be found within the revitalized DDS that now has community representation. Or it may become a more independent local organization with fewer ties to the Catholic Secretariat of Nigeria.

Finally, the provision of the non-financial services specified or alluded to above may lie beyond the scope of DDS even though they are badly needed by the producers in Igalaland. DDS may prefer to stick to what it does best and to stay within its comfort zone. In this case, it is possible to look to other organizations in the area for a co-ordinated provision of related services. In other words, rather than trying to do everything in one project, a program approach may be more effective.

My re-visioning of the micro-lending project has shifted our focus away from the damage ostensibly done by the World Bank. The authors of the article do say, "Indeed, since that time, DDS has been very careful to avoid a single donor becoming so dominant in its affairs, and has successfully undertaken a policy of diversification."[9] So the World Bank has at least been helpful in teaching DDS to diversify its lines of development income. Implied, but not stated, is the lesson that organizations like DDS need to avoid donor dependency. But DDS has only temporarily resolved its dilemma by becoming dependent on many donors instead of one and has not developed the exit strategy to free the producers from DDS-dependency.

It was counter-productive and unnecessary to "potify" the target population in the first place by offering them small loans because low interest rates restricted the growth potential of the loan fund and because DDS was allergic to higher interest rates required to offer larger loans. The original project strategies perpetuated subsistence production and mere sustainability of the DDS loan fund on the grounds that the Igala people are impoverished and lacking in competitive skills. The redesigned project allows the producers to evolve away from dependencies. It first imagines full participation of the Igala producers in Nigeria's development and renewal of the natural environment. Then it works backwards to the needed practical change strategy.

Project 2: Bicycle Messenger Service—Khartoum, Sudan

Peter Dalglish, the Canadian founder of Street Kids International, reports a remarkably successful project that involves mostly southern Dinka and Nuer street children in Khartoum, the Sudanese capital, which is located in the predominantly Arab north.[10] Poverty, language and colour made them easily identifiable and they were feared, rejected and badly mistreated by ordinary citizens, public officials and law enforcers alike. From the outset, Dalglish comprehended the essentials of the demand-led approach to development:

> For kids with an entrepreneurial bent, I knew that a small business could be their ticket out of the garbage dump and along the road to self-sufficiency. They needed something that required little or no infrastructure and that allowed them to be their own bosses. I thought of various kinds of enterprises.... They depended on continuous injections of money and expertise by their non-profit sponsors, and sold most of their production to sympathetic members of the expatriate community. My idea was to design a project for Khartoum's street children that was modelled after a business rather than a charity. The challenge was to identify an enterprise the kids could run themselves, that met the needs of the local market economy, and that ultimately could be self-supporting.[11]

The project was designed to be self-sustaining and hence, entrepreneurial. In consequence, Dalglish was forced to design a project that was responsive to the environment of Khartoum, where other communications and transportation systems had broken down and where, as a result, the business community badly needed an efficient and effective courier system. It was the perfect project niche once he discovered it. For the most part, Dalglish employed participatory methods, but the identification of this niche was his own discovery and a function of his own training and experience. His target group, the mostly Dinka and Nuer street boys (girls are less often forced by their starving and desperate families to fend for themselves) were unfamiliar with the bicycle courier concept. Similarly, Dalglish took the lead in identifying seven aid agencies and embassies that agreed to try the service to deliver bulk mailings of little importance to them. Similarly, a fledgling but burgeoning English-language paper made a tentative agreement. The editor would open a subscription/delivery service. If papers weren't delivered across Khartoum by 10 AM each day, the courier service would not have to be paid. In this way, Dalglish reduced the risk for clients.

He himself incurred greater risk as the temporary benevolent dictator. He purchased three used bicycles and put his reputation on the line. The first three bike couriers could prove unable to finish their delivery routes before 10 AM or steal his bicycles. As Dalglish remarks, "Surely they had already done the calculation themselves and knew that they could abscond with the bikes and make a tidy profit."[12] Neither event occurred and the street boys stuck with the courier business and completed their routes within the deadline.

Success came quickly after that. Other street boys joined the collectively owned company, new clients purchased service from it and the boys bought bicycles and uniforms out of the surplus income that was generated by their business. In fact, three new bicycles were purchased out of earnings within the first 14 delivery days. Eventually, stories printed or filmed about them brought Street Kids Incorporated and SKI Courier service some recognition in western countries.

Dalglish insisted on participatory decision-making almost from the first. The kids decided who could join their business and how to punish those who disobeyed the rules they established. They were taught how to make the financial decisions and how to manage the funds. If Dalglish was a benign dictator for the purposes of selecting an effective project, marketing the idea to the street kids and making a gift of the first three courier bikes, his power was very quickly delegated to the business owners, and they very quickly opened a legitimate economic niche for themselves in the economy of Khartoum.

Other benefits accrued automatically, too. For example, when one of the three original couriers sold his SKI Couriers bike for a profit, the other couriers decided that he had to replace it or be expelled from the courier service. He simply stole it back. When colour coding became too complex to guide illiterate boys to their destinations, they themselves insisted on learning to read and write and even threatened their tutor with her job to ensure that she stop showing up late for classes. In this manner, they behaved exactly like the fishermen from San Andrés Island, Colombia, who initially had no interest in co-operative regulations, but who insisted on a workshop to develop operational regulations for their co-operative only after some members had appeared at meetings high on drugs or alcohol. Enforcement of such regulations was never a problem after that, nor was there a problem formulating co-operative bylaws and registering their organization.

Dalglish reports a surprising piece of information. He says:

> In one important aspect, we differed from most businesses: our goal was not
> to keep our employees but to lose them. We designed SKI Courier as a step-
> ping-stone for street children along the road to self-sufficiency. We paid the
> kids a wage they could live on, but not so much that they would want to make
> a career out of riding a bicycle around town. We wanted them to learn some
> basic social skills and then move on. [13]

I do not disagree with this decision. After all, as Dalglish had explained in
his book, the Dinka and Nuer children had every intent of returning to their villages after the war to find their surviving family members and to return to their
pastoral livelihoods. Their hearts lay in the south. I need also observe that I
know nothing more of the facts than those reported by Dalglish himself. The
probability is great that moving the street children beyond SKI was the wisest
decision.

Still, I can't help but wonder whether Dalglish and those around him,
including the street kids, had taken that inventive model to its limits and
obtained all of its potential benefits. I do note that not all the children were
from the south, that not all the southerners would likely return. The children
did not necessarily need to remain bike couriers after all. There may have been
other entrepreneurial opportunities available to them that developed as spin-
offs from SKI. As I attempt to show in the CAT$ scenario below, it might have
been possible to make a going concern of Street Kids Incorporated in such a
manner as to offer win-win-win opportunities for the street kids moving into
their own businesses, for other kids moving into the SKI Courier business, and
for SKI itself. Perhaps the sky could have been the limit.

Had such a route successfully been taken, I also wonder whether SKI had
yet to discover untapped political-economic potential. Dalglish talks about the
abusive treatment street boys suffered in the streets and jails of Khartoum. He
also reports on the lack of response he experienced from the international aid
agencies and on the difficulties he encountered in assisting boys jailed in adult
prisons. One wonders whether SKI wasn't on the cusp of achieving some
improvements in the treatment to which street children in Khartoum were
being subjected. The couriers had established pragmatic business relationships
in that city and had succeeded in changing the opinions of the owners and managers of each of those businesses about the value of Dinka and Nuer street kids.
One is encouraged to speculate. Perhaps SKI could have expanded opportuni-

ties for its young courier business "graduates." Perhaps SKI could then have increased its financial and business clout by selling business services (e.g. bulk purchasing, packaging, advertising, loan facilitation) to those new businesses. Would that, in turn have escalated the rate at which it could have absorbed more street kids into the courier business and into new business niches that suited this target group? As the SKI mini-empire expanded, would it not have been able to solidify business relationships with established companies owned by recognized civic leaders with connections in government? If all of that came about, might it not have been easier to move conservative (i.e. "establishmentarian" development) organizations into promoting humanitarian treatment of street children where, until then, they had feared offending the Sudanese government? Might such a network also have been willing and able to encourage enforcing bodies to offer better treatment to imprisoned youth?

Again, I want to emphasize that I raise these questions not to undercut Dalglish's impressive successes, but to encourage our willingness to play with ideas such as his. We may be able to build upon the thinking of pioneers like Dalglish and accomplish far more than we dreamed to hope for.

Project 3: Street-Corner Youth—Belize (an invented scenario)

This project is designed to respond to a reality I see daily. On many of the street corners of the six or seven lower income neighbourhoods of Belize City, one passes youth in their late teens and early twenties. They have been called delinquents and base-boys. The present euphemism is "unattached youth." They have left school and have no jobs. Some of them sell cigarettes, alcohol, marijuana, crack or cocaine to people in the neighbourhoods or to Belizeans from the "nicer" parts of town who slip past these street corners by night. Some of them belong to the local Crips or Bloods, gangs that were imported from the United States and that control "turf" in neighbourhoods for the purpose of selling drugs, carrying out robberies or cat burglaries, or doing favours, it is broadly believed, for corrupt police officers or politicians.

A number of supply-led projects have been attempted with this target group over the years—usually with very limited results. Some of the churches have tried outreach by preaching righteous behaviour and by castigating the youth for their backsliding. At times, the police have attempted repressive measures to keep the lid on the neighbourhood rowdiness and violence. Youth have been picked up for loitering or because they are suspected for reported crimes.

The government supported a project called the "Conscious Youth

Development Project" (CYDP) that had success for a while. The CYDP negotiated a truce between Crips and Bloods and in return, it offered the youths construction jobs. There was a foreign-financed street improvement project at the time and CYDP was given a contract with the contractors. Youth who agreed to the truce made pre-cast sidewalk sections to cover the improved drainage ditches along the newly paved, but narrow streets of the older neighbourhoods. By attracting youth to these income-generating jobs, it was possible to offer literacy, basic math and other opportunities to this target group. The hope was that the youth would outgrow their allegiance to the "red" and "blue" gangs and that making sidewalk sections and training would serve as stepping stones to other jobs and to participation in legitimate social activity. There was a tendency, it was claimed, to extend the majority of these opportunities to youth whose families were affiliated with the party in power. Coincidentally, their party colour was red.

The contracts eventually ended and were not replaced, and the red party was replaced by the party whose colour coincidentally, was blue. The blue party, perhaps not wishing to be associated with a good initiative of their opponents, cancelled the CYDP project. Over time, gang strife re-emerged. Eventually, an analogous program called "Youth For the Future" (YFF) was begun by the blue party. It offers similar opportunities to targeted youth. Again, there are claims that youth whose relatives are loyal to the current party have easier access to the opportunities. One wit has observed that the red and blue parties represent gangs for grown-ups.

Both CYDP and YFF represent variants of demand-led projects, though both may have been tainted by party politics. However, the training and welfare-to-work initiatives included in these projects are useful and become important elements in our next scenario, a project called CAT$ that is designed to operate independently of Belizean politics. It introduces other ideas, too, such as savings and credit opportunities, opportunities to move the ownership of CAT$ into the hands of the street corner youth, opportunities for the youth to build up the economic clout of CAT$, and opportunities for CAT$ to begin negotiating with the established political-economic system on behalf of its growing membership of street corner youth.

To create a demand-led project for such a target group, let's start by imagining that a teen from a low income neighbourhood in Belize has gotten his girlfriend pregnant and is desperate for cash. He is unemployed, lives with his mother, frequently guilt-trips her into giving him cash and once out on the streets, he hustles for more with friends who find themselves in similar circumstances. Like his friends, he is a fast talker, adept at taking advantage, extremely wary, and quick to assume slights. He likes basketball, watches the NBA, cares less about baseball except for the World Series, and "seets," that is, he hisses and then tosses suggestive remarks to eligible girls who pass him and his giddy friends.

His power fantasies vary. He sees himself as a hip-hop star. He knows the lyrics to a number of the hits and he's got down all the appropriate bobbing, weaving and finger jabbing. At other moments, he sees himself as an NBA star. Sometimes, he pretends he's giving an after-game interview because he's been MVP in a televised game. When he's in a pick-up game on the neighbourhood court, he's not much interested in passing the ball—he's driven to finish the play with a brilliant slam dunk amidst the shrieks of the girls. He's less of a team player than a wanna-be star because this is the court where he is judged. Having little independence, his sense of self is bound to what the girls and his male peers think of his performance. This is his stage: he is a player and he can't afford to let his team-mates make the impressive plays.

Frequently, he's the perfect lover, and once again, a legend in his own mind. His mythical partner washes and cooks for him and buys him rings and chains. He swoops her into his arms and she melts. He also fancies himself a thug. The tough guy living on the edge of the law, whose don't-give-a-damn-and-don't-need-anybody attitude puts a positive romantic spin on his desperation. It's all about respect (or, among the youth on the streets of Belize City, "re-SPEC") and ultimately, about having a reputation—good or bad—and about being somebody instead of an unknown kid who believes the better part of himself dribbled down his unknown father's leg.

If he had money, he'd spend it on clothes, drinks with his friends, a shiny "drive," and on women. But he does feel love and concern for his pregnant girl-friend. He sees them sharing a nice space of their own, dressing the new baby in sharp outfits and parading him (sic) about in a new stroller. He sees himself as a provider, head of a family and daddy to his expected boy.

He and his friends have complex dependency relationships with the police and the gate-keepers to the politicians and moneyed financiers. They operate on the edge of legality and when caught on the wrong side of the law, they may avoid imprisonment or parole violation by co-operating. They may then be used to finger other perpetrators, intimidate political opposition supporters, or to do favours for individuals with unusual tastes who have him at a disadvantage.

Periodically, there are special opportunities. For example, prior to elections, he may be paid to keep things quiet when this is valuable to the division incumbent; or contrarily, he may pick up a few dollars by making things hot for the incumbent's political competitor.

This young man, in other words, embodies static, modal behaviour. He subsists and spins his fantasy wheels, just as his friends do. He has plenty of wants and several genuine needs. Lots of the goals sound unrealistic: he's got no income of his own, no marketable skills and only sporadic access to illicit sources of income. His fantasies focus on having and spending money and on feeling good by being admired.

But he doesn't have any clear strategy for achieving his dreams, and not much confidence behind all the cool posing.[14] Some of the dreams, like becoming an NBA star, are pretty unattainable. This existential vacuum is common enough. Such a personal desert is frequently all a developer has to work with—a few conceivably attainable objectives, few means to attain them, and not much belief they can be realized.

There are, however, enough real ambitions and demands to spur this youth and his friends into risk-taking behaviours—at least for quick money. In the case of this youth, there also is a desire to help the pregnant woman he cares for, and a not too impossible fantasy about stability: the shared quarters, the man coming home from the hunt with a fistful of dollars,[15] the grateful woman with a baby and a full plate of food on one hand; a folded pile of his laundry on the other, and her face all made up and her hair nicely straightened.

He also has his youth, humour, energy, slick mouth and daring going for him. He's quick to figure things out, too. If his life is to change, and if his changing life is to generate a positive opportunity for his peers, some of his demands have to be gratified pretty quickly. Otherwise he'll lose patience, turn away and scavenge in other directions. So, in fact, might project donors. Walsh and Brinkerhoff say, "Many health professionals advocate taking on limited, high-priority goals first, partly in the interest of having a widespread effect quickly, which can then be used as a lever to raise more resources to sustain additional activities."[16]

In many ways, this youth typifies many of the urban youth of Belize City. But there are a range of distinctions to be made on the basis ethnicity, skin colour, age, gender, religion and neighbourhood. Some of the distinctions are significant and call for special design features capable of making the project targeted at youths like this one, attractive to ones less like him.

Let's assume there is a storefront NGO in his neighbourhood called "Ca$h for Any Thug with $pirit" (CAT$ for short). CAT$ has received a three-year community development grant from a foreign donor and must show progress towards economic sustainability to qualify for a second phase of funding. One of the first things CAT$ did was to use Participatory Learning and Action (PLA) methods with high risk youth to make its presence known to them, earn their confidence, and map out their principal incentives and objectives.[17]

Based on what we know of the youth, the dollar signs and the possibility are appropriate incentives to dangle in the neighbourhood. So is the word "Thug" on the storefront sign. It suggests the people inside may not be entirely square, not intent on judging him and exposing his obvious hollowness.

The youth enters CAT$ one morning and brazenly asks for a handout from the young woman at a desk. His name is taken. He's told to return at 6:00 PM for his money, given a rag and told to go out the door with a motley troop of other young guys and a couple of not-too-bad looking young ladies in similar predicaments. They are accompanied by a youth worker. Going with them is one condition. Satisfying the youth worker of his ability to work well and to behave decently in public are the others, and he's been told so. The youth worker looks more like a drill sergeant than a minister. CAT$ is not playing around, he sees, but he's desperate. He rolls his eyes, sucks his teeth but heads out the door with the others, trying to sidle up to one of the girls.

CAT$ holds a number of contracts with local merchants for periodic service. This work crew is off to wash windows; others wash cars. The city has offered a contract to keep the parks clean. There's another crew doing yard cleaning for individual home owners; and another that paints houses. All the young men and women are doing unskilled tasks. It's work for squares as far as the youth in question is concerned, except that the other kids are wanna-be Thugs like him, and they've been standing at the front door making stupid jokes and talking to the girls. The youth assures himself that it won't be too much like having a job.

This youth and the others in his work team agreed to the terms set out by CAT$, though most do not. This was expected and although CAT$ can survive during the life of the project on the donor grant, it has been carefully costed for post-project sustainability. CAT$ knows how many productive teams it has to employ over the three years to be able to cover its eventual operating costs. These will include the storefront that is also used for meetings and dances, a desk, phone and some chairs, a computer and filing cabinet. Personnel will include the receptionist and some team leaders, one of whom is the co-ordinator. CAT$ also knows that the greater the number of youth who succeed in moving out of their situation, the greater the number of new youth who will come to benefit from CAT$. So the few initial entrepreneurs are enough to start with.

When the youth returns at 6.00 PM, he's given a choice: take all your cash now and don't come back for three weeks, or take half your cash and come back tomorrow to join another work crew. There is a plan for the other half of the cash which is explained to him: if he chooses to go ahead tomorrow and sticks with the program for four working days, he qualifies for a Friday interview with a counsellor. The team leaders double as counsellors at Friday counselling sessions.

At the interview, the counsellor continues a series of discussions with the youth that were begun casually at the work sites. The counsellor is learning about this youth's background and current situation. The counselling sessions with all the youth continue back at the work sites during breaks and at lunch time. The counsellor develops a written profile on each youth and works up a Personal Development Game Plan for each of them. This Game Plan is reshaped in discussion with the youth on Fridays. Part of the value of the profile sheet on each youth and of the personalized development plan is that it provides the project with baseline data for later comparison. The baseline data from project participants can be generalized to characterize their modal behaviour and, if needed, the range of behaviours on a number of questions. A later profile on the same youths can offer a means of verifying modal behaviour shift.

The personal plan is intended to allow this particular youth to become head of his new family. The change in this youth is rapid and astounding, except perhaps to youth workers who see the change happen to a lot of kids like this one. He is not being discouraged or dissuaded. He's got a couple of dollars in his pocket at the end of each day. His personal dream is being treated like a sensible ambition and he's part of the process to formulate the strategy to attain it. He pretty quickly starts to work with the opportunities and to make productive plans for the loan he intends to obtain in a few months.

He is not an instant model citizen, however. He has been late for work once and has been caught trying to steal another youth's watch. His punishment was exclusion. He lost a day of work each time and missed out on being with a new gang of wanna-be Thugs and a lot of stupid jokes. He thought of quitting. But he has half the income he's earning at the end of each day to entice him, and the growing excitement about a personal development plan. The protective layer of cynicism, it turns out, is not yet that thick. There's an impressionable and optimistic kid just below the surface.

With the team leader/counsellor he has figured out that he needs to do something about his reading and basic math skills. He gets into a lot of fights and wants to get into the anger management group too. He wants to find out how to protect his girlfriend from AIDS because he plans to continue "shopping around." He claims he's not concerned about using drugs, but says he wants to know more about drugs "to protect my woman and because of my little brother."

What social services cannot be offered by CAT$ (e.g. remedial reading and basic arithmetic, drug counselling, health check-up) is organized with other NGOs or with government services. Belize already has incipient interorganizational referral programs.

What became of the half-payment that was withheld at the end of each working day? Half of it, as was explained to the youth, was taken by CAT$ and invested in their own sustainability fund.[18] The other half was deposited into a new account in the neighbourhood credit union in the name of the youth. Of that money, half is to be available immediately for withdrawal, but half is held as a share deposit and refunded when the youth has saved $500 in shares. The young man has been told that when he reaches $500 in saved shares, he may also choose to leave the amount in the local credit union and qualify for a $1,000 loan at 12 per cent per annum. So far, he doesn't like the idea and thinks he's being "ripped off" by CAT$. However, he's resigned. All the big-shots he's had to deal with have been on the take. So far as he's concerned, CAT$ is just like all the rest—except maybe they promise a bit more and they give you cash every day. He still has the evening and night time hours to hustle at the street corner—except for Tuesday and Thursday evenings, because that's when he's doing the remedial math and reading thing and the anger-management thing.

Youth (male and female) making it through four weeks of the program without being late or in trouble are invited to a Friday night dance. Food and soft drinks are served there. There is one catch, however—there will always be one catch with CAT$. This time, the catch is that the doors to the dance are locked at 8.00 PM and there is a meeting and a short film before the dance. Youth who make it through the door before 8.00 PM get a bonus paid at the end of work on Monday. That's the reward, and there will always be a reward whenever there is a catch.

The meeting is about explaining ownership of CAT$. It is offered to program participants who have completed their skills improvement courses and who have held a job for six months, or who qualified for the micro-enterprise loan described below and operated a micro-business for six months. Basic skills include literacy, numeracy and a certificate from the local Sexual and Reproductive Health (S&RH) NGO on "S&RH Decision-Making for Mature Adolescents," etc. They must also purchase shares in CAT$. Dividends are paid on shares according to the surplus that is generated.

There is a speaker for the evening: a woman from the neighbourhood credit union who gets 20 minutes to explain how the credit union works. The presentation is extended another 20 minutes because of the number of questions coming from the youth present. Some of the youth are angry because some of their money is locked into their share deposits. They want access to all of it and they want the right to get it if they want it. The rule, however, is not changed. All are hungry to get at the loan funds, so nobody bolts for the door.

The film for the evening is on how the HIV virus invades the male and female reproductive systems and the importance of abstaining from sex or using a condom for protection. The meeting runs late because of the discussion and the giggling that ensues. And the dance is successful. CAT$ thinks of everything: there are even condoms available in the male and female bathrooms with a small sign saying, "An Aspirin Between the Knees is Safer—Try Abstinence!!"

After three months of participation in work gangs, savings and attendance at meeting-dances, each youth is offered the opportunity to enter a career skills program from a limited menu of choices: refrigeration, perhaps, or air conditioning. Again, and always, there is one little catch, and one special incentive. As seen in the tomato vendors example, program participants will have to pay to study refrigeration. Fortunately, they now earn money. A couple have saved some of it in the non-share account at the credit union, as the counsellors had recommended. The related bonus is that CAT$ and a micro-lending NGO will help the career skills participants prepare a micro-entrepreneurship loan application. For graduates of the skills-training courses (e.g. refrigeration), these loans will be necessary to purchase tools.

The CAT$ project for street corner youth is summarized in Figure 9.1. For simplicity, it focuses on the sub-group of urban male youth. A similar system can be drawn for young female members of CAT$ as well. The lower half of the diagram represents the clientelistic system of limited alternatives available to

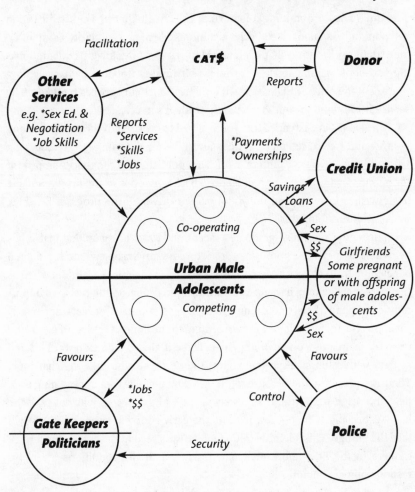

Figure 9.1
Collective Action Made Possible by CAT$

the youth. This diagram has already been presented (see Figure 2.1). The upper half of the diagram is new and summarizes the system introduced by CAT$ that enables youth to co-operate and to develop independent economic alternatives. The diagram suggests that the old clientelistic dependencies can continue while the independent alternatives gather strength.

The NGO (i.e. CAT$) offers basic business training to loan applicants. It is a requirement for obtaining a loan from the Credit Union. The Credit Union will pool individual loans and offer a combined loan to a solidarity group of no more than four youth if that is preferred. CAT$ will offer advertisement, booking and bookkeeping services for micro-businesses initiated by participating youth, but the catch is that CAT$ will hold back a fee for services rendered. The service is only sold to youth who purchase shares in CAT$.

Until loans are extended, the youth is free to drop out of the program along the way and free to re-enter. There is a penalty for dropping out, of course, a kind of public censure. Quitters' names are published on the NGO's storefront for public viewing. The youth must drop back two levels in the program if she or he wishes to rejoin and the youth may not re-enter the program for three weeks after dropping out.

Through a system of graduated incentives, CAT$ has gambled that it has been able to provide appropriate opportunities to elicit new entrepreneurial behaviours from street hustlers—entrepreneurs in their own right. But whereas the current behaviours have proved limiting to marginal youth, the CAT$ opportunities expand their opportunity matrix. The program attracts apparently irresponsible individuals seeking something for nothing. It trades off greed and operates in an atmosphere of low trust. There is always a quick reward offered as bait, with a longer term bonus available to those who take the challenge. There are penalties and censure for those who quit. The cost of obtaining each new and larger opportunity is always a little higher. Most will not take the bait—especially at first; a few will. As the early adopters succeed, others will take the plunge. This "demonstration effect" was seen in the case of the terrace farmers in the hills above Medellín, Colombia. If the conditions are right, responsibility is catching.

In the initial stages, co-operation with peers is not required. Trust is too low for that. Each individual works for him- or herself; the program offers the conditions and the rewards as would a patron. The co-operation opportunities are offered later. The youth may enter solidarity groups and they may invest in CAT$ and be elected to its Board. The organization is structured, well-regulated and audited. By the time youth can help run the organization, the desire to assist the work of CAT$ has increased.

The CAT$ program starts with a grant, but becomes self-sustaining. The break-even point has been calculated. Because its program is pre-defined, it's costs are predictable. Therefore, it is also possible to calculate fees and rewards. It can always absorb new participants at the first level, and can retain those who have progressed through its system. It develops owner/members by selling services and offering investment and policy-making opportunities. It can retain its original members by inventing new services to sell them as the need arises.

It begins as a benign dictatorship and becomes a peer-owned and operated democratic enterprise. Its progress towards sustainability and its setbacks are objective and verifiable, as are the gains of its participants.

From the first, the formula engages merchants and government officials in business transactions (not shown in Figure 9.1). These are nearly charitable at first. But as CAT$ begins producing members with better training, tougher deals can be made. For example, graduates with air conditioning experience may wish a contract to service government units or take jobs with the private sector. A special deal between a private company (whose owner is a personal friend of the relevant Minister) and the government may have been the standard arrangement. However, the increasing ability of CAT$ to absorb indigent youth may have growing importance to the Government. CAT$ may eventually win government contracts. Like the fishermen in Colombia, CAT$ begins to represent votes to politicians. If it plays its cards right, it can operate between competing political parties (the way the bigger capitalists do), throwing its support where its Directors see the best opportunities for CAT$.

The above proposal takes account of the dynamic alliance strategies of the youth being targeted. They respond to opportunities and constraints directed at them by politicians, police and the private sector. The CAT$ approach is incremental. It does not compete with the existing opportunity environment. Instead, it offers an additional choice. Youth are able to stick with their hustle, at least initially, and participate in the CAT$ program. The advantage of CAT$ is that the youth can achieve increasing benefits by sticking with the incremental program that engages them in positive interdependencies. They have the opportunity to change in the process of becoming. And they have diminishing need for the self-destructive alliances.

CAT$ is designed as an urban response and is not involved in activities affecting the natural environment. It does, however, have the potential for initiating agricultural programs, and is able to relate with the environment in a creative manner.

From the outset, CAT$ linked itself to other organizations providing necessary services such as savings and loans, literacy, and sexual and reproductive health information and alternatives to youth. The lateral linkages broaden and deepen opportunities which CAT$ is able to extend to youth. It is able to increase these linkages, integrating the CAT$ project into a youth-responsive program.

CAT$' design allows it to let youth opt into strengthening their economic and skills level over time, and, if it succeeds, CAT$ flourishes in the process. It uses a strategy with the potential for long-term impact on the target population. Because it is organizing a constituency with economic clout and business interests, CAT$ and participating youth are also positioning themselves for more egalitarian transactions with the current patron class.

Finally, CAT$' design contemplates an exit strategy for donor organizations who can either withdraw as CAT$ and the participants reach a level of sustainable interdependence, or can shift their focus to promote the long-term impact strategies such as entrepreneurial negotiations with former patrons or profitable alliances with other demand-led development initiatives. Finally, donors can withdraw entirely, since successful initiatives are able to attract alternative donor organizations.

Thus, CAT$ represents a mechanism to help unravel clientelism. The more of these organizations are operating, or the broader their participating clientele (e.g. single parents, small farmers, immigrant Latino families from neighbouring countries), the more individuals are breaking free of patron dependency and weakening the hegemony of the clientelistic system.

Project 4: Forest Poachers and Conservation NGO (an invented scenario)

Belize has an active environmental program with a number of forest reserves. Some are managed by non-governmental organizations (NGOs). There are a number of small villages on the periphery of one of the large reserves. Villagers have been illegally poaching animals and hardwood trees to augment their meagre income from agriculture. The NGO management is concerned about preserving the forest ecology, but recognizes the villagers' survival (i.e. dependency) needs as well. A mapping exercise with villagers has helped make their interests and priorities clear to the NGO. They are also dependent upon national politicians travelling to Belmopan and Belize City to attend weekly representative "clinics" where favours are sought (rent-extraction) and where continued loyalty is promised.

The NGO's objective is to get the villagers to leave the hardwood trees alone and to stop killing the larger animals and edible birds. Briefly, I suggest, the NGO would have tried supply-led solutions. At first, they would have used police from the nearby town to arrest villagers until they realized that this caused much resentment and that continued policing was too costly a burden for government to sustain.

Through a development grant, the NGO might next have supplied educational sessions on environmental protection in the village primary schools and at community meetings among the adults. By using brief before and after tests, they would have been able to complete these supply-side initiatives with objective evidence that their message was understood. However, if many such attempts are any indicator, my prediction is that the NGO will have been disappointed with the results of their educational efforts: the level of environmental degradation would have remained about the same for reasons cited earlier—so long as peasants on the edge of reserves depend on poaching reserve resources to survive, they will continue to do so.

This time, let us pretend that the NGO plans to develop a more responsive approach and has turned to a demand-based community development model. Belizean villagers on the edge of the sub-tropical rainforests are already experimenting with a range of survival strategies—with varying degrees of success. They have to be doing this if they are attempting to improve their survival chances. The NGO can make a scan of these strategies. They are seeking the ones with the best chance of providing sustainable payback, those where the payback can increase over time without causing environmental degradation.

Some kind of trade-off is going to be required. Let's assume that preliminary research has suggested, for a number of reasons, that agricultural diversification outside the reserve will have trouble bringing increased income to the villagers. Perhaps farmers lack the land; production loan programs are flawed; technologies are rudimentary; or the cost of labour and other inputs cannot compete with neighbouring Guatemala and Mexico. Farmers are stuck growing corn and a range of fruits and vegetables, mostly for subsistence.

There are a few exceptions. There can be value added to corn by operating a tortilleria.[19] The process for making corn masa (dough) from harvested corn is well-known to this Maya population and a "factory" consists only of a small cinder-block building and an electric and gas mechanism, sold in Mexico, that rolls the masa, cuts it into disks, and toasts it over flames. The hot tortillas are then weighed and sold in plain newsprint to local consumers. There is a constant demand for tortillas in the villages: they are eaten at every meal, and their preparation is labour intensive. Women from each village have been wanting to make clubs for years to run tortillerias. With very small donations, the NGO can organize women in each village and establish tortillerias. Each will generate enough surplus to cover costs, amass reserves and pay a small dividend to each woman.

However, the forest and tourism will have to provide the rest of the strategy. Part of the forest can be reserved for sustainable exploitation such as the collection of chicle (chewing gum) from the sapodilla tree, and edible nuts and fruits for the market. This will help a bit, but not much. Furthermore, it isn't a very elastic opportunity.

There are howler monkeys. The howler monkeys are endangered because they require a "highway" of trees to connect them to the rivers in the reserve. The villagers have been destroying their lifeline. There are poisonwood trees and other hostile plants, and near them, natural antidotes. There are considerable plants of known medicinal value familiar to the Maya population. There are wild orchids and brilliant bromeliads. There are healthy sapodilla trees, and experienced chicle collectors and processors could be allowed to harvest their gum. Near each village, there are minor Mayan ruins in the forest as well. There are Mayan recipes by the score in the village households and many talented cooks.

In other words, there is enough in the forests and villages to enchant the eco-tourists coming to Belize in increasing numbers. Besides, the villages are connected by a peripheral all-weather road to the forest reserve entrance, where the NGO operates an ecology educational centre. The villagers have a natural, hospitable grace but need skills as tourist guides. Fortunately, the government operates a training program that could be brought to the villagers.

All that is need is a focal point to attract the tourists and some improvements (sanitary latrines, screened-in, thatched porches attached to the villagers' thatched houses) to entice them to dine at the villagers' homes. In discussion with the villagers, it is decided that a forest "museum" can be opened at the furthest of the villages. From that location, tourists—those from the NGO's ecology centre and others found from advertising locally and from use of the NGO's website—will be assigned to tourist guides for forest walks and a home-cooked meal with the guide's family. A number system is to be used to ensure that tourists are assigned fairly to the guides. The NGO's mini-bus is used to bring its own tourists to the museum, and to bring tourists with their guides to the respective villages along the road back to the NGO's ecology centre. After their forest walk and meal, the bus retrieves them and returns them to the ecology centre. The return is timed to meet the public bus that runs from the centre back to Belize City. An overnight bed and breakfast arrangement can also be made with the guide's family.

Villagers from all the villages who join the community museum organization can qualify to participate in the various opportunities being provided (e.g. tour guides, handicraft production and sales, bed and meals opportunities). There are specific requirements for entering into and continuing with any of the specific opportunities. But the elected Board of Directors of the museum organization are in a position to speak on behalf of the villagers and to negotiate with the local ecology NGO and with purveyors of other services to villagers (e.g. financing, training). Many villagers will approach the museum organization because it will be known that it is legitimized by its affiliation with the environmental NGO and the foreign funding organization and by the allure of the opportunities being made available.

Funds for improvements (e.g. screened-in verandahs) may be borrowed by project participants. They must first go through training in general tourism, sanitation, tortilla production, home-restaurant operation and guides' training. The courses are offered after working hours for men who farm, and in the afternoons for women, when the babies sleep. Borrowers for the improvements must also have opened an account at the credit union in the farm town which services all the villages, and must have saved up BZ$500.

When new organizations are created—in this case the museum organization—the old system of constraints and dependencies does not evaporate.[20] Furthermore, the board of the new entity may ostensibly operate democratically, but may be peopled by village gatekeepers for powerful landowners or political party representatives. McNamara et al. have urged donors to limit interventions into project management (of micro-finance projects) because they may punish participants in their anxiety to achieve sustainability of the local institution.[21] The local environmental NGO can also serve as an honest broker on behalf of project participants to be sure that the conditions for their participation are just and their application uniform across such factors as gender, ethnicity or party affiliation. The participation of multiple donors can serve to balance concerns for the viability of the local populations, their organization, the environment and the local environmental NGO. Other strategies to empower end users have been devised by Platteau and Gaspart and have already been described.[22]

Careful project design by multiple stakeholders can ensure the inclusion of appropriate checks and balances. But part of the design must still include the costing of an economically sustainable mechanism based on the interdependence of the environmental NGO, the museum organization and villagers in tourism, forest income-generation activities and bed and breakfast tourism.

An appropriate design can bring a range of sustainable benefits to female and male villagers and different age groups (including youth), to their properties, to their health and to the sustainability of the forests. It is achievable by defining key incentives and then combining them in such a way that sustainable mechanisms emerge. For example, tourists will come to see the howler monkeys. They are large and tribal and actively defend the borders of their territory from other groups by uttering ear-shattering howls that can be heard for miles. The local village population knows how to make the sound that gets the howlers going. To the local population, the value of the tourists' dollars is greater than that of the trees the monkeys use. Where a very similar approach to this idea has been attempted in Belize, local populations have left the "treeways" standing and do their farming around them.

Like the CAT$ and the DDS projects above, this environmental project is amenable to a program approach. It already brings together the local environmental NGO, a museum organization of villagers, individual village micro-entrepreneurs, a savings and loans organization and relevant technical assistance extension personnel from various Ministries. Furthermore, the Government of Belize, together with some NGOs, has initiated District-level committees which work towards coordinated provision of services related to agriculture, education and health (e.g. HIV/AIDS). The development of an entrepreneurial body of stakeholders involved in this environmental project provides good opportunities for the district-level committees to extend their services to villagers. On the other side, it offers the stakeholders the opportunity to obtain needed relevant technical assistance and to get it on a non-partisan basis, if the donor organizations are included among the stakeholders.

The consideration of entrepreneurial alliances between the CAT$ and the environmental project makes the issue of long-term impact really interesting. CAT$, for example, may be positioned to function as an urban retailer for products developed by individual entrepreneurs in the environmental project and marketed through their museum organization. On the other hand, new project funds may be attracted to permit CAT$ youth to learn about forest ecology and to be trained in tourism in the villages. Tourism packages might be developed offering an urban/rural experience to tourists—not to the cruise tourists already co-opted by the "tourist village"/ruins excursion packages, but to those arriving overland and by air.

Prolonged interdependencies between donors and the other environmental project direct stakeholders can be avoided through break-even costing of the sustainable mechanism. From the first, the termination of funding targeted at achieving sustainable interdependence among the environmental NGO, local participating villagers and their museum organization can be planned. Iterative Results-Based Management (RBM), including annual roll-up evaluations of scheduled outputs and outcomes, and corrective redesign of outputs and activities for the coming year, help ensure that targets are met on schedule.

Project 5: Underpaid Lecturers and University Development (an invented scenario)

Finally, let me present an imaginary project designed to resolve a number of problems faced by the University of Belize. Salaries for lecturers at the University of Belize (UB) are tight. The university's budget is 80 per cent dependent on Government of Belize grants, and the government faces serious constraints of its own. Faculty are tempted to seek independent grants or leave the university to work for the private sector or live abroad. Faculty represent the target population for this project, and their behaviours reflect the distribution discussed by Greenfield and Strickon.[23] The mean behaviour of faculty is to offer grudging obedience to the mandates of university administrators to keep one's job. Authoritarian management methods have been used to maintain discipline because administration must remain responsive to governmental priorities to avoid biting the feeding hand.[24] The result has been tension between faculty and administrators, the former complaining of administrative deafness and insensitivity; the latter, of poor co-operation on the part of faculty. Faculty members believe that administrators think that they are not very capable because they lack academic qualifications. Faculty observe that their poverty and political favouritism have blockaded their access to advanced degrees. But part of the intransigence of faculty may stem from its resentment of the administration's authoritarian operating style. The more inflexible faculty are seen to be, the greater the temptation by administration can become to resort to the best known management system throughout Belize's history of slavery and colonialism—that is, increased authoritarianism.

In past, the administration has also offered awards to honour outstanding faculty members, with indifferent results. Faculty's position is that awards do not resolve their issues.

The University is in another bind. UB, an amalgamation of five small tertiary-level institutions, is only four years old. It offers a two-year associate and a four-year bachelor degree only. UB therefore competes with foreign institutions for the best students who finish high school. UB requires academic recognition to attract the best students and to enable its undergraduates to continue their studies at more established institutions. To gain accreditation from American and Central American university associations, UB has tended to model itself after the prestigious University of the West Indies, and well-known institutions in Britain and the USA. It attempts to conform to the organizational and instructional approaches used elsewhere as well. As a result, it finds itself establishing formats and forms and curricula to suit foreign bodies and enforcing compliance among faculty. In other words, UB administrators may not have made sufficient distinction between the ends sought by the institution (i.e. accreditation) on one hand and the unique programs and didactic methods it needs to be using in Belize, on the other. Given the pressures applied by Government on one hand and by faculty on the other, limited vision and creativity are understandable—although ultimately, they restrict UB's utility to its students, to its urban and rural populations, and to the Government of a nation attempting to hasten the process of development.

Ironically, the University is situated in a unique and exciting environment that, in part, consists of sub-tropical rainforest, wetlands and an enormous barrier reef; tropical logging, agro-industry, fisheries and animal husbandry; archaeological wonders; complex cultural and geo-political relationships bridging the US, the Caribbean and Central America; an ethnically and culturally varied population; challenges facing social service delivery; finance, productivity and development policy challenges; and, the challenges of political clientelism and corruption.

UB offers only the standard range of undergraduate courses and generally relies on imported—usually American—textbooks. But by shaping programs and didactic methods so as to conform with external accreditation standards, the University reduces its ability to respond to the challenges and opportunities provided by its student body, its under-prepared faculty, the natural environment, and the social, economic and political realities of a developing nation.

In fairness, it needs to be said that UB does attempt responses to its reality within the severe constraints of limited budget and overworked personnel. Where needed, UB students are offered remedial courses in basic English and math skills. Also, UB seeks opportunities to augment its GOB subsidies through that might be of interest to foreign students. At its new Belmopan campus, for example, it operates a language lab, teaching English to Spanish-speaking students from Central America and to some students from non-Spanish speaking countries. It is considering opportunities in marine biology too which can be extended to foreign students.

The majority of UB's faculty have first degrees from tertiary institutions. There are still a few with secondary school diplomas only. A few have Masters' degrees, and fewer than a dozen have PhDs—and of these, many are non-Belizeans. The creation of Galen University, a private institution in Belize, and some foreign medical universities further complicates the situation for UB as some of the better-prepared faculty are being attracted to institutions that are less constricted by political pressure and are externally subsidized, small, and responsive to faculty ideas. Hence, the pool of well prepared faculty has been reduced and may continue to shrink.

UB's attempts to recruit better prepared faculty have not been effective. At one point, the government of Belize offered special salaries to repatriate newly graduated Belizean PhDs, although it still offered less than what is paid in the US. Two Belizeans came home. But, neither UB nor the government of Belize was able to sustain this costly initiative. An attempt was then made to recruit Jamaican PhDs, but salaries were too low to be attractive. As a result, some sort of on-the-job, low-cost upgrading of current staff may become an attractive alternative except that paying for a foreign education is terribly costly.

The UB administration runs the risk of intensifying the authoritarian relationship with its poorly prepared, underpaid and unmotivated faculty in its efforts to gain external accreditation from US and Central American academic bodies, while ignoring the genuine academic needs of students and the pressing research needs for the development of this nation.

Is there a single strategy that can satisfy the dual need of UB to offer more responsive research and education to Belize while opening itself to additional income opportunities? And can it do so in a way which helps its faculty increase income and upgrade skills? A demand-based community development model is suggested next. Again, sub-groupings among administrators, faculty and students, for example, based on political affiliation, gender, training, academic interests, available time and so forth, are not presented.

With the University so dependent upon Government for financing, the ability of administrators to contemplate creative alternatives can become limited. Nevertheless, UB administration might be willing to turn to its handful of PhDs to work the following project.

Each PhD would be asked to devise a research proposal in a distinct discipline that the University will help market. Each proposal should have several characteristics: the research should address an issue of importance to Belize's development and within the PhDs' field of specialization; the research is to be applied—that is, as a part of the project, results of the research are to be integrated into some practical, beneficial and sustainable activity in Belize; where possible, the applied activity should involve government Ministries or Departments, NGOs and community members.[25]

The research and/or applied components of the project are to involve non-PhD faculty of UB in a learning capacity as a means of upgrading their skills. Formal training and assessment components for faculty are to be included and credit towards a Masters degree is to be awarded; non-PhD faculty who receive the on-the-job experience are to involve their students in field activities. They are to make the field experience part of course requirements, and the co-ordinating PhD is to guide them in this process.

The proposal is to be financed by foreign academic and/or research-oriented organizations. It is to be designed to allow research/training opportunities for foreign faculty and students. The University's in-kind contribution is to include existing facilities, the co-ordination services of its PhDs, and the field time of its non-PhD faculty and students; and, the budget is to include fees for participating faculty and students, and a fee for the University to be paid by the foreign institution.

However, what is to be done if administrators are unable to consider such a radical departure from the standard model university they are attempting to replicate? Because they have been unable to attract or adequately pay newly graduated Belizean PhDs from US institutions, nor to import Jamaican PhDs to Belize, the local PhDs are put in a strong negotiating position. Furthermore, they number only a few. As observed by Olson and other scholars interested in the logic of collective action, it is easy for small groups to use approbation and censure to hold an alliance together. Such an alliance is able to organize a proposal and attract donor support, bringing the new mechanism for sustainability and increasing academic relevance to the administrators—not as an alternative to current operations, but as an experimental addition to present initiatives. The potential for increased income to PhDs can unite them around the concept.

The potential bargaining strength makes it an attractive organization. And the potential for the same PhDs to operate the concept outside the University functions as a counter-incentive to encourage administrators to consider the idea. Similarly, the ease with which the PhDs can attract donor financing to an external applied development research company acts as an incentive to forestall any desire by the administrators to introduce regulations outlawing such an action.

From the outset, the proposal intends to do environmental good by allowing UB, faculty and students to do well both economically and intellectually. By design, it intends to couple social and environmental benefits. Because it includes a (limited) number of PhDs from a broad range of academic areas, its funding proposals may also allow UB to broaden its developmental work into other areas including the social, political, cultural and economic. Socio-economic interdependence (i.e. among UB, Government of Belize and NGO initiatives at the community level) as well as the achievement of a program approach become possible.

The function of a supportive administration (or failing them, the PhDs themselves) would be to ensure as many lateral and beneficial linkages as possible across the individual proposals. For this reason, the idea has additional potential for moving this sustainable mechanism from a project to a program mentality: the separate proposals also bring UB into co-operation with Governmental and or NGOs and community members.

The project design is built around a long-term impact strategy. With this strategic approach, the university is able to move its best educated faculty into research and leadership capacities, break into more innovative education for its students or offer educational opportunities to its under-prepared faculty. It can also provide practical research findings to the nation or participate in applied research activities, strengthening other organizations, or establish linkages with other educational bodies and profit from advances in research or earn income for itself. The university could provide additional income opportunities to its faculty and open opportunities for entrepreneurial alliances between UB and other demand-led development projects in Belize such as CAT$ and the environmental project.

Finally, a reassuring exit strategy for donors can be integrated into a project designed for iterative Results-Based Management (RBM) which includes annual roll-up evaluations of scheduled outputs and outcomes, and corrective re-organization of outcomes and activities in the roll out of an annual plan for the coming year.

The immediate objective of this project is to offer a win-win partnership to the University faculty and the University itself. But an innovative and effective design becomes possible by looking beyond the University by way of its Mission Statement. The University does not exist only to exist, nor to offer tertiary education in Belize because one expects to find a university in a modern nation. The UB mission calls for the institution to use research and study for the purpose of contributing to Belizean students and to nation building. By responding to the nation's needs and those of the University's administration and faculty simultaneously, it becomes possible to help resolve each problem by helping to resolve them all.

* * *

In each of the project descriptions above, an incentives-based, three-way interdependency has been established:

a) between a member of a target group and a collective action mechanism;

b) between that individual and others similarly attracted to the mechanism; and,

c) between the mechanism and such individuals.

The use of incentives to pull together interdependent individuals and to hold them to a sustainable and expandable collective action mechanism eliminates the need to push people into sacrificing for the greater good; they do it to do better for themselves. But in so doing, they allow others to do the same. Each project is designed so that individuals may opt into an opportunity if s/he desires, or ignore it—the onus is upon the project initiators not to cajole, but to ensure that sufficiently attractive incentives are being offered.

The mechanism for each project is designed so that it can co-exist with the current system of dependency. But it can also expand without difficulty so that patron dependency can lessen or be forgotten altogether. Each mechanism is also designed so that individuals participating can take ownership (both moral and economic) of the expandable alternative. It is amenable to the determination of objectively verifiable indicators and means of verification, and designed so that donor dependency can be removed or re-targeted at a definable point in time.

Solidarity with members sharing one's class interests may even occur—not as the basis for class action to combat a ruling class, but the opposite way: as a by-product of protracted peer exchanges of mutual benefit. Perhaps affection is a function of need.

10

Conclusion

Origins of the Demand-Led Model

I STARTED THINKING ABOUT moral and economic models of development from the time I began organizing production and consumer co-operatives in San Andrés Island, Colombia in 1966. This coconut-covered island, shaped very much like a sea-horse, is located in the southwest Caribbean, about 300 miles north of the fortified coastal city of Cartagena de Indias, and about 180 miles to the east of Bluefields, Nicaragua. I was a volunteer with the Canadian University Service (CUSO) back then, teaching English at the *Colegio Bolivariano* on Slave Hill—an aptly named place, I have always thought. A surprising number of students fell asleep in my class, but I convinced myself that malnutrition was more of a factor than boredom.

In San Andrés, I had been watching a tourist economy replace the coconut export economy that brought diminishing income to the Islander families whose sons were sleeping in my English classes. As their economy languished, the local population were being supplanted by Middle Eastern merchants who ran the tourist shops, restaurants and hotels and by mainlanders from the mountain cities who ran the banks and bureaucracies. Their sons remained alert in class. They were also being replaced by black, coastal mainlanders who

233

did menial labour for the new economy. The members of the third group were not on their own land like the Islanders were; they were also much poorer, and hence, were more eager to accept the low wages. They were also willing to endure the insults that accompanied the menial pay. Few of their children were in school at all. Many Islanders, bewildered and depressed by the loss of the old ways and the old standards of decency, were selling their properties and living off the cash, or moving away.

I wondered what sort of opportunity might allow the Islander group to avoid cultural extinction and loss of their homeland. They were black, Baptist and English-Creole speakers in a largely white and mestizo, Catholic and Spanish-speaking nation. Tourism was almost like a gold rush experience for the government and for the new populations that invaded San Andrés. These newcomers had little interest in commiserating with the plight of the Islanders and the new economy that was crowding onto an island only 7 miles by 2 miles was not going to leave room for them. They had to have a productive niche of their own to be taken seriously and would have to create it for themselves. If an entire population was being economically marginalized and seeking a survival opportunity, the most efficient mechanism would have to be one with economic characteristics and with income-generating potential for a whole population. That is how I became interested in production co-operatives.

I had considered the alternatives discussed during training and orientation by other volunteers heading for CUSO assignments throughout the Caribbean and the Spanish Americas. Some of them were enthusiastic about the potential for a class-based revolution and a fresh and more egalitarian start. Cuba had successfully thumbed its nose at the United States, Ché had at least alarmed them again in Bolivia, and Allende's presence in Chile promised a less class-dominated future for the Southern Cone. I was interested in such ideas, but thought that a realistic initial challenge in San Andrés would be to keep my students awake for a 50-minute English class.

Since at that time I had also decided that my students slept because of poverty and not because of my poor English teaching, I determined I would try an experiment. I recruited volunteer members of my *cuarto bachillerato* (i.e. 2nd Form, or Grade 10) class for a tomato-growing co-operative that we called "SAC"—an acronym for the "Students' Agricultural Co-operative." SAC would produce tomatoes on an acre of land loaned to us by the father of one of the students. In about 90 days, we'd sell the tomatoes, hold back a re-investment fund and divide the remainder. The students would purchase food to energize them during my classes and I would have proven to be a valuable CUSO volunteer.

My enthusiasm for the production co-op idea was huge. I showed up on the appointed Saturday to open the donated acre of land. Most of the volunteers appeared as well—at least they did on the first Saturday. I worked up huge blisters on my urban, chalky hands, much to the amusement of the students. Student participation dwindled rapidly from one week to the next over the growing season even as my blisters hardened into calluses and my neck reddened. There were occasions when only two or three of the students appeared to weed or "back" water for the plants. A couple of times, I think I was out there alone, and I was stuck making the arrangements to get rid of the ripe tomatoes. However, the students were back again when we shared out the profits. I don't know whether they used the cash for healthy meals. Somehow, I doubt it. That their enthusiasm was greater for the cash than for the hard work did not bother me particularly. I guess I noticed all of this, but considered the experiment a moderate success anyway. We had harvested the tomatoes and earned more than we spent in the process.

On the basis of the qualified success, I returned to Canada and then took a Master of Social Welfare in the US, concentrating on community organization and the economics of poverty. The thesis I wrote used research data I had collected back in San Andrés Island. The thesis was essentially a project proposal for community development to be built around a range of production and consumer co-operatives as a way of enabling San Andrés Islanders to increase their income and to decrease their costs.

A friend and colleague from my CUSO days was employed at the Canadian International Development Agency (CIDA) at that time. He was shown my thesis by a mutual friend and was excited by what he saw. At the time, Quebec was aflame with one of its periodical rages for independence. He, being Quebecois, may have thought the San Andrés/Colombia cultural and economic relationship was analogous to that of Quebec and Canada and probably decided that it was valuable and safer to experiment in the Caribbean. He called one summer morning and made me an offer: if I could interest two or three Canadian Non-Governmental Organizations (NGOs) to finance the project, he would support the proposal for a matching grant from CUSO.

Unbelievably, OXFAM-Canada, CCODP and CUSO were talked into my mad proposal and CIDA went along with the experiment. My wife—who had wanted to marry an MD (but had to settle for a PhD) and wanted to live in the suburbs and purchase wall-to-wall carpeting—helped me pack our belongings and came to live with me in a tiny, sweltering house beneath the coconut palms in San Andrés. I had by then talked a multi-denominational set of priests and preachers into registering an ecumenical foundation, letting me sit on its board and also hiring me as its first executive director in order to receive the grant monies from Canada. My wife helped me train a set of extension workers—the brightest and most enthusiastic of my former students (and generally the ones who stayed awake)—and to organize a co-ordinating office. Then, night after night, she (and eventually our first-born son) accompanied me on our under-powered motorbike to community meetings all around the island.

After four years, we had organized seven consumer co-operatives that vended food staples, a water-taxi drivers' co-operative regulating the dispatch of tourist-laden boats and renting snorkelling equipment, and a fishermen's co-operative purchasing the daily catch, operating a fried fish restaurant on the beach and even operating a mini sickness payment plan for their membership. All of the co-operatives were generating annual surpluses.

At that point we left. One of the Islander extension workers was hired as the replacement executive director of the foundation and the other extension work-ers decided to stick with the foundation. This looked like the beginning of a tremendous success—the very opportunity I had hoped might emerge for Islanders.

But something was wrong. There were odd anomalies. The fishermen's co-operative was robust. It was diversifying its means of production and re-establishing its power relationship with the politicians. But the fishermen's loyalty to the co-operative that was bringing real change and new opportunities to their lives was questionable. Most of the members continued selling fish to family members at the shore and to taxi drivers and to the hotels. The co-op was supposed to do all that for them, keeping them united and protected from all the opportunists. But doing the honourable thing for the whole was sacrificed in favour of opportunism for many of the individuals. As things developed, the fishermen were playing both with their co-op and against it. The water-taxi dri-vers used their co-op like a police corps. Members continually cheated on the co-op, sneaking off boatloads of tourists to the cays. Other members were enraged by those who cheated and then proceeded to cheat themselves. The consumer co-operative members loaned their membership cards to relatives who refused to join and then bought basic foodstuffs at bargain prices. The girls hired to run the shops didn't stop them. Worse, even though there were regulations against the practice, they extended credit to buyers.

In all the co-operatives, the anomaly I observed was that the people frequently engaged in ignoble behaviours when they appeared to have the chance to opt for idealism. I remember a co-operative banquet where all of us came together to celebrate a year of progress. To my chagrin, a food fight broke out in the midst of this celebration of co-operation. People had brought socks to stuff with bread and pots to fill with food. One large woman was elbowing her way to the front of the melee shouting, "Me no get!"

"But Miss Gladys," (not her real name, of course) I rationally explained, "we're not here to eat. We're here to celebrate co-operation and unity!"

"That's why you come, Mr. Roastpork," (nobody got my name right) was her angry retort, "I come fi *nyam*" (that is, to chow down).

And she pushed herself forward again, shouting, "Me no get!"

She and I—in fact, many of the co-operative members and I—were separated by our ways of seeing the world. I intervened as an idealist. Miss Gladys and many of the others were pragmatists.

Later, I did international project officer work with the Canadian Co-operative Association for a number of years. And later still, after the PhD, I was their Director of Project Management. I have also worked as a development consultant for many years. Together with the extended field experience in San Andrés Island, Colombia, I was exposed to hundreds of development programs and projects in the Caribbean and Latin America, in Africa and in Asia, studying production, consumption, education and health projects. Some of them took the form of co-operatives; many did not. And across this sectoral and geographical range of experiences, the observations that I made in San Andrés have been reinforced with fair consistency: in the short- and long-term, participants in development projects appear to be subject to both moral and economic pressures. They had to make decisions that could hurt or benefit themselves, ones that had consequences either positive or negative for others involved in the project. With good consistency, they were opting for short-term personal benefits. When project participants opted for the long-term benefits that would benefit others, it was because they themselves were usually benefiting personally in the short-run. That is, when they did good for others, they were also doing well for themselves. It usually took the personal opportunity to make the social one possible. When they couldn't benefit on their own terms, they seldom made efforts to benefit others.

Over the same period, I have been impressed by the gap that often appears to exist between the targets of development and the developers themselves. The project beneficiaries are bent upon doing well for themselves, but we, the developers, are hell-bent upon doing good for others—even upon getting them to do good for one another. I suppose the gap is to be expected. After all, poverty is the mother of invention; sympathy on the other hand elicits decency. Decency and generosity may bring us into development work, but when we expect others to live by our purported altruistic standards we undercut our own ability to be effective. The more I observe troubled development projects on the ground and the more I observe and read about their failures to achieve sustainability and to challenge the *status quo*, the more I come to suspect that we developers have been hampered by a problem in our mindset.

I believe that our moral mindset has been our major development obstacle: we have inherited and have been taught to employ a counter-productive way of looking at the world. This book has proposed that we would do better to stop supplying solutions to the developing world. It has recommended that we suspect idealism though we have been taught to value it. It has contended that we respond to the greedy demands of the people we intend to assist where we have understood that their greed, not our opposition to it, has been the obstacle. It has even suggested we include the very tormentors of marginalized populations in such responsive strategies. We know the talents of such people and the resources they command. Nevertheless, we seldom question our tendency to turn away from creative interaction with them because of the suffering they cause the poor. In short, this book has maintained that we shift our development paradigm from one that is moral to one that is economic.

We have been encouraged to label people as either friends or enemies, as progressives or reactionaries. We have been encouraged to disapprove of behaviours we observe among our enemies and even to apply moral valuations to the behaviours of the people we assist. The whole development world is divided into two camps: Good dwells in one; Evil in the other. Development work, we have been encouraged to think, is a battle to make a heaven of hell, and life is a morality play. We are either part of the problem, we have been told, or part of the solution. Peter Dalglish puts it in a different context: "Street children divide the world into two: those who help them, and those who hurt them."[1] But it's more complicated than that. Dalglish praises the National Film Board[2] of Canada because they can make a wonderful animated cartoon to teach street children around the world about the need to take precautions against AIDS. He also blames Toronto entrepreneurs for building a world class stadium with a retractable roof for a world class city where, only blocks away, he sees aboriginal children high on gasoline fumes, staggering between the lamp posts. Yet it was the businessmen's taxes that helped to fund the National Film Board. Circumstances have caused businessmen to contribute to one Good and to one Evil.

Moral categories require little reflection once they have been established. We can ignore the fact that contradictory realities shape complicated circumstances and fight, rather naïvely, for the side we've taken—punching at our noses to spite our faces. Moral categories free us to devise plans of betterment and to turn our plans to action. We ally with friends and oppose our enemies— or theirs. We support progressive causes and decry or battle reactionary ones. We condemn greed, but we laud and encourage co-operation, selflessness and other-centeredness. And because we have come to think that we have sided with Good and taken action against Evil, we do our development work with will (and perhaps with little pay), but nonetheless with great will and with an absolute sense of righteousness.

In general, we have learned to participate in two categories of moral development initiatives: where we encounter Evil, we have learnt to mount barricades and to convince others to join us. Where there is suffering, we have been encouraged to help those who are victimized to find ways of opposing evildoers for themselves. Marx claimed that evildoers inculcate false consciousness among those they victimize and for that reason, victims will lick the boots of the powerful and battle each other to the detriment of their class interests. Alternatively, they will be kept ignorant of the skills they need to do better for themselves as individuals and as members of a class. And we have been taught it is our responsibility to help them understand the deceit, to apprise them of their ignorance, and to get them to appreciate and to struggle for their true class interests. Too often, we have proceeded in this manner without reflecting upon the accuracy and the utility of the categories to which we react and that form the bases for our activism—categories such as "friend" or "enemy," "progressive" or "reactionary," "generous" or "greedy."

In this book, I have said that what we need to be wary of more than anything else, is this very sort of moral bifurcation of the world. Nobody's consciousness is completely false or true; nobody achieves total solidarity across class nor total enmity with all members of their own class. The world really doesn't fall neatly into two camps. Of course we really know this but we have been encouraged, nevertheless, to proceed with our development work as though we didn't.

I have labelled as "greedy" such behaviours as false consciousness, intra-class battling and cross-class alliance-making. And I have argued that greed need not be relegated to the camp of Evil. Since we really know that nothing is wholly good or evil, then perhaps we need not discard greed just because it has been dismissed as a behaviour unworthy of the people we intend to assist.

My reasons for having recommended a re-evaluation of greed are twofold. For one thing, greed motivates many individuals to act. Many of us would say it motivates too many—perhaps because we disrespect so many of the actions taken because of greed. Greed can hurt others, but it can nonetheless be useful as a development tool. In contrast, sermons motivate few people to leap into action. Development workers deal with change and I see greater potential for change in greed than in sermons.

In the second place, action motivated by greed represents an individual's movement towards some kind of improvement. Flawed as this unilateral definition of improvement may be, we should not be troubled by it—only make use of it in positive ways. As community developers, we need only to identify with those individuals who coincidentally show potential for opening up choices to others who also suffer limited opportunities. We need not endorse those greedy actions that restrict alternatives.

According to this reasoning, greed need not be defined using moral categories as "a bad or evil thing." It may be defined using economic categories as "a force that motivates an individual towards a change she or he considers an improvement, and possibly one that opens new opportunities to others."

When moral thinking dominates our approach to development, our alternatives are confined by our belief system, that is to say, by our prejudices. In contrast, when we apply economic-based thinking, we can make use of more scientific, more objective methods. Thus, an economic examination of human behaviour allows us to generate behavioural theories and to use hypotheses (i.e. predictions) to test them.

Prejudgement of people and actions and siding with those we deem good denies us the ability to learn from our development work. As anti-establishmentarian development workers, for instance, we cannot cost good and evil. There is no range of alternatives between these extremes. We can assure ourselves that the progressive struggle will eventually bring progress; but the real point of being anti-establishmentarian is to be engaged in the struggle against evil, to be against it. However, we have had no way of measuring the status of the class struggle. I have heard Scientific Socialists refer to these as "the latter days of capitalism." But how would we know until later?

As establishmentarian development workers we can oppose wrong procedures when we identify them in the government offices and businesses in the developing world. We can try to replace them with proper ones. But we've generally failed at this approach too, because, as Amartya Sen observed, we persist in measuring indicators of growth instead of measures of human freedom.[3] Human freedom is a multi-dimensional phenomenon. It has to do with the world of relative advantages and with the multiple alliances we must engage in to achieve these advantages. That is, we need to apply an economic model.

Consequently, this book has suggested that, as developers, we should do better by paying greater attention to people's objectives and to the strategies they employ to attain them, than to forming an opinion of their attitudes and encouraging them to adopt ones we like better. Behaviours that open opportunities to others are efficient. Behaviours that limit others are not—not for those who are denied the opportunities, nor for the developers who intend to assist them; nor, ultimately, for those employing the strategies profitably in the short-term. Attractive strategies are more rewarding to their users and therefore developers need to work with those who are denied access to opportunities to define incentives that will attract them towards more rewarding strategies. Of all the attractive incentives, the ones that coincidentally increase others' opportunities are the incentives developers should offer. The old, restrictive strategies can then be abandoned for ones that are of greater utility to the decision-maker and to others.

The usual approach to promoting collective action is to coerce people who are suspicious of a neighbourhood, caste or class members into contributing more to the greater good. The ploy fails if it implies less for the individual. But in this book, we have suggested that for the poor person the moral course of action will be more difficult to adopt than the win-win strategy that rewards him or her as well as others. Furthermore, we have suggested that the strategy that can succeed over time is the win-win-win formula that rewards individuals and their collective action organization while bringing mutual rewards to other individuals.

Does the Model Suit Projects Not Designed for Co-operatives?

Much of my career has involved producer, consumer, service and credit co-operatives. So some of the examples I have used and many of the principles I have drawn on in this book on collective action bear their stamp. From the co-operative model I have learned about the central role of production, consumption, credit and savings in eradicating the dependency relationships that keep the poor beholden to patrons and gatekeepers. By observing co-operatives I have identified the critical three-way inter-relationship that is required to sustain productive interaction among populations usually reduced to suspicion, hostility and competition by patronage. I have attempted to apply the lessons I learned from co-operative work more broadly to collective action work in general.

The logic put forward suggests that community organization work by itself—for example, the creation of political advocacy groups—is not adequate because moral indignation spawned by injustice will not sustain group unity and protest for very long. A hungry man is an angry man, as Bob Marley said. But a sufficiently angry man will stop demonstrating when he has enough to eat. Group unity and protest, in other words, must be fed. If the hungry man or woman cannot feed it, donor agencies must. That limits the size of the protest organization to the limited resources of the donors and undermines its vigour. Besides, foreign donors come to replace local patrons if the protesters cannot nurture their own rebellion.

The mere provision of social services such as prenatal care, anti-HIV/AIDS measures, literacy efforts or teacher training are not adequate by themselves. These activities are conducted in contexts of low productivity and those who need these services the most are usually the ones who are least able to pay for them; those who can pay are usually least interested. Social service projects per se don't have to be put on a self-financing basis. That is usually not possible because the poor cannot cover their cost. But to achieve the provision of social services on a continuing basis without depending on foreign donor agencies requires a program approach—one that includes measures to increase user productivity as well as user advocacy directed at government. So I have argued that responsible development work of any sort—including advocacy and social service provision—cannot ignore the critical role of productivity, cost-reduction and the provision of credit and savings opportunities.

There are certain advantages to following a critical role that is associated with the co-operative and credit union models. Developers often have plenty of experience with such projects and there is an existing network of organizations from world to local level with which local collective action initiatives can associate. That network possesses an impressive wealth of experience and a track record of successful technical assistance—much of which has been objectively verified. The World Council of Credit Unions (WOCCU) and the International Co-operative Alliance (ICA) are available for community developers interested in taking the co-operative development route. Similarly, there are international co-operative development organizations in many industrialized countries that are furnished with much expertise and with access to technical assistance and some financing of their own. Canada, for example, boasts a number of such institutions including the International Development Department of the Canadian Co-operative Association and also of the Conseil des Coöperatives du Canada (CCC) as well as the Societé de Developpment International Déjardins of the Movement Déjardins of Québec. And within the developing world, there are regional and national co-operative organizations affiliated upwards and downwards so that technical assistance and finance can be efficiently co-ordinated and channelled.

However, even with the co-operative examples I presented, I have included some efficient alternatives not based on the co-operative model. The organized Philippine valley of peasants that co-invested in a feed mill with their former patron was one such example of a model that never registered co-operatives. Among the demand-led models in the previous chapter, the Nuer and Dinka street boys' bicycle courier service was another example of successful collective action that operated without co-operatives. So were the scenarios I created that involved street-corner youth, the forest poachers and the university lecturers. The demand-led model does not have to be limited to co-ops and credit unions. In fact, one of the major points I am trying to make in this book is that we might do well to consider income-generation for project sustainability in any community-level project we undertake. We might also think about linking non-productive initiatives to productive undertakings so that they can remain viable after the funded project ends. The catch, however, is that if there is no real demand for the service supplied in the first instance, new resources generated by a productive component of a program will be spent on other things. That may have been the case among the sleepy students who offered little help when I was in the tomato business and who may not have spent their portion of the income on wholesome meals.

My Participation in Demand-Led Projects

The full concept of demand-led development work came together for me only in the course of writing this book, so I cannot claim to have been involved in a completely demand-led type of project. I had identified some of the anomalies of the moral approaches to development even while engaged in creating, administering, monitoring and evaluating projects that were based on these principles. I have also observed some of their consistent weaknesses. When possible, I have experimented with elements of the demand-led project. For example, the technique of withholding technical assistance for management and leadership until the leaders demanded it (which I used when helping the fishermen's co-operative in San Andrés Island to organize) proved to be so valuable that I repeated it with other projects and even incorporated such tactics into my university lecturing work. Like many people before me, I have learned that a question is worth hundreds of statements. Socrates figured that out before any of us, didn't he? And now far fewer of my students sleep in my classes.

In Belize I reworked the power relationship between local management and production assistance organizations and the agricultural collective co-operatives they assisted. There were two such organizations, each of which may have had political connections to the two major Belizean parties. Their main source of finance came from a Canadian organization for which I worked, but that appeared to compete to organize farmers into co-operatives. Perhaps this was done to assist politicians with extending small favours to groups instead of individuals, collecting blocs of votes in return. There appeared to be more co-operative organizing and registering than actual provision of management and production assistance. The two organizations were even setting aside project funds intended for the producer co-operatives and setting up revolving loan funds even though the farmers had little real control over the organizations. As a result, the members of ostensibly independent co-operatives were rapidly being reduced to a dependent clientele that was eager for the approbation of, and the loan funds controlled by, the officers of the organizations.

A simple change on the part of the Canadian donor reversed the power structure. We began extending contracts directly to the producer co-operatives. They, in turn, were free to choose the assistance organization that offered them the better service package. A contract was then signed between the co-operative and the organization it preferred. That contract specified the services that were to be offered and the number of visits to be completed by the organization providing technical assistance (TA) each year. The TA organizations had to sign an attendance book at each co-operative they serviced and had to provide records of services delivered. When the co-operatives gave us permission we channelled payments directly to the TA organization. The choice was made in Canada to deal with the co-operatives. The TA organizations had the choice between agreeing to the new terms and signing contracts with the co-operatives or taking direct service contracts with other foreign donors.

When the co-operatives eventually opted for their own federation, they organized their own revolving fund through a local credit union. The affiliated producer co-operatives used these loans to build locally designed grain dryers. This project operated prior to the development of Results-Based Management, so there was little monitoring of movement towards the economic and political independence of the federation or its members beyond the attendance books at the co-ops and the written technical visit reports. Nevertheless, the project was demand-driven to the extent that the Belizean service providers and the Canadian donors began to respond to the agenda set by the producer groups.

I have also worked closely with the Americas Program Director of the Canadian Co-operative Association on the design and monitoring of demand-led programs that operated in Colombia, El Salvador and regionally in Central America. This individual, a Costa Rican, shared much of my development philosophy and has been supportive of my project and program design work with local counterpart organizations. He far surpasses my skills in the areas of negotiation and project monitoring. He is a trained accountant and is comfortable working in Brazil, the Hispanic Americas and in the English-speaking Caribbean. The successes of these programs were his more than mine, as I confined my contribution to the design and to a bit of the assessment work.

The Central American program supported the development of a regional marketing consortium and the gist of its demand-led elements of success was provided earlier in the book when describing the Guatemalan peapod exporters. In Colombia, a sizeable association of co-operatives was sustained by the payments of its largest affiliates and burdened by the cost of aiding its weakest ones through its technical assistance department. Together, we (the developers) and the association organized a system that allowed the association's technical assistance department to offer production and management training to selected production co-operatives that had the potential to become economically viable—at first as a funded venture, but later on a paying basis.

Over a five year period, that department moved from something like 18 per cent to more than 100 per cent sustainability on the basis of the sale of services to such co-operatives. Its ability to sustain itself through the sale of services was the result of the inclusion of one element of the demand-led model. Previously, the association had visited co-operatives, deciding for them what they needed to be told. They were not becoming economically viable on the basis of lectures on co-operative legislation and members' rights and duties. But when the department became dependent on services purchased by the co-operatives themselves for its income, it was motivated to offer services the co-operatives wanted to pay for, or to lose their patronage. The co-operatives only wanted to pay for the services that moved them to sustainability.

This project was designed in El Salvador; I was involved in planning a project for Results-Based Management and all of its achievements were statistically and verifiably indicated. Following the cessation of hostilities in the region, the army created a consortium of cashew-producing co-operatives in the east end of the country. The new owner-members were the illiterate *campesinos* that lived on large estates that had belonged to members of the 14 families that had formerly ruled that nation. After their lands were expropriated by the army, the families succeeded in getting legislation approved that allowed individual *campesino* co-operative members to sell their parcel of the co-operative lands. Because the co-operatives were unproductive for lack of production and management skills among the *campesinos*, the old owners were re-purchasing their holdings piece by piece. When enough pieces were gone, the whole co-operative would collapse and the remaining *campesinos* would hurriedly sell off their holdings for a song.

With the co-ordinated assistance of Salvadoran and Canadian co-operative federations, the cashew producers' co-operative consortium learned to improve management practices, increase productivity and reduce production costs while converting their lands to organic cashew farming. They built and now operate a small processing plant and began exporting the more valuable organic nuts to organic consumer co-operatives in Canada before diversifying their market. Through the efforts of their consortium, many of the women (and the men too) have become literate. Previously, housebound women without incomes had not been involved in the co-operative. Most entered co-operative employment as labourers in the processing plant thanks to the day care the consortium organized and operates. Some, who had the ability, became administrators of the consortium production/processing organization. The program was also extended to youth so that families would not lose children to the cities. A bussing service operates to get the youth to the district high school. But the youth are also entering the production co-operatives and the consortium as producers and administrators.

The opportunities that open for members of the cashew growers' co-operative consortium are sustainable because they all operate on a paying basis. The consortium initiates what services its organic cashew sales make affordable. And all of the opportunities are provided in response to the demands of the producers who want to increase the volume of their sales, the youth who want to obtain jobs, and the women who want to gain entrance to schools and co-operative opportunities. Finally, the sale of lands by individual producer members has ceased in that consortium.

Many development projects described in this book have included elements of income generation and have been concerned with sustainability. The bike couriers and the Nigerian production credit projects were two examples. But without the adjustments I suggested earlier, I maintain that only the courier project is demand-led. Peter Dalglish had come up with the idea, not the street boys. However, that project was demand-led because it responded to what the boys were really after. Dalglish himself reported that the boys were entrepreneurial; one, at least, told the writer he wanted to become a big man some day.[4] The boys wanted brilliant yellow and blue uniforms and they wanted to be able to read and write. Dalglish explains this demand-led element as follows:

> When the children of ski Courier decided they wanted to learn to read and write, they were not trying to make me happy, or UNICEF happy, or even their clients happy. They were making themselves happy. We had already set up an incentive system that rewarded kids for their efforts. The kids earned points in five different categories: punctuality, appearance, bicycle maintenance, helping other kids, and performance.... At the end of each week, the points were translated into a cash bonus. The more letters the kids delivered, the more money they earned each day. Poi, Moj and Sunday scored more points than the other children because they didn't have to consult the dispatcher or another adult in the street to determine where a letter was to be delivered. They could read, and they were getting rich as a result. That did the trick.[5]

Characteristics of the Demand-led Model

Some, but not all, of the characteristics of truly demand-led projects can be found in each of the projects just mentioned. There are four characteristics to the demand-led model and some, but not all, of these characteristics can be found in the projects we have just discussed.

Characteristic 1: Projects are Demand-Responsive

A project operates via a collective action mechanism that responds to the survival demands of its users—or dies as an institution. The incentive system had to respond to the street boys' own objective (i.e. money) or it would have gone up in flames. Dalglish could only be effective by responding to legitimate demands. That is one of the essential characteristics of the model. Any project that does not meet that criterion—even a project that intends to be self-sustaining—is not a demand-led project.

Characteristic 2: Projects must Benefit Others

The second essential criterion is that the demand-led strategy must not only respond to the demand of individuals within the targeted population, but must also open opportunities for other similarly excluded individuals. As it was operating, the Nigerian production loan credit union did not represent a *bona fide* demand-led project because it was not financially sustainable without continued external grants. The micro-loans given to individual producers were too small to enable a farmer to realize more income and a greater margin of profit than she or he was used to earning. That obstacle limited the interest rate of the credit union. In turn, the credit union was proving to be too unproductive to allow new producers to join, save and obtain meaningful loans of their own.

Characteristic 3: Reduces Patron-Dependency

The central collective action mechanism does not just extend a product or service to its users (as does a co-operative or credit union), but deliberately extends that service for the purpose of reducing the dependency of the user upon one or more patrons and gatekeepers. This may or may not be a function of a collective action organization, but it does need to be a function of one that is designed on the demand-led model.

Characteristic 4: Permits Improved Cross-Class Social Relations of Production

As part of their design and implementation, projects based on the demand-led model are deliberately used to reposition the owners of the new income generation collective action mechanism. The mechanism may be the dairy or fishing or water taxi co-operative. It may be the bicycle courier organization or

a multiple-village forest museum organization that facilitates individual vil-
lager tourism businesses. But in all cases, that mechanism (or another its
owners created for the purpose) is developing the clout and the skills to renegotiate the social relations of production with those who formerly held them
and who had used them to subordinate people and to create dependent relationships of class, cash and status. This renegotiation takes place on the basis
of mutual benefit.

The difference between this characteristic of a demand-led model and the
previous one is subtle, but important. By increasing the individual's ability to
depend on the collective action organization, the individual described in the
previous characteristic may reduce his or her individual dependency on one or
several clients if this is what is desired. In this fourth instance, the collective
action organization itself is designed to renegotiate with one or more clients on
behalf of all of the members of that collective action mechanism.

In the *Communist Manifesto*, Frederich Engels and Karl Marx called on the
workers to unite and destroy the bourgeoisie. More than a century later, I think
we can admit that their advice has been ineffective. Frequently, the workers have
been too competitive to unite. When conditions have occasionally supported
enough unity to sustain a successful revolution, the emerging people's state
deteriorated into a horribly inefficient dictatorship of the socialist state bureaucrats, one riddled with corruption as individuals were forced to purchase
special favours to prosper (or just subsist).

I am suggesting that the demand-led development model can at least facilitate the emergence of a sustainable—even expandable—three-way mechanism
among individuals and between individuals and the mechanism itself. That
relationship is analogous to the unity sought by the revolutionaries, except that
it is not built on the basis of moral indignation, but on economic need. And
unlike the unattained enduring unity of class, this interdependency does not
ultimately attempt to smash the bourgeoisie but to co-invest with it. When,
through repositioning, a former opponent becomes an ally, why destroy him?
Marx's intransigent enmity towards the bourgeoisie was based upon the
assumption that the bourgeoisie has no option whatever except to survive
through the extraction of surplus labour from the proletariat. As with most generalized inevitabilities, this is not exactly true in the case of some individuals,
like the former patron investing in the Philippine peons' feed mill. We have recommended seeking the exceptional cases where co-investment becomes a more
attractive option for old exploiters than lost opportunities. From an economic

perspective, moral intransigence may prove to be like clinging to a sinking ship: ultimately, the cost becomes too dear.

Is the Demand-Led Model a Panacea?

Is the true demand-led development model recommended as a community development panacea? I think it is generally a better approach to take than ones based on moral indignation and idealism. I think we can expect to find better response rates among target groups, longer periods of participation in collective action organizations, longer periods of sustainability among those organizations and more concrete indicators of interaction with authority individuals and institutions.

However, there are some conditions under which a demand-led model is not appropriate. These are situations that call for a residual approach to social work as a way of dealing with cases of great urgency and/or with individuals who are unable to assist. The other obstacle to the implementation of demand-led models include situations where the need of the poor to obtain social services is greater than their ability to pay. Also, structural constraints imposed by local patrons or national (or even global) regulations may be such that a demand-led model may not be equal to the magnitude of barriers encountered. In this latter case, I recommend an iterative approach of repeated repositioning of client populations and of pragmatic association (that is mutually beneficial alliances of client populations) with more and more demand-led organizations.

Even with the above exceptions, I would say that we still cannot know whether the demand-led model offers us a panacea. There may be situations that we have not encountered and for which the model is not appropriate. We also have to attempt to reposition clients vis-à-vis the patrons and gatekeepers by using incentives that attract clients into new behaviours and limit the incentives to those behaviours that, as a by-product, yield opportunities for other clients. Then we have to identify incentives that bring mutual benefit to collective action organizations and to former patrons. I have to admit that I do not know whether enough such incentives exist to make the difference we as developers desire.

By the same token, when I told my mother I didn't like broccoli, she replied, "Well, how will you know unless you try?" I had no answer to that either.

Recommendations

The first recommendation is simple: we have to at least try this alternative. This means trying to see development from the perspective of multiple opportunists. It is not just that the rich exploit the poor. Because the poor are exploited, they have developed defensive, exploitative strategies of their own to hold the line against the rich and to protect themselves from one another. We are witnessing a multi-dimensional chess game and we have to determine our own best move. We wish to participate because we care, because we believe that the multiple passive/aggressive behaviours are usually destructive to all those involved and most destructive to those people who are least able to withstand further losses. But we are trying to intervene in a manner that is highly strategic and with the expectation that we are being observed by those who wish to take advantage if they can. Realizing this can help us to shape our intervention.

New projects can be designed using the demand-led model. Where our development interventions used to suffer at the hands of those who related to us in an opportunistic fashion, they now stand to benefit. Where other potential project beneficiaries used to suffer because of the greed of the most aggressively opportunistic, they too can now benefit. We will relate to our target population with strategies of our own, ones that allow the takers to benefit, but that also enable others to take, to benefit and to open doors to still more people in the process. Our strategy will need to be built around an economic relationship. Frequently, we are using a business mechanism and economic means money. But not always. The mechanism can be modelled on the basis of barter: more rice for your ducks and pigs, more manure for my rice paddies. The barter can even exist between humans and natural resources: more Brazil nuts for my basket, more Brazil trees for the forest.

Second, there will be value in reviewing on-going projects to understand which characteristics of the demand-led model they already possess, which are lacking and what might be done to improve them. Perhaps the costs of not having included the additional demand-led elements can be estimated as a way of determining whether moral measures have short-changed our intended project beneficiaries. Where current projects cannot be changed, the lesson will still prove valuable.

Our projects will need to weaken the bonds of dependency between patrons and clients. The more Brazil nuts the project participants collect from the forest and the more trees they plant, the fewer visits they need to make to their political Area Representative's "clinic" where they have to beg for handouts and offer up their votes and those of their relatives.

Our projects will need to strengthen the central, participant-controlled mechanism. The stronger the mechanism becomes, the greater the services it can offer to the participants. In turn, as more participants benefit, more people will join. Furthermore, the stronger the central mechanism becomes, the greater the likelihood that it can enter into win-win relationships with other such mechanisms and the greater the chances that erstwhile clients can enter into win-win relationships with their former patrons.

Finally, our assessment of projects allows us to ask new questions. We used to be concerned that activities were completed on schedule. Results-Based Management (RBM) brought some improvement to the process. We were able to ask whether sets of activities (e.g. workshops completed) achieved the expected direct outputs (e.g. improved understanding of technical issues) and to measure such results against objectively verifiable indicators using pre-determined means of verification (e.g. before and after knowledge quizzes). We were also able to ask whether sets of outputs achieved the broader expected outcomes (e.g. improved institutional management), with the expectation that achieving such outcomes would increase the likelihood that the overall impact of the project (e.g. reduced operating costs of a fishermen's co-operative) would similarly be achieved.

Without consciously using a demand-led model we may not have been asking questions about the ability of our projects to 1) increase lateral, practical inter-dependencies of members of our target group; 2) reduce the need for such individuals to lessen their dependence on key patrons and their stakeholders; 3) increase the ability of these individuals to increase their mutually profitable dependence upon their own collective action organization; and, 4) increase the ability of the collective action organization to negotiate win-win relationships with other collective action organizations and with former patrons. Now we are able to do so.

Finally, I would recommend discussions among development assistance organizations in First and Third World nations and in the public and civil sectors to consider the ramifications of demand-led development. The participants in these discussions should also consider strategies that might hasten mutually profitable lateral linkages across demand-led collective action organizations and between them and former patrons.

* * *

For Community Developers, there has always been the danger that solidarity with the most marginalized people of this world could come to represent a search for that comfortable place where the anguish of our own littleness might be reduced. The monstrous successes of capitalist initiatives that have consistently benefited few and that have punished many have surely diminished us all. Perhaps by setting the poor against the rich, we have been attempting to lessen the inevitable personal pain. It is always elating to see defiance among the oppressed, though we have never really been able to demonstrate sustainable development resulting from such dangerous behaviours.

It is true that we can earn respectable fees for institutional strengthening or capacity development contracts in the developing world while ignoring the conditions within that environment that nullify our efforts. No one can deny that we make strenuous attempts to help, but at some level we must know full well that our development assistance actions will not endure or achieve meaningful shifts in the social relations of production. Perhaps we even know why they will fail. For years, anti-establishmentarian development workers have made much noise about eliminating the root-causes of development, yet the assessment and evaluation work we do—on both sides of the moral development model divide—has paid little heed to demonstrable improvements in mutually profitable and lateral interdependence among the target groups or between them and their collective action mechanism. We have not looked at improvements among collective action organizations, or at improvements between such mechanisms and former patrons. Surprisingly, when we look for indications of improved sustainability of development projects we find the depressing data collected by the World Bank and by USAID—organizations considered to be their nemesis by anti-establishmentarian organizations. The evidence, therefore, suggests that we do not know whether we are eliminating the root causes of injustice, nor are we making an effort to find out. We have not fundamentally changed our methods, nor have we made attempts to assess our progress. We therefore stand accused either of taking our salaries and making a profession of ineffective practices (ones that show poor results when assessed), or of being too blindsided by our moral philosophy, or of being too timid to make a fresh start.

Better to be braver. Dare I say, more altruistic? Ultimately, the committed developer's greatest reward is demonstrable development. Beyond solidarity, a nobler, a more responsible, and a more gratifying task for us is to ensure that development is profitable for the target populations as well as for ourselves. Our sense of meaning would then come, not from using others to assuage our own pain, but from choosing strategies which work.

Earlier, we observed that morality is an economic issue. However ironic this may seem, an economic model that is more successful therefore represents a more profound sort of morality—one that values community development above our personal need to feel righteous because of our solidarity with the masses. Cost and benefit thinking; pre-costed collective actions; incentives and disincentives: these may not appear to be attractive tools to employ, notwithstanding their utility. Nevertheless, it may be time to pick them up and set to work.

* * *

Mind you, I should talk. It's hurricane season again. This week, the roofers appeared. My wife and I have been after them since Hurricane Keith left bald patches atop our house more than a year ago. But they said they've been busy. Plus ça change....

And the screws are still missing from my front window. But, you see, I have screws in my toolbox. And those screwdrivers are right there, still wedged into the wall. My front window won't fix itself and I'm not very good with screwdrivers. But the hurricanes will return and it all starts with me. Maybe I'd better unwedge one of those screwdrivers and do something practical to change our own condition.

Think globally; act locally.

Notes

Introduction

[1] At the worst point, one fourth of the US workforce was unemployed.

[2] Joseph E. Stiglitz, *Globalization and its Discontents* (New York: Norton, 2002), 11.

[3] Several decades later substantial amounts of capital and intentional organizational efforts brought the model to South Korea when it was "(re)built" in the wake of Western (primarily US) military involvement in the standoff against the Soviet Union in the peninsula.

[4] Stiglitz, *Globalization*, 11.

[5] Stiglitz, *Globalization*, 16ff.

[6] Now including the IMF, which the World Bank and the World Trade Organization (WTO) finally created half a century after Bretton Woods.

[7] Stiglitz, *Globalization*, 18.

[8] See Sidney M. Greenfield, "The Patrimonial State and Patron Client Relations in Iberia and Latin America: Sources of 'The System' in the Fifteenth Century Writings of the Infante D. Pedro of Portugal," *Ethnohistory* 24, no. 2 (1977): 163–78.

[9] Robert Ricard, "L'Infant D. Pedro de Portugal et 'O Livro da Virtuosa Bemfeitoria'," *Bulletin des Etudes Portugaise et de l'Istitut Français au Portugal* 17, (1953): 17.

[10] Dom Pedro, *O Livro da Virtuosa Bemfeitoria*, Ed. Joaquim Costa (Porto, Portugal, 1946), Book II, ch. 7.

[11] Pedro, *Livro da Virtuosa*, Book I.

[12] Roberto DaMatta, *Carnivals, Rogues, and Heroes: An Interpretation of the Brazilian Dilemma*, trans. John Drury (Notre Dame, IN and London: University of Notre Dame Press, 1991).

[13] Note that in both languages, the same word is used for the terms "boss" and "patron."

[14] Glen C. Dealy, *The Latin Americans: Spirit and Ethos* (Boulder, CO: Westview Press, 1992).

[15] It also may explain instances such as the recent case of the former mayor of São Paulo having been shown to have deposited millions of dollars in overseas banks during the period of his tenure in office, not only not being arrested, but running for the office again.

[16] See Sidney M. Greenfield, and Arnold Strickon, "Entrepreneurship and Social Change: Towards a Populational, Decision-Making Approach," in *Entrepreneurs in Cultural Context*, ed. Sidney M. Greenfield, Arnold Strickon and Robert T. Aubey (Albuquerque, NM: The University of New Mexico Press, 1979), 329–50; Sidney M. Greenfield, and Arnold Strickon, "A New Paradigm for the Study of Entrepreneurship and Social Change," *Economic Development and Cultural Change* 29, no. 3 (1981): 469–99; Sidney M. Greenfield, and Arnold Strickon, eds., *Entrepreneurship and Social Change* (Washington, DC: University Press of America, 1985); Sidney M. Greenfield, Arnold Strickon and Robert T. Aubey, eds., *Entrepreneurs in Cultural Context* (Albuquerque, NM: The University of New Mexico Press, 1979).

[17] Robert A. Nisbet, *Social Change and History* (London: Oxford University Press, 1969).

[18] Joseph Schumpeter, *The Theory of Economic Development* (Cambridge, MA: Harvard University Press, 1959).

[19] Greenfield and Strickon "A New Paradigm," 479.

[20] Colin M. Turbayne, *The Myth of Metaphor* (Columbia, SC: University of South Carolina Press, 1971).

[21] Sidney M. Greenfield, and Arnold Strickon, eds., *Structure and Process in Latin America* (Albuquerque, NM: The University of New Mexico Press, 1972).

[22] Ernst Mayr, *Evolution and the Diversity of Life* (Cambridge, MA: Harvard University Press, Belknap Press, 1976), 27–28.

[23] Goals may be taken to reflect what an individual values and desires that lead to his (or her) making actual choices of action in specific social situations.

[24] Greenfield and Strickon, "A New Paradigm," 489.

[25] Greenfield and Strickon, "A New Paradigm," 490.

[26] Sidney M. Greenfield, "On Monkeys, Fish, and Brazilian Agricultural Development: Some Questions and Suggestions," *The Journal of Developing Areas* 5, no. 4 (1971): 507–15.

1 Morality is Blinding Us

[1] Everett M. Rogers, "Motivation, Values and Attitudes of Subsistence Farmers: Towards a Subculture of Peasantry," in *Subsistence Agriculture and Economic Development*, ed. Clifton R. Wharton (Chicago: Aldine, 1969), 111–35 .

[2] Editorial, *The Guardian* (Belize), 25 January 2004.

[3] Meb Cutlack, Editorial, *The Reporter* (Belize), 25 January 2004.

[4] S. Baogang, "Preventive Health Care Services in poor rural areas of China, Institute of Development Studies," *(IDS) Bulletin* 28, no. 1 (1997): 53–60.

[5] In his article, "International Cooperation against Corruption" SPAN (Sept/Oct 1998): 38, the macro-economist, Robert Klitgaard, explains "corruption" in the following way:

> Consider two analytical points. First, corruption may be represented as following a formula: $C = M + D - A$
>
> Corruption equals monopoly plus discretion minus accountability. Whether the activity is public, private or non-profit, and whether it is carried out in Ouagadougou or Washington, one will tend to find corruption when an organization or person has a monopoly power over a good or service, has the discretion to decide who will receive it and how much that person will get, and is not accountable.
>
> Second, corruption is a crime of calculation, not passion. True there are both saints who resist all temptation and honest officials who resist most. But when bribes are large, the chances of being caught small, and the penalties if caught meagre, many officials will succumb.

[6] David Schrock, "Debt Causes...Hunger And The Borrower Is The Slave Of The Lender," http://www.mcc.org/us/globalization/resources/hunger.html (accessed 12 August 2004).

[7] Letter to the Editor, *The Guardian* (Belize), 25 January 2004.

[8] See Francis B. Arana, *It Used To Be That* (Belize City: Amandala Press, 1992).

[9] M. Rosberg, "'I Know These People': The Paradox Of Authoritarian Management," paper presented at Developing Countries; The Case Of Belize 23rd Conference of the Caribbean Studies Association, Princess Hotel, Belize, 29–31 May 2003.

A number of writers consider authoritarian management to be one of the characteristics of the Caribbean. See: G.M. Draper, *The Civil Service in Latin America and the Caribbean: Situation and Future Challenges: The Caribbean Perspective* August 2001 (draft working paper); Keith M. Miller, "Advantages & Disadvantages Of Local Government Decentralization," paper presented at the Caribbean Conference On Local government & Decentralization, Ocean View International Hotel Georgetown, Guyana, 25 June 2002.

[10] John Saldivar, "Shadowing the Ministry of Finance: Corruption and the

International Financial Community, *The Guardian* (Belize), 25 January 2004.

[11] In this book, "Community Development" is used to mean changes deliberately introduced to increase quality of life opportunities available to individuals with lower than mean scores on broadly accepted (e.g. UNDP) indicators of human development. "Community Development" also means that community members are in a stronger position to contribute to national development (e.g. through increased tax payments, peer education, increased productivity, and policy formulation).

"Community" is less easily defined than community development, given the inter-connectedness of people across class, status and geographical location. For this book, "community" includes participants in a collective action intended to improve their quality of life—according to their own definition of the term. Inclusion need not be restricted by status, class or geographical location.

[12] Both the guilty and the innocent are protected, in this book, by changing enough of the details (such as names, organizations and locations), to make identification impossible.

[13] M. Rosberg, "Pragmatic Adaptations and Idealistic Interventions: An Analytical Description Of Development Agencies Within A Context of Political Clientelism in San Andrés Island, Colombia" (PhD diss., University of Wisconsin-Madison, 1980).

[14] See Iyo, Joseph and Michael Rosberg. "Theoretical Perspectives on the Stasis of Class Relations in the Caribbean: The Belize Case Study," paper read at the 23rd Conference of the Caribbean Studies Association, Princess Hotel, Belize 30 May 2003.

[15] Sperber and Hirschfeld make this observation about culture: "The human mind... is viewed as the basis for an extra somatic adaptation—culture—that has fundamentally changed the relationship between humans and their environment. Culture permits humans to transcend physical and cognitive limitations through the development and use of acquired skills and artifacts. Thus, humans can fly, scale trees, eat chocolate, and perform advanced mathematical calculus despite the fact that humans are not equipped with wings, claws, natural sonars, or advanced calculus abilities. Cultural adaptations trump cognitive ones in the sense that cultural skills and artifacts can achieve outcomes unpredicted by human cognitive architecture." (D. Sperber and L. Hirschfeld, "Culture, Cognition, and Evolution," in *MIT Encyclopedia of the Cognitive Sciences*, vol. CXI, ed. R. Wilson and R. Keil, III [Cambridge, MA: MIT Press, 1999].)

[16] For examples of what I call the establishment approach, see David Stoesz, David, C. Guzzetta, and M.W. Lusk, *International Development* (Boston: Allyn & Bacon, 1998); Albert O. Hirschman, *Development Projects Observed* (Washington, DC: Brookings Institution Press, 1967); Carl K. Eicher and John M.. Staatz, eds., *International Agricultural Development*, 3rd ed. (Baltimore: Johns Hopkins University Press, 1998); John Boli and George M. Thomas, eds., *Constructing World Culture: International Nongovernmental Organizations since 1875* (Palo Alto: Stanford University Press, 1999);

World Bank, World Development Report: Attacking Poverty (Oxford: Oxford University Press, 2000).

[17] See Derrick W. Brinkerhoff and Arthur A. Goldsmith. "Promoting the Sustainability of Development Institutions: A Framework for Strategy," World Development 20 (1992): 369–83.

[18] For examples of what I call the anti-establishmentarian approach, see David C. Korten, Getting to the 21st Century, Voluntary Action and the Global Agenda (Ann Arbor: Kumarian Press, 1990), esp. pp. 185–212; D.C. Korten, Globalizing Civil Society: Reclaiming Our Right to Power (New York: Seven Stories Press, 1997); D.C. Korten, When Corporations Rule the World (Ann Arbor: Kumarian Press); Sarah Anderson, ed., Views from the South: The effects of Globalization and the WTO on Third World Countries (Oakland, CA: Food Firs/Institute for Food & Development Policy, 2000); Robin Brood, ed., Global Backlash: Citizen Initiatives for a Just World Economy (Lanham, MD: Rowman & Littlefield, 2002); Jerry Mander, and Edward Goldsmith, eds., The Case against the Global Economy: And for a Turn toward the Local (San Francisco: Sierra Club Books, 1997); R.M. O'Brien, M. Williams, A.M. Goetz, and J.A. Scholte, Contesting Global Governance (Cambridge: Cambridge University Press, 2000).

[19] Amartya Sen, Development as Freedom (New York: Knopf, 1999).

[20] United Nations Department of Public Information, http://www.unhchr.ch/-udhr/lang/eng.htm (accessed 12 August 2004).

[21] United Nations, Annual Report of the Secretary-General 16 July 1997.

[22] Claudio Schuftan, "The new UN human rights approach Hanoi, Vietnam," AFRO-NETS, http://www.afronets.org/archive/200102/msg00015.php (accessed 4 Feb 2001).

[23] See D.C. Korten, Globalizing Civil Society; Amartya Sen, Development as Freedom; and William Easterly, The Elusive Quest for Growth: Economists' Adventures and Misadventures in the Tropics (Cambridge, MA: MIT Press, 2001).

[24] Brinkerhoff and Goldsmith, "Promoting the Sustainability," 369.

[25] Binkerhoff and Goldsmith, "Promoting the Sustainability," 379–80.

[26] Robert Klitgaard, "International Cooperation Against Corruption."

[27] See M. Rosberg, "Pragmatic Adaptations."

[28] Tahira M. Probst, Peter J. Carnevale and Harry C. Triandis, "Cultural Values in Intergroup and Single-Group Social Dilemmas," Organizational Behavior and Human Decision Processes 77, no. 3 (March 1999): 71–91. Incidentally, sacrificers tended to defect somewhat away from their own group if it was in competition with another faction. However, this last finding is complicated by the fact that members of either group were equally unknown to participants in the experiment. Perhaps the sacrificers wished to see everybody in both the alliance and the faction benefit. Not much behavioural difference existed between individualists or sacrificers who saw others in their group to be peers, or who accepted a hierarchy within their group

[29] Rhett Butler, "Saving What Remains, Chapter 10: Solutions," http://www.-

mongabay.com/1001.htm (accessed 21 September 2004).

[30] See Oscar Lewis, *La Vida: A Puerto Rican Family in the Culture of Poverty in San Juan and New York* (New York: Random House, 1966).

[31] "Stop 'n Look at What's Going Down," Special Report: Corruption (Public Life), http://members.tripod.com/sankalpa/stop/so4stop.html (accessed 3 Oct 1998).

[32] David D. Korten, *Getting to the Twenty-First Century*, 185; see also W. Harman, *Global Mind Change: The Promise of the Last Years of the Twentieth Century* (Indianapolis: Knowledge Systems, 1988).

[33] Baha'i International Community, "Sustainable Development and the Human Spirit: Bahá'í International Community," Adapted from the statement delivered to the Plenary of The Earth Summit, Rio de Janeiro, Brazil, 4 June 1992. http://www.bcca.org/ief/bicrio.htm (accessed 21 December 2004).

[34] John Dewey, "Theory of Valuation," *Foundations of the Unity of Science, Toward an International Encyclopedia of Unified Science*, vol. II, no. 4. (Chicago: University of Chicago Press, 1966).

[35] J. Iyo, and M. Rosberg, "Theoretical Perspectives on the Stasis of Class Relations in the Caribbean: the Belize Case Study," paper presented at Beyond Walls: Multi-Disciplinary Perspectives, Country Conference Series, University of the West Indies, November 2001, 2.

[36] See David Potts, "Project Identification and Formulation," *Economic Development* (Boulder, CO: Lynne Reinner, 2002), 23–46.

[37] A number of scholars support an approach to community development that is decentralized and inclusive. See, for instance, R. Picciotto, R. and R. Weaving. "A New Project Cycle for the World Bank?" *Finance and Development* 30 (Dec 1994): 42–44. Such an approach also needs to be iterative, responsive and process (rather than blueprint) oriented. See David Potts, "Project Identification and Formulation," *Economic Development*, Chapter 7).

2 Decision-Making and Responsibility

[1] Viktor Frankl, *Man's Search for Meaning* (New York: Washington Square Press, 1959), 131.

[2] Viktor Frankl, *Man's Search for Meaning*, 129–30.

[3] John D. Martz, *The Politics of Clientelism: Democracy & the State in Columbia* (Somerset, NJ: Transaction Publishers, 1996), 10.

[4] Fred S. McChesney, *Money for Nothing: Politicians, Rent Extraction, and Political Extortion* (Cambridge: Harvard University Press, 1996).

[5] D. Eric Schansberg, "Review of *Money for Nothing; Politicians, Rent Extraction, and Political Extortion*," *The Independent Review* 3, no. 1 (Summer 1998). http://www.independent.org/publications/tir/article.asp?issueID=29&articleID=363.

[6] V. Brusco, et. al. "Clientelism and Democracy: Evidence from Argentina," presen-

tation to the Conference on Political Parties and Legislative Organization in Parliamentary and Presidential Regimes, Yale University, March 2002.

[7] See Jean-Francois Bayart, *The State In Africa: The Politics Of The Belly* (New York: Longman, 1993).

[8] Paul Yoo Hyung-Gon, "Corruption, Rule of Law, and Civil Society: Why Patronage Politics is Good for Developing Markets and Democracies," *International Affairs Review* 12, no. 1 (2003): 30.

[9] The debate remains open regarding Hyung-Gon's attempt to distinguish between clientelism and corruption. He does not, for example, confront the additional problem of achieving a transition to fully functional democracy once the legitimacy of patrons has been enshrined—a problem that may even confront Korea.

[10] Carlene Edie, "From Manley to Seaga: The persistence of Clientelist Politics in Jamaica." *Social and Economic Studies* 38, no. 1 (March 1989): 1.

[11] Samuel Agere, Promoting Good Governance: Principles, Practices and Perspectives (London: Commonwealth Secretariat, 2000), ??.

[12] Other mechanisms may be used to maintain the *status quo* such as the respect for authority taught by schools and churches. See Assad Shoman, *Party Politics in Belize, 1950–1986* (Belize: Cabola Productions, 1987), 88–89.

[13] Susan Sontag, *Illness as Metaphor and Aids and Its Metaphors* (New York: Picador, 2001).

[14] It is said that at his death, Morter left only one dollar to his wife, and the rest to the UNIA.

[15] Derrick W. Brinkerhoff, and Arthur A. Goldsmith, "Promoting the Sustainability of Development Institutions: A Framework for Strategy," *World Development* 20, no. 3 (1992): 370.

[16] Thomas S. Szasz, *The Myth Of Mental Illness: Foundations Of A Theory of Personal Conduct*, rev. ed. (New York: Harper & Row, 1974), 2.

[17] Karl Marx, *Eighteenth Brumaire of Louis Bonaparte* (New York: International Publishers Company,1990), http://www.marxists.org/archive/marx/works/1852/-18thbrumaire/-cho7.htm (accessed 13 August 2004).

[18] Oscar Lewis, *The Children of Sanchez* (New York: Vintage Books, 1979), 6.

[19] Edward Banfield, *The Unheavenly City* (New York: Little, Brown and Company, 1970), 215–24.

[20] Emile Durkheim, *The Division of Labor in Society* (New York: The Free Press, 1947).

[21] See R.J. Hernstein and Charles Murray, *The Bell Curve: Intelligence and Class Structure in American Life* (New York: Simon & Schuster Adult Publishing Group, 1995); see also J.P. Rushton, *Race, Evolution, and Behavior* (New Brunswick, NJ: Transaction Publishers, 1997).

[22] P.T. Schoenemann, et al., "Brain size, head size, and intelligence quotient in monozygotic twins," *Neurology* 50, no. 5 (May 1998): 1246–52, http://pubpages.-

unh.edu/~jel/brainIQ.html (accessed 20 July 2004).

[23] D.A. Kinsley, and R.E.L. Masters, *The Cradle of Erotica: a Study of Afro-Asian Sexual Expression and an Analysis of Erotic Freedom in Social Relationships* (New York: Julian Press, 1962).

[24] In this regard, see also Norman Girvan, "Societies at Risk? The Caribbean and global Change," Management of Social Transformations Discussion Paper Series No. 17, revised version of a paper presented at the Caribbean regional Consultation on the Management of Social Transformations (MOST) Program of UNESCO, Kingston, Jamaica, February 1997, http://www.unesco.org/most/girvan.htm (accessed 13 September 2004); *Samuel Agere, Promoting Good Governance: Principles, Practices and Perspectives* (London: Commonwealth Secretariat, 2000); G.M. Draper, The Civil Service In Latin America And The Caribbean: Situation And Future Challenges: The Caribbean Perspective (Draft Working Paper)," August 2001, http://unpan1.-un.org/intradoc/groups/-public/documents/CARICAD/UNPAN005729.pdf (accessed 22 September 2004); K. Miller, "Advantages & Disadvantages Of Local Government Decentralization" (paper presented at the Caribbean Conference On Local Government and Decentralization, Georgetown, Guyana, 25 June 2002).

[25] Joanna Gualtier, "We Must Protect Whistle-Blowers. Government Accountability Will Only be Assured if Officials Can Safely Reveal Misdeeds," *The Ottawa Citizen*, Wednesday, 25 June 2003, A17.

[26] This prediction is extrapolated from a frequently demonstrated positive relationship that exists between the level of authoritarianism and the externality of the locus of control. See for example C.L. Ray, and L.M. Subich, "Staff Assaults and Injuries in a Psychiatric Hospital as a Function of Three Attitudinal Variables," *Issues Mental Health Nursing* 19, no. 3 (1998): 291–300: "Associations also were noted between both locus of control and authoritarianism and employees' frequency of assault and injury experiences" and "... an external locus of control was related to authoritarianism in the mother and workaholism in both parents."

[27] H.D. Seibel, and U. Parhusip, "Attaining Outreach with Sustainability. A Case Study of a Private Micro Finance Institution in Indonesia," *Institute of Development Studies (IDS) Bulletin* 29, no. 4 (1998): 81–90.

[28] Pretty and Shah quoted in M. Ahluwalia, "Representing Communitities: The case of a community-based watershed management project in Rajasthan, India," *Institute of Development Studies (IDS) Bulletin* 28, no. 4 (1997): 24.

[29] V. Sibanda, "Corruption in the Private Sector: Its Causes, Extent and Effects," *Reports–Seminar on Corruption in the Private Sector*, 5 June 2001, http://www.kubatana.-net/tiz/html/reports/rep_fs.htm?corrps010605.htm (accessed 22 September 2004).

[30] Paul Constance, IDB *América*, "May the Best Bureaucrat Win!," March 2002, vol. 27 no. 9–10, http://www.iadb.org/idbamerica/index.cfm?thisid=437 (accessed 21 December 2004). The part about budgets absorbed mostly by the payroll is true in

Belize too. After paying administration, salaries and emoluments, the budget left for programs in the Ministry of Education is 8 per cent. It is 4 per cent in the Ministry of Human Community development. See M. Rosberg, and M. Johnson, *Belize, Human Development Report* (Belize: National Human Development Advisory Council/UNDP, 2001), 24.

[31] Quoted in Charo Quesada, "First, close the democratic deficit." *IDB América* March 2001, www.iaab.org/idbamerica (accessed 22 September 2004).

[32] Ibid.

[33] *IDB América*, (accessed 18 June 1999).

[34] Kark Marx, "Effect of Capitalist Competition on the Capitalist Class, the Middle Class and the Working Class," in *Wage Labour and Capital*, Fredrick Engels trans., ed., 1891.

3 The Emergence of Expediency in the Caribbean Region

[1] O. Nigel Bolland, and Assad Shoman, *Land in Belize, 1765–1871: The Origins of Land Tenure, Use and Distribution in a Dependent Economy* (Mona: Institute of Social and Economic Research, University of the West Indies, 1977), foreword.

[2] Ibid.

[3] Richard B Sheridan, *Sugar and Slavery: An Economic History of the British West Indies 1623–1775* (Great Britain: A. Wheaton and Co. Ltd, 1974), 246.

[4] Sheridan, *Sugar and Slavery*, 248.

[5] Sheridan, *Sugar and Slavery*, 254, parentheses added.

[6] Sheridan, *Sugar and Slavery*, 255.

[7] Sheridan, *Sugar and Slavery*, 256.

[8] Sheridan, *Sugar and Slavery*, 260.

[9] Sheridan, *Sugar and Slavery*, 261.

[10] Sheridan, *Sugar and Slavery*, 479–80.

[11] Sheridan, *Sugar and Slavery*, 241.

[12] Bolland and Shoman, *Land in Belize*, 55.

[13] Bolland and Shoman, *Land in Belize*, 56, parentheses added.

[14] Ibid.

[15] Bolland and Shoman, *Land in Belize*, 72.

[16] Arthur to Bathurst, 15 May 1820, CO 123/33 in Bolland and Shoman, *Land in Belize*, 72, emphasis is added.

[17] Bolland and Shoman, *Land in Belize*, 73.

[18] O. Nigel Bolland, *The Formation of a Colonial Society: Belize, from Conquest to Crown Colony* Baltimore: Johns Hopkins University Press, 1977.

[19] Bolland, *The Formation of a Colonial Society*, 66.

[20] Bolland, *The Formation of a Colonial Society*, 69.

[21] Bolland, *The Formation of a Colonial Society*, 70.

[22] Bolland, *The Formation of a Colonial Society*, 64.

[23] Ibid.

[24] Bolland, *The Formation of a Colonial Society*, 71.

[25] Bolland, *The Formation of a Colonial Society*, 124.

[26] Bolland, *The Formation of a Colonial Society*, 189.

[27] Bolland, *The Formation of a Colonial Society*, 190.

[28] Bolland, *The Formation of a Colonial Society*, 132.

[29] Bolland, *The Formation of a Colonial Society*, 132–33.

[30] Bolland, *The Formation of a Colonial Society*, 139.

[31] Ibid.

[32] Bolland, *The Formation of a Colonial Society*, 156.

[33] Bolland, *The Formation of a Colonial Society*, 160.

[34] Carla Barnett summarizes the system: "Under 'advance' and 'truck' systems, labourers were advanced a portion of their wages in cash and kind prior to going into the forests at the beginning of the cutting season. While in the forests, indebtedness to the lumber company was increased through further advances of food and supplies from the company stores. At the end of the woodcutting season, when advances were deducted from wages, labourers were often left with very little cash or with outstanding debt to be carried forward to the next season." ("Aspects of State Policy on Land Distribution and Use in the Crown Colonial Period and After" Fourth Annual Studies on Belize Conference. SPEA*Reports* 7 [Belize City: Society for the Promotion of Education and Research, 1991], 73).

[35] See G.W.T. Allport, *Nature Of Prejudice* (Cambridge: Addison-Wesley, 1954). According to Allport, the authoritarian personality will defer to superiors and exact obedience from those below. Hence, the education of hewers of wood and of lumber barons would not have to differ essentially.

[36] Even today, many Belizeans own no land, and most own little. Foreigners own about 90 per cent of all private lands. Belizeans own only 4.1% of all land, and 10 per cent of it is private. As much as 91 per cent of all private landowners hold only 1 per cent of all private land and foreigners own 93 per cent of all private land over 100 acres. See Bolland and Shoman, *Land in Belize*, 103.

[37] Bolland, *The Formation of a Colonial Society*, 178.

[38] Bolland, *The Formation of a Colonial Society*, 180–81.

[39] Ibid.

[40] Bolland, *The Formation of a Colonial Society*, 163.

[41] Bolland, *The Formation of a Colonial Society*, 166.

[42] Bolland, *The Formation of a Colonial Society*, 188, emphasis mine.

[43] Bolland, *The Formation of a Colonial Society*, 147 identifies the alternative major strategy for Belizeans: flight. The proximity of impenetrable and hostile inland forests, and of freedom in neighbouring Mexico during slavery, and of better income in the United

States during the hundred years of debt peonage that followed it and into the present era, allowed avenues of escape for some Belizeans unwilling to tolerate the indignities of authoritarian rule. Although brief and aggressive rebellions have also occurred, the possibility of escape may explain why overt rebellion figures less prominently in Belize than elsewhere. See also O. Nigel Bolland, *Colonialism and Resistance in Belize* (Benque Vierjo: Cubola/SPEAR, 1988), 147.

[44] Bolland, *The Formation of a Colonial Society*, 191.

[45] Franklin W. Knight, *The Caribbean: The Genesis of a Fragmented Nationalism* (New York: The Oxford University Press, 1976).

[46] Knight, *The Caribbean*, 177–78.

[47] Knight, *The Caribbean*, 178.

[48] Ibid.

[49] Ibid.

[50] Assad Shoman, *Party Politics in Belize, 1950–1986* (Belize: Cubola Productions, 1987), 8; 12; 88–89.

[51] Shoman, *Party Politics*, 59.

[52] Gordon K. Lewis, *The Growth of the Modern West Indies* (New York: Monthly Review Press, 1968), 343–86.

[53] Knight, *The Caribbean*, title page.

[54] Lewis, *The Growth of the Modern West Indies*, 343.

[55] Knight, *The Caribbean*, 203

[56] Ibid.

[57] Knight, *The Caribbean*, 204.

[58] Knight, *The Caribbean*, 205.

[59] Knight, *The Caribbean*, 205–206.

[60] Knight, *The Caribbean*, 206, emphasis added.

[61] Knight, *The Caribbean*, 206.

[62] Bolland, *The Formation of a Colonial Society*, 270–71.

[63] Bolland, *The Formation of a Colonial Society*, 275.

[64] Bolland, *The Formation of a Colonial Society*, 277.

[65] Ibid.

[66] Bolland, *The Formation of a Colonial Society*, 282.

[67] Bolland, *The Formation of a Colonial Society*, 283.

[68] Shoman, *Party Politics in Belize*, 183–184.

[69] Shoman, *Party Politics in Belize*, 185.

[70] Shoman, *Party Politics in Belize*, 186–187.

[71] Shoman, *Party Politics in Belize*, 187.

[72] Ibid.

[73] Shoman, *Party Politics in Belize*, 188.

[74] Shoman, *Party Politics in Belize*, 189.

[75] Ibid.

[76] Ibid.

[77] Shoman, *Party Politics in Belize*, 190.

[78] Shoman, *Party Politics in Belize*, 191.

[79] Ibid.

[80] Ibid.

[81] Macpherson in Shoman, *Party Politics in Belize*, 191.

[82] Shoman, *Party Politics in Belize*, 193.

[83] Shoman, Ibid.

[84] Shoman, *Party Politics in Belize*, 194.

[85] Shoman, *Party Politics in Belize*, 195–96.

[86] Shoman, *Party Politics in Belize*, 195.

[87] Shoman, *Party Politics in Belize*, 196.

[88] Fanon in Shoman, *Party Politics in Belize*, 203.

[89] Shoman, *Party Politics in Belize*, 203.

[90] Shoman, *Party Politics in Belize*, 203–4.

[91] Shoman, *Party Politics in Belize*, 246.

[92] Shoman, *Party Politics in Belize*, 249.

[93] Shoman, *Party Politics in Belize*, 262.

[94] Shoman, *Party Politics in Belize*, 263.

[95] Shoman, *Party Politics in Belize*, 264.

[96] Ibid.

[97] Ibid.

[98] Shoman, *Party Politics in Belize*, 265.

[99] Shoman, *Party Politics in Belize*, 266.

[100] Ibid.

[101] Shoman, *Party Politics in Belize*, 267.

[102] Shoman, *Party Politics in Belize*, 268.

4 Clientelism Versus Moral Community Development

[1] Edgar H. Schein, "The Impact of Transnational Institutions on Cultural Values and Vice Versa." *Reflections: The SOL Journal*, 3, no. 1 (2001): 46.

[2] See Cornia et al., *Adjustment with a Human Face: Protecting the Vulnerable and Promoting Growth* (Oxford: Clarendon Press, 1987).

[3] Ngugi, 1999, emphasis added.

[4] For a delightful presentation of an American macro-economist vs. Ministers of Government employing very similar ploys in Equatorial Guinea, see Robert Klitgaard, *Tropical Gangsters: One Man's Experience with Development and Decadence in Deepest Africa* (New York: Basic Books, 1991).

[5] Michael Richman, "Uncle Tom's Montgomery Cabin," *Washington Post*, 10 December 1997, H05.

[6] Irma McClurin, *Women of Belize: Gender and Change in Central America* (New Jersey: Rutgers University Press, 1966), 92–93; 98–101.

[7] Bullard in McClurin, *Women of Belize*, 103.

[8] In contrast, and as seen with the fisherman described above who had no boat or outboard, the person with very few assets may be the very person to spend liberally when money comes his/her way: it feels good to be somebody; it can be spent on peers as a way of cancelling debts and obligating others; and, it's a useful way of indicating superior rank in a group. See: Marcel Mauss, *The Gift: The Form and Reason for Exchange in Archaic Societies* (New York: W.W. & Norton, 2000).

[9] Except, of course, for the time Bra Hanansi met the beautiful princess and outsmarted the king—but that's another tail....

[10] See Peter J. Wilson, *Crab Antics: The Social Anthropology of English-Speaking Negro Societies in the Caribbean* (Long Grove, IL: Waveland Press, 1995).

5 Structural Theories and Related Strategies

[1] Meenakshi Ahluwalia, "Representing Communities: The Case of a Community-Based Watershed Management Project in Rajasthan, India," *Institute of Development Studies Bulletin (IDS)* 28, no. 4 (1997): 34.

[2] Tang, Kwong-Leung, "The Marginalization of Social Welfare in Developing Countries: A Study of Four Theories of Social Policy Development," *Journal of Sociology and Social Welfare* 23, no. 2 (1996): 41–58.

[3] Emile Durkheim, *Sociology*, trans. George Simpson (The Division of Labor in Society, New York: The Free Press, 1947).

[4] Emile Durkheim, Emile (Translator, George Simpson). *Suicide*, trans. George Simpson (New York: Simon & Schuster Adult Publishing Group, January 1997).

[5] Walter W. Rostow, *The Stages of Economic Growth* (Cambridge: Cambridge University Press, 1960), 4–16.

[6] Though the basic notion of a five-stage schema is still subject to criticism, in fairness to Rostow, it should be observed that his own use of the schema was subtler than that of many of his admirers and critics. He paid close attention to a range of factors, which could function to distort any of the five "impressionistic" stages he described.

[7] Peter J. Wilson, *Crab Antics: The Social Anthropology of English-Speaking Negro Societies in the Caribbean* (Long Grove, IL: Waveland Press, 1995).

[8] These criticisms don't actually de-legitimize Rostow's model. When socio-economies "misuse" blue jeans and KFC, he would argue, the basic stages of development remain unchallenged; it's just that "normal" societal evolution has been distorted by local historical anomalies and current realities. He would in all likelihood argue that as ideal types, the underlying stages still have validity. The exogenous fac-

tors make them difficult to see and it is these factors we must labour to rectify. The problem with Rostow's approach may have more to do with the fact that he has no way of integrating these "exogenous" realities into his basic theory—it becomes a matter of constant back filling to explain why the theory doesn't apply to any given situation. Marx faced this problem too.

[9] Robert A. Nisbet, *Social Change and History: Aspects of the Western Theory of Development* (London: Oxford University Press, 1969).

[10] Nisbet, *Social Change and History*.

[11] See Melville J. Herskovits, *Life in a Haitian Valley* (New York: Knopf Publishing Group, 1937).

[12] Joseph Iyo, *A Cultural History of Belize* (Belize: The Angelus Press, 2001).

[13] Karl Marx, *Eighteenth Brumaire of Louis Bonaparte* (New York: International Publishers, November 1990).

[14] Louis A. Woods, and Joseph M. Perry, "Regional Integration, Foreign Trade and Economic Development: Caricom and Belize." Fourth Annual Studies on Belize Conference. SPEAReports 7 (Belize City: Society for the Promotion of Education and Research, 1991), 25–47.

6 The Development Potential of Process Theories

[1] Sidney M. Greenfield, and Arnold Strickon, *Structure and Process* (University of New Mexico Press, 1971).

[2] Greenfield and Strickon, *Structure and Process*, 338.

[3] So far as I know, no Social Scientist has made serious use of Darwinian adaptation since Herbert Spencer who, in 1873, published *The Study of Sociology*, comparing society to a giant organism (an idea used by Durkheim) and that civilizations, like organisms adapt and evolve. The process was apparently finite to Spencer, who thought Britain represented the apogee of development and the paragon which more primitive nations should emulate.

[4] Greenfield and Strickon, *Structure and Process*, 46–47.

[5] Greenfield and Strickon, *Structure and Process*, 50.

[6] Candy P. S. Fong and Robert S. Wyer, "Cultural, Social, and Emotional Determinants of Decisions Under Uncertainty," *Organizational Behavior and Human Decision Processes* 90, no. 2 (2003): 304.

[7] Samuel Popkin, *The Rational Peasant in Vietnam: The Political Economy of Rural Society in Vietnam* (Berkeley: The University of California Press, 1977), 14.

[8] Joseph A. Schumpeter, *Capitalism, Socialism and Democracy* (New York: HarperCollins, 1976), 132.

[9] Strickon used to observe that Aranda tribes-persons ("Aboriginees") from Australia were often called primitive and compared negatively to the 'modern' Europeans whose ability to exploit the urban environment was so much greater. But,

he pointed out, following an atomic holocaust, with urban infrastructure destroyed, the former urbanites would become the new primitives. Modern and primitive, he would conclude, are dependent upon the environment.

[10] Clark, G.L. and John C. Marshall, *Decision-Making: Models Of The Real-World and Expertise Neurophsychology Unit* (Oxford: Radcliffe Infirmary, 2002).

[11] Vilfredo Pareto, *Manual of Political Economy* (New York: Augustus M. Kelley, 1971).

[12] Usually, the x and the y axis of a graph like this would be situated across the bottom and left sides of the diagram, respectively. I've deliberately placed them this way in preparation for the next two figures.

[13] Mancur Olson, *The Logic of Collective Action: Public Goods and the Theory of Groups* (Cambridge, MA: Harvard University Press, 1971).

[14] See Gerald Marwell and Pamela Oliver, *The Critical Mass in Collective Action: A Micro-Social Theory* (Cambridge: Cambridge University Press, 1993), 6.

[15] Olson writes: "...but it is not in fact true that the idea that groups will act in their own interest follows logically from the premise of rational and self-interested behaviour. Indeed, unless the number of individuals in a group is quite small, or unless there is coercion or some other special device to make individuals act in their common interest, rational self-interested individuals will not act to achieve their common or group interest." (*The Logic of Collective Action*, 1–2).

[16] Marwell and Oliver, *The Critical Mass in Collective Action*.

[17] Elinor Ostrom, "A Behavioral Approach to the Rational Choice Theory of Collective Action," *American Political Science Review* 92, no. 1 (1998): 1–22.

[18] Ibid.

[19] Ibid.

[20] Daniel Klein, "The Voluntary Provision of Public Goods: The Turnpike Companies of Early America," *Economic Inquiry* 28, no. 4 (1990): 788–812.

[21] Klein, "The Voluntary Provision of Public Goods" 10. Klein also cites a relevant passage by de Tocqueville: "Local freedom...that leads a great number of citizens to value the affection of their neighbours and of their kindred, perpetually brings men together and forces them to help one another in spite of the propensities that sever them" (14).

[22] Klein, "The Voluntary Provision of Public Goods," 14.

[23] It should not be expected that back-to-work welfare reform will have the results conservatives may desire. Simply reversing welfare assistance may not reverse the level of dependency within welfare clients. The escape from heightened dependency is not necessarily a reversal up the road initially taken. Though welfare roles may shorten and welfare payments, diminish, careful investigation may reveal that clients ejected from the system may have developed their own alternative strategies such as eating less, drinking more or using drugs, thereby becoming dependents of the health system, or may have turned to begging more or engaging in crime and becoming clients of law

enforcement. They may also have created new alliances and social dependencies. The additional costs to society of these behavioural adjustments may be higher than the cost of maintaining the welfare system. In other words, the alternatives selected by former welfare clients will be the ones which make sense to them, which result from their experience (not the experience of conservative policy makers) and which are also a function of the new environment into which welfare rejects are being thrust.

[24] Mel Huang, "The Amber Coast: Ten Years After," *Central Europe Review* 1, no. 9 (1999): 1.

[25] Marwell and Oliver, *The Critical Mass in Collective Action*, 10.

7 Greed Can Dismantle Clientelism

[1] Seibel provides an Indonesian example of private bank services effectively extended to the poor. One of his conclusions is especially worthy of note. He says that no single model is adequate: a systems approach to micro-finance is needed. See H.D. Seibel , and U. Parhusip, "Attaining Outreach with Sustainability, A Case Study of a Private Micro Finance Institution in Indonesia," *Institute of Development Studies (IDS) Bulletin* 29, no. 4 (1998): 81–90.

[2] Seibel and Parhusip, "Attaining Outreach with Sustainability."

[3] S. Guhan, "Social Security Options for Developing Countries," *International Labour Review* 133, no.1 (1994): 35-51.

[4] It is true, however, that participants in such schemes come with a great list of needs and problems. This may include everything from illiteracy to health needs; or from issues of abuse to ones of land tenure. The income directly derived from a brilliant program, like the one devised and operated by the credit union in Bogotá, will never be sufficient to provide for the range of services needed. And unless much of them are offered, ultimately, the core program will be overwhelmed by everything else. Co-ordinating and financing those needs will be discussed below.

[5] In fact, many micro-credit and micro-finance projects report loan repayment rates of nearly 100%. Women tend to have lower delinquency rates and their success tends to have more positive impact on family indicators of nutrition, health and the education of children. The responsibility of caring for children may be one factor affecting their performance. Some developers favour assisting women to the exclusion of men. However, increasing the responsibility of men remains a worthy community development challenge.

[6] "Micro-finance" is used to distinguish this credit union approach from the less effective 'micro-credit' programs used by many NGOs. The latter offer credit only which has to be granted to the NGOs by a donor organization. The micro-finance approach includes a savings component. Like all credit unions, loans are extended—not from grants from donor organizations—but from participants' savings.

Micro-credit programs have frequently not been able to continue after donor funds are discontinued; credit unions are self-sustaining. Borrowers often have little or no interest in the management of the micro-credit program so long as it gets them cash; they invest in the credit union, on the other hand, and are more motivated to supervise it closely.

[7] A. Rahman, "Micro-Credit Initiatives for Equitable and Sustainable Development: Who Pays?" World Development 27, no. 1 (1999): 67–82.

[8] Rahman, "Micro-Credit Initiatives," 67.

[9] In contrast, none of the fishermen without boats and outboards joined the co-operative. It offered them no benefit. Upon return from sea, they received a cash payment from the owner of the dugout. Many of them used their earnings to share "run-down" (a local fish dinner), cigarettes and beer with other dependent friends, and to play dominoes with them. When cash was scarce, these instrumental friends saw them through hard times.

[10] Ahluwalia, "Representing Communities," 23, 25.

[11] Since this was written, CCA has organized a project between the consortium and one of Canada's two wholesale co-operative federations for the sale of Canadian dry goods to Central American consumer co-operatives.

[12] T. Dichter, "Questioning the Future of NGOs in Micro-Finance," Journal of International Development 8, no. 2 (1996): 185–89; L.D. Brown, and D. Ashman, "Participation, Social Capital, and Intersectoral Problem Solving: African and Asian Cases," World Development 24, no. 9 (1996): 1467–79.

[13] See Peter Morgan, and Victoria Carlan, eds., "Capacity Development, an Introduction," in Emerging Issues in Capacity Development: Proceedings of a Workshop, 7–17 (Ottawa: Institute on Governance, 1994).

[14] N. McNamara, and S. Morse, "Donors and Sustainability in the Provision of Financial Services in Nigeria," Institute of Development Studies (IDS) Bulletin 29, no. 4 (1998): 91–101. For discussions on donor competition and resolving competition, refer to B.G. Grey, Collaboration: Finding Common Ground for Multiparty Problems (San Francisco: Jossey-Bass, 1989); and Brown, and Ashman, "Participation, Social Capital, and Intersectoral Problem Solving."

8 The Development Project as a Creative Response to Greed

[1] S. Guhan, "Social Security Options for Developing Countries," International Labour Review 133, no. 1 (1994):38.

[2] Guhan, "Social Security Options," 51.

[3] Hernando de Soto, "Dead Capital and the Poor," SAIS Review 21, no. 1 (2001): 14.

[4] See H.R. Jackelen, and E. Rhyne, "Towards a More Market-Orientated Approach to Credit and Savings for the Poor." Small Enterprise Development 2, no. 4 (1991): 14–26; J. Yaron, Successful Rural Finance Institutions, World Bank Discussion Paper, no. 150

(Washington, DC: World Bank, 1992); L. Bennett and C.E. Cuevas, "Sustainable Banking with the Poor," *Journal of International Development* 8, no. 2 (1996): 15–52; Dichter, "Questioning the Future of NGOs."

[5] See Seibel and Parhusip, "Attaining Outreach with Sustainability," 82. Others have argued for greater involvement in capacity development of the NGOs providing credit and other services to ensure the achievement of sustainability (See R.H. and C-P. Zeitinger Schmidt, "Prospects, Problems and Potential of Credit-Granting NGOs," *Journal of International Development* 8, no. 2 (1996): 241–58.

[6] Shahid Khandker, "Does Micro-finance Really Benefit the Poor? Evidence from Bangladesh," 15, paper presented at the Asia and Pacific Forum on Poverty: Reforming Policies and Institutions for Poverty Reduction, Asian Development Bank, Manila, 5–9 February 2001, http://www.adb.org/Poverty/forum/pdf/Khandker.pdf.

[7] Verónica González Aguilar, "Micro-Finance Reaching The Poor? An Overview Of Poverty Targeting Methods," *ADA Dialogue* (October 1999). http://www.globe-net.org/horizon-local/ada/c18.html.

[8] Martin Ravallion, Gaurav Datt, and Shubham Chaudhuri, "Does Maharastra's Employment Guarantee Scheme Guarantee Employment?" *Economic Development and Cultural Change* 41, no. 2 (January 1993): 251–75.

[9] Michael Andrew McPherson and Carl Liedholm, "Determinants of Small and Micro Enterprise Registration: Results From Surveys in Niger and Swaziland," *World Development*, vol. 24, no. 3 (March 1996): 481–87, we define a micro-enterprise as a firm with no more than 10 employees, and a small enterprise as one with 11–50 employees.

[10] J. Davis, et al., "How Important Is Improved Water Infrastructure to Microenterprises? Evidence from Uganda," *World Development* 29, 10 (Oct., 2001): 2.

[11] Ibid.

[12] P. Wickramasekara, "Rural Employment Generation Schemes: Review of Asian Experience." *Indian Journal of Industrial Relations* 25, no. 4 (April 1990): 108–9.

[13] Wickramasekara, "Rural Employment Generation Schemes," 103.

[14] Wickramasekara, "Rural Employment Generation Schemes," 108–9, emphases added.

[15] See Robert Michels, *Political Parties. A Sociological Study of the Oligarchical Tendencies of Modern Democracy*, trans. Eden Paul and Cedar Paul (New York: The Free Press, 1962).

[16] Ahluwalia, "Representing Communities."

[17] cf. Ravillion et al, 1993; Seibel, 1998; Rahman, 1999; Khandker, 2001; Miller, 2002)

[18] T. Kepe, "Communities, Entitlements and Nature Reserves, the Case of the Wild Coast, South Africa," *IDS Bulletin* 28, no. 4 (1997): 47–58.

[19] Kepe, "Communities," 47, parentheses added.

[20] Norman T. Uphoff, "Grassroots Organizations and NGOs in Rural Development: Opportunities with Diminishing States and Expanding Markets," World Development

21, no. 4 (1993): 607.

[21] L.D. Brown, and D. Ashman, "Participation, Social Capital, and Intersectoral Problem Solving: African and Asian Cases." *World Development* 24, no. 9 (1996): 1476.

[22] Ibid., parentheses added.

[23] M. Leach, R. Mearns, and Ian Scoones, "Environmental entitlements: a framework for understanding the institutional dynamics of environmental change," *IDS Discussion Paper* No. 369, 90–91 (Brighton: Institute of Development Studies, 1997).

[24] Charles Tilly, "War Making and State Making as Organized Crime," in *Bringing the State Back In*, ed. P.B. Evans, D. Reuschemeyer and T. Skocpol, (Cambridge: Cambridge University Press, 1985), 169–91.

[25] Jean-Philippe Platteau, and Frederic Gaspart, "The Risk of Resource Misappropriation In Community-Driven Development," *World Development* 31, no. 10 (October 2003): 1688.

[26] Platteau and Gaspart, "The Risk of Resource Misappropriation," 1692.

[27] Platteau and Gaspart, "The Risk of Resource Misappropriation," 1693.

[28] Errol Alexis, "Ensuring Male Responsibility In Reproductive Health." *Insight* (2002).

[29] Errol Miller, *Men At Risk* (Kingston: Jamaica Publishing House, 1991).

[30] For instructive discussions of formal (objective) and informal (participatory) methods to project design and development, see K. Kumar, ed., *Rapid Appraisal Methods* (Washington, DC: World Bank, 1993), 8–22; R. Weaving and R. Picciotto, "A New Project Cycle for the World Bank?" *Finance and Development* (December 1994), 42–44; Meera Kaul Shah, with Rose Zambezi. and Mary Simasiku, *Listening to Young Voices: Facilitating Participatory Appraisals on Reproductive Health with Adolescents* (Lusaka, Zambia: CARE International, June 1999); and David Potts, *Project Identification and Formulation* (Boulder: L. Reinner, 2002).

[31] For an explanation of, and application to an analysis of the institutional dynamics of environmental change of the endowments and entitlements framework, see Leach, (1997), Kepe (1997), and Meenakshi Ahluwalia (1997) respectively.

9 Five Scenarios of Demand-Led Projects

[1] N. McNamara, and S. Morse, "Donors and Sustainability in the Provision of Financial Services in Nigeria," *Institute of Development Studies (IDS) Bulletin* 29, no. 4 (1998): 91–101.

[2] McNamara and S. Morse, "Donors and Sustainability," 97.

[3] McNamara and S. Morse, "Donors and Sustainability," 99.

[4] McNamara and S. Morse, "Donors and Sustainability," 98–99.

[5] McNamara and S. Morse, "Donors and Sustainability," 97.

[6] My wife occasionally amazes me with Creole vocabulary, and "PO' ting-fy," as she pronounces it, is a word I first heard her use. We were approached by a well-known

panhandler, when I was taught it. To my surprise, she refused him money for she is usually generous and considerate in such cases. When he walked away, she turned to me and, with some irritation, said in Creole, "That fellow been 'po' ting-fy' (that is, poor-thing-i-fied)!"

And then she continued in Standard English, "Everybody looks at him and says, 'Ah! Po-ting!' But he's no Poor Thing. I know him and I know his family; I taught him in school—there's not a thing wrong with him except that he's been victimized by everybody's 'Po' thing-i-fication.'" He was, in other words, made helpless because everybody acted on the assumption that he couldn't do better. I tried the word out on my UB students, initially drawing a blank. Eventually they "corrected" PO-tingfy to PO-tify. By their generation, the word has no etymology.

[7] See, Chapter 8, "Elite Capture-Resource Misappropriation."

[8] See T. Kepe, "Communities, Entitlements and Nature Reserves, the case of the Wild Coast, South Africa." *Institute of Development Studies (IDS) Bulletin*, 28, no. 4 (1997): 47–58.

[9] McNamara and S. Morse, "Donors and Sustainability," 97.

[10] Peter Dalglish, *The Courage of Children: My Life with the World's Poorest Kids* (Toronto: Harper-Collins, 1998), 238–52.

[11] Dalglish, *The Courage of Children*, 238–39.

[12] Dalglish, *The Courage of Children*, 243.

[13] Dalglish, *The Courage of Children*, 250.

[14] Janet Mancini Billson, *Cool Pose: The Dilemma of Black Manhood in America* (New York: Simon & Schuster, 1993).

[15] The Belizean dollar is currently pegged to the US dollar at BZ$2 = US$1.

[16] Walsh, cited in Derrick W. Brinkerhoff and Arthur A. Goldsmith, "Promoting the Sustainability of Development Institutions: A Framework for Strategy," *World Development* 20, no. 3 (1992): 378.

[17] See Shah, Zambezi and Simasiku, *Listening to Young Voices*.

[18] As with the Tomato Vendor project in Bogotá, the hold-back is a calculation based on the costs to be covered against the number of youth who can be enticed into the program.

[19] Tortilla factory. pronounced: 'tore-tea-ya-REE-ahs' locally.

[20] As we have read above (Leach, 1997).

[21] McNamara and S. Morse, "Donors and Sustainability," 92.

[22] above (see Chapter 7, Elite Capture).

[23] Ibid.

[24] Michael Rosberg, "'I Know These People': The Paradox of Authoritarian Management in Developing Countries; The Case Of Belize," 10, paper presented at the 23rd Conference of the Caribbean Studies Association. Princess Hotel, Belize: 29–31 May 2003.

[25] The term "community members" is used instead of Grassroots Organizations (GROs). There are effective NGOs operating in Belize. There are some cultural GROs (such as the cultural councils) operating as well. At the level of Belizeans with low education, however, much of the community organization work is undertaken by the elected Village Councils. Concerns have been raised about the degree of political control over these Councils exerted by the major political parties in Belize. If extensive, coordination of development work with these Councils might involve the University in partisan squabbles at the local level, jeopardizing good relations with Government.

Conclusion

[1] Dalglish, *The Courage of Children*, 295.

[2] Dalglish, *The Courage of Children*, 297.

[3] Amartya Sen, *Development as Freedom* (New York: Knopf, 2000).

[4] Dalglish, *The Courage of Children*, 238.

[5] Dalglish, *The Courage of Children*, 247–48.

Bibliography

Adams, Don. "The Monkey and the Fish: Cultural Pitfalls of an Educational Advisor." *International Development Review* 2, no. 2 (1960): 22–28.

Agere, Samuel. *Promoting Good Governance: Principles, Practices and Perspectives.* London: Commonwealth Secretariat, 2000.

Ahluwalia, Meenakshi. "Representing Communitities: The Case of a Community-Based Watershed Management Project in Rajasthan, India." Paper presented at the Crossing Boundaries conference of the International Association for the Study of Common Property, Vancouver, BC Canada, 10–14 June 1998.

Alexis, Errol. "Ensuring Male Responsibility In Reproductive Health." *Insight*, (2002).

Allport, G.W.T. *Nature Of Prejudice.* Cambridge: Addison-Wesley, 1954.

Anderson, Sarah, ed. *Views from the South: The Effects of Globalization and the WTO on Third World Countries.* Oakland, CA: Institute for Food & Development Policy/Food First Books, September 2000.

Arana, Francis B. *It Used To Be That.* Belize City: Amandala Press, 1992.

Banfield, Edward C. *The Unheavenly City.* New York: Little, Brown and Company, 1970.

Baogang, S and Baogang, Y. "Preventive Health Care Services in poor rural areas of China." *Institute of Development Studies (IDS) Bulletin* 28, no. 1 (June 1997): 53–60.

Barnett, Carla. "Aspects of State Policy on Land Distribution and Use in the Crown Colonial Period and After." *Fourth Annual Studies on Belize Conference. SPEAReports* 7.

Belize City: Society for the Promotion of Education and Research, 1991.

Bayart, Jean-Francois. *The State in Africa: The Politics of the Belly.* New York: Longman, 1993.

Bennett, L. and C.E. Cuevas. "Sustainable Banking with the Poor." *Journal of International Development.* 8, no. 2 (1996): 145–52.

Billson, Janet Mancini. *Cool Pose: The Dilemma of Black Manhood in America.* New York: Simon & Schuster, 1993.

Boli, John and George M. Thomas, eds. *Constructing World Culture: International Nongovernmental Organizations Since 1875.* Palo Alto: Stanford University Press, 1999.

Bolland, O. Nigel. *Colonialism and Resistance in Belize: Essays on Historical Sociology.* Benque Viejo, Belize: Cubola Publications, 1988.

———. *The Formation of a Colonial Society: Belize, from Conquest to Crown Colony.* Baltimore: Johns Hopkins University Press, 1977.

Bolland, O. Nigel and Assad Shoman. *Land in Belize, 1765–1871: The Origins of Land Tenure, Use and Distribution in a Dependent Economy.* Mona: Institute of Social and Economic Research, University of the West Indies, 1977.

Brinkerhoff, Derrick W. and Arthur A. Goldsmith. "Promoting the Sustainability of Development Institutions: A Framework for Strategy." *World Development* 20, no. 3 (1992): 369–83.

Brood, Robin, ed. *Global Backlash: Citizen Initiatives for a Just World Economy.* Landham, MD: Rowman & Littlefield, 2002.

Brown, Deryck B. "Sustainability is not About Money!: The Case of the Belize Chamber of Commerce and Industry."*Development in Practice* 7, no. 2 (1997): 185–89.

Brown, L.D. and D. Ashman. "Participation, Social Capital, and Intersectoral Problem Solving: African and Asian Cases." *World Development* 24, no. 9 (1996): 1467–79.

Brusco, V, Marcelo Nazareno, and Susan C. Stokes. "Clientelism and Democracy: Evidence from Argentina." Presentation to the Conference on Political Parties and Legislative Organization in Parliamentary and Presidential Regimes, Yale University, March 2002.

Clark, G.L. and John C. Marshall. *Decision-Making: Models Of The Real-World And Expertise Neurophsychology Unit.* Oxford: Radcliffe Infirmary, 2002.

Constance, Paul. "May the Best Bureaucrat Win." *IDBAmérica.* March 2002. www.iaab.-org/idbamerica.

Cooper, Allison. "Young Adult Children of Workaholics as Compared to Young Adult Children of Authoritarian Parents: Long Term Mental Ramifications and Subsequent Implications," Honors Diss., Syracuse University, n.d.

Cornia, Giovanni Andrea, Richard Jolly, Frances Stewart, eds. *Adjustment with a Human Face: Protecting the Vulnerable and Promoting Growth.* Oxford: Clarendon Press, 1987.

Dalglish, Peter. *The Courage of Children: My Life with the Worldy's Poorest Kids.* Toronto: Harper-Collins, 1998.

DaMatta, Roberto. *Carnivals, Rogues, and Heroes: An Interpretation of the Brazilian Dilemma.*

Trans. John Drury. Notre Dame, IN: University of Notre Dame Press, 1991.

Darwin, Charles. *The Origin of Species*. (1859). Reprint, New York: Philosophical Library, 1951.

Davis, Jennifer, Alice Kang, Jeffrey Vincent, Dale Whittington. "How Important Is Improved Water Infrastructure to Microenterprises? Evidence from Uganda." *World Development* 29, no. 10 (Oct. 2001): 1753–67.

Dealy, Glen C. *The Latin Americans: Spirit and Ethos*. Boulder, CO: Westview Press, 1992.

De Soto, Hernando. "Dead Capital and the Poor." *SAIS Review* 21, no. 1 (2001): 13–44.

Dewey, John. "Theory of Valuation, Foundations of the Unity of Science." *Towards a Theory of Unified Science*. Vol. 2, no. 4. Chicago: University of Chicago Press, 1966.

Dichter, T. "Questioning the Future of NGOs in Micro-Finance." *Journal of International Development* 8, no. 2 (1996): 185–89.

Draper, G.M. "The Civil Service In Latin America And The Caribbean: Situation and Future Challenges: The Caribbean Perspective (Draft Working Paper), August 2001. http://unpan1.un.org/intradoc/groups/public/documents/CARICAD/UNPAN005729 .pdf.

Durkheim, Emile. *Suicide*. Trans. George Simpson. New York: Simon & Schuster, 1997.

———. *The Division of Labor in Society*. Trans. George Simpson. New York: The Free Press, 1947.

Easterly, William. *The Elusive Quest for Growth: Economists' Adventures and Misadventures in the Tropics*. Cambridge, Mass: MIT Press, 2001.

Edie, Carlene. J. "From Manley to Seaga: The persistence of Clientelist Politics in Jamaica." *Social and Economic Studies* 38, no. 1 (March 1989): 1–35.

Eicher, Carl K., and John M. Staatz, eds. International Agricultural Development. 3rd ed. Baltimore, MD: Johns Hopkins University Press, 1998.

Fong, Candy P.S. and Robert S.Wyer. "Cultural, Social, and Emotional Determinants of Decisions Under Uncertainty." *Organizational Behavior and Human Decision Processes* 90, no. 2 (2003): 304–22.

Foster, George M. *Traditional Cultures and the Impact of Technological Change*. New York: Harper and Row, 1962.

Frankl, Viktor E. *Man's Search for Meaning*. New York: Washington Square Press, 1959.

Girvan, Norman. "Societies at Risk? The Caribbean and Global Change." Management of Social Transformations Discussion Paper Series No. 17. Revised version of a paper presented at the Caribbean regional Consultation on the Management of Social Transformations (MOST) Program of UNESCO, Kingston, Jamaica, February 1997. http://www.unesco.org/most/girvan.htm.

Glade, William P. "Approaches to the theory of Entrepreneurial Formation." *Explorations in Entrepreneurial History*, 2d ser., 4, no. 3 (1967): 245–59.

González Aguilar, Verónica. "Micro-Finance Reaching The Poor? An Overview Of

Poverty Targeting Methods." *ADA Dialogue* (October 1999). http://www.globe-net.org/horizon-local/ada/c18.html.

Greenfield, Sidney M. "The Patrimonial State and Patron Client Relations in Iberia and Latin America: Sources of 'The System' in the Fifteenth Century Writings of the Infante D. Pedro of Portugal." *Ethnohistory* 24, no. 2 (1977): 163–78.

———. "On Monkeys, Fish, and Brazilian Agricultural Development: Some Questions and Suggestions." *The Journal of Developing Areas* 5, no. 4 (1971): 507–15.

Greenfield, Sidney M. and Arnold Strickon. "Entrepreneurship and Social Change: Towards a Populational, Decision-Making Approach." In *Entrepreneurs in Cultural Context*, ed. Sidney M. Greenfield, Arnold Strickon and Robert T. Aubey (Albuquerque, NM: The University of New Mexico Press, 1979)329–50.

———, *Entrepreneurship and Social Change*. Washington, DC: University Press of America, 1985.

———, *Structure and Process in Latin America*. Albuquerque, NM: The University of New Mexico Press, 1972.

———. "A New Paradigm for the Study of Entrepreneurship and Social Change." *Economic Development and Cultural Change* 29, no. 3 (1981): 469–99.

Greenfield, Sidney M., Arnold Strickon and Robert T. Aubrey, eds. *Entrepreneurs in Cultural Context*. Albuquerque, NM: The University of New Mexico Press, 1979.

Grey, B.G. *Collaboration: Finding Common Ground for Multiparty Problems*. San Francisco: Jossey-Bass, 1989.

Guhan, S. "Social Security Options for Developing Countries." *International Labour Review* 133, no. 1 (1994): 35–51.

Harman, W. *Global Mind Change: The Promise of the Last Years of the Twentieth Century*. Indianapolis: Knowledge Systems, Inc., 1988.

Hernstein, R.J. and Charles Murray. *The Bell Curve: Intelligence and Class Structure in American Life*. New York: Simon & Schuster, 1995.

Herskovits, Melville J. *Life in a Haitian Valley*. New York: Knopf, 1937.

Hirschman, Albert O. *Development Projects Observed*. Washington, DC: Brookings Institution Press, 1967.

Huang, Mel. "The Amber Coast: Ten Years After." *Central Europe Review* 1, no. 9 (August 1999). www.ce-review.org/99/9/voice9.html.

Hyung-Gon, Paul Yoo, "Corruption, Rule of Law, and Civil Society: Why Patronage Politics Is Good for Developing Markets and Democracies." *International Affairs Review* 12, no. 1 (2003): 24–45.

Iyo, Joseph. *A Cultural History of Belize*. Belize: The Angelus Press, 2001.

Iyo, J. and Rosberg, M. "Theoretical Perspectives on the Stasis of Class Relations in the Caribbean: the Belize Case Study." Paper presented at the Beyond Walls: Multi-

Disciplinary Perspectives Country Conference Series, University of the West Indies, November 2001.

Jackelen, H.R. and E. Rhyne. "Towards a More Market-Orientated Approach to Credit and Savings for the Poor."*Small Enterprise Development* 2, no. 4 (1991): 14–26.

Kepe, Thembela. "Communities, Entitlements and Nature Reserves, the case of the Wild Coast, South Africa." *IDS Bulletin*, 28, no. 4 (1997): 47–58.

Khandker, Shahid. "Does Micro-finance Really Benefit the Poor? Evidence from Bangladesh." Paper presented at the Asia and Pacific Forum on Poverty: Reforming Policies and Institutions for Poverty Reduction, Asian Development Bank, Manila, 5–9 February 2001. http://www.adb.org/Poverty/forum/pdf/Khandker.pdf.

Kinsley, D.A., and R.E.L. Masters. *The Cradle of Erotica. A Study of Afro-Asian Sexual Expression and an Analysis of Erotic Freedom in Social Relationships*. New York: Julian Press, 1962.

Klein, Daniel. "The Voluntary Provision of Public Goods? The Turnpike Companies of Early America." *Economic Inquiry* 28, no. 4 (October, 1990): 788–812.

Klitgaard, Robert. "Excerpts from 'International Cooperation against Corruption.'" Stop 'n Look at What's Going Down. Special Report: Corruption (Public Life). http://members.tripod.com/sankalpa/stop/s4corr.html. 3 October, 1998.

Klitgaard, Robert. "International Cooperation Against Corruption." SPAN (Sept/Oct 1998): 38.

———. *Tropical Gangsters: One Man's Experience with Development and Decadence in Deepest Africa*. New York: Basic Books, June 1991.

Knight, Franklin W. *The Caribbean: The Genesis of a Fragmented Nationalism*. New York: The Oxford University Press, 1976.

Korten, D.C. *Getting to the 21st Century, Voluntary Action and the Global Agenda*. Ann Arbor: Kumarian Press, 1990.

———. *Globalizing Civil Society: Reclaiming Our Right to Power*. New York: Seven Stories Press, 1997.

———. *When Corporations Rule the World*. Ann Arbor: Kumarian Press, 2001.

Kumar, K., ed. *Rapid Appraisal Methods*. Washington, DC: World Bank, 1993.

Leach, M., R. Mearns, and Ian Scoones. "Environmental entitlements: a framework for understanding the institutional dynamics of environmental change." *IDS Discussion Paper*. No. 369. Brighton: Institute of Development Studies. 1997.

———. "Institutions, Consensus and Conflict: Implications for Policy and Practice." *IDS Bulletin* 28, no. 4 (1997): 90–95.

Lewis, Gordon K. *The Growth of the Modern West Indies*. New York: Monthly Review Press, 1968.

Lewis, Oscar. *The Children of Sanchez*. USA: Vintage Books, 1979.

Mander, Jerry and Edward Goldsmith, eds. *The Case against the Global Economy: And for a Turn Toward the Local*. San Francisco: Sierra Club Books, 1997.

Bibliography

Martz, John D. *The Politics of Clientelism: Democracy & the State in Colombia.* Somerset, NJ: Transaction Publishers, 1996.

Marwell, Gerald and Pamela Oliver. *The Critical Mass in Collective Action: a Micro-Social Theory.* Cambridge: Cambridge University Press, 1993.

Marx, Karl. *Eighteenth Brumaire of Louis Bonaparte.* New York: International Publishers Company, 1990.

Mauss, Marcel. *The Gift: The Form and Reason for Exchange in Archaic Societies.* Trans. W.D. Halls. New York: W.W. Norton, July 2000.

Mayr, Ernst. *Evolution and the Diversity of Life.* Cambridge, MA: Harvard University Press, Belknap Press, 1976.

McChesney, Fred S. *Money for Nothing: Politicians, Rent Extraction, and Political Extortion.* Cambridge, MA: Harvard University Press, 1996.

McClurin, Irma. *Women of Belize: Gender and Change in Central America.* NJ: Rutgers University Press, 1966.

McNamara, N., and S. Morse. "Donors and Sustainability in the Provision of Financial Services in Nigeria." *Institute of Development Studies (IDS) Bulletin* 29, no. 4 (1998): 91–101.

McPherson, Michael Andrew and Carl Liedholm. "Determinants of Small and Micro Enterprise Registration: Results From Surveys in Niger and Swaziland." *World Development* 24, no. 3 (1996): 481–87.

Mead, Don. *Medium Micro Enterprise Developments in KwaZulu-Natal and Northern Province.* Pietermaritzburg, South Africa: University of Natal, 1998.

Michels, Robert. *Political Parties. A Sociological Study of the Oligarchical Tendencies of Modern Democracy.* Trans. Eden Paul and Cedar Paul. New York: The Free Press, 1962.

Miller, Errol. *Men at Risk.* Kingston: Jamaica Publishing House, 1991.

Miller, Keith M. "Advantages and Disadvantages of Local Government Decentralization." Paper presented at the Caribbean Conference On Local Government & Decentralization, Georgetown, Guyana, 25–28 June 2002.

Morgan, Peter and Victoria Carlan, eds. "Capacity Development, an Introduction." In *Emerging Issues in Capacity Development: Proceedings of a Workshop,* 7–17. Ottawa: Institute on Governance, 1994.

Ngugi, Rose. *Health-Seeking Behaviour in the Reform Process for Rural Households: The Case of Mwea Division, Kirinyaga District, Kenya.* Nairobi, Kenya: African Economic Research Consortium, 1999.

Nisbet, Robert A. *Social Change and History: Aspects of the Western Theory of Development.* London: Oxford University Press, 1969.

O'Brien, R., M. Williams, A.M. Goetz, and J.A. Scholte. *Contesting Global Governance.* Cambridge: Cambridge University Press, 2000.

Olson, Mancur. *The Logic of Collective Action: Public Goods and the Theory of Groups.* Cambridge, MA: Harvard University Press, 1971.

Ostrom, Elinor. "A Behavioral Approach to the Rational Choice Theory of Collective Action." *American Political Science Review* 92, no. 1 (March 1998): 1–22.

Pareto, Vilfredo. *Manual of Political Economy.* New York: Augustus M. Kelley, 1971.

Pedro, Dom. *O Livro da Virtuosa Bemfeitoria.* Ed. Joaquim Costa. Porto, Portugal, 1946.

Picciotto, R. and R. Weaving. "A New Project Cycle for the World Bank?" *Finance and Development* 30 (December 1994): 42–44.

Platteau, Jean-Philippe and Frederic Gaspart. "The Risk of Resource Misappropriation In Community-Driven Development." *World Development* 31, no. 10 (October 2003): 1687–1703.

Popkin, Samuel. *The Rational Peasant in Vietnam: The Political Economy of Rural Society in Vietnam.* Berkeley: The University of California Press, 1977.

Potts, David. *Project Identification and Formulation.* Boulder: L. Reinner, 2002.

Probst, Tahira M., Peter J. Carnevale and Harry C. Triandis. "Cultural Values in Intergroup and Single-Group Social Dilemmas." *Organizational Behavior and Human Decision Processes* 77, no. 3 (March 1999): 171–91.

Quesada, Charo. "First, close the democratic deficit." *IDBAmérica* March 2001. www.iaab.org/idbamerica.

Rahman, A. "Micro-Credit Initiatives for Equitable and Sustainable Development: Who Pays?" *World Development* 27, no. 1 (1999): 67–82.

Ravallion, Martin, Gaurav Datt, and Shubham Chaudhuri. "Does Maharastra's Employment Guarantee Scheme Guarantee Employment?" *Economic Development and Cultural Change* 41, no. 2 (January 1993): 251–75.

Ray C.L., and L.M. Subich. "Staff Assaults and Injuries in a Psychiatric Hospital as a Function of Three Attitudinal Variables." *Issues Mental Health Nursing* 19, no. 1 (1998): 291–300.

Ricard, Robert. "L'Infant D. Pedro de Portugal et 'O Livro da Virtuosa Bemfeitoria'." In *Études sur L'Histoire Morale et Religieuse du Portugal,* Paris: Fundaçaõ Calouste Gulbenkian. Centro Cultural Português, 1970. 87–136.

Rogers, Everett M. "Motivation, Values and Attitudes of Subsistence Farmers: Towards a Subculture of Peasantry." In *Subsistence Agriculture and Economic Development.* Ed. Clifton R. Wharton, 111–35. Chicago: Aldine, 1969.

Rosberg, M. "Pragmatic Adaptations and Idealistic Interventions: An Analytical Description Of Development Agencies Within A Context of Political Clientelism In San Andrés Island, Colombia." Ph.D. diss, University of Wisconsin-Madison, 1980.

Rosberg, Michael and Melvina Johnson. *Preparing for the New Millennium: Human Development Report, 1999.* Belize: National Human Development Advisory Council/UNDP, 2001.

Rosberg, Michael. "'I Know These People': The Paradox of Authoritarian Management in Developing Countries; The Case Of Belize." Paper presented at the 23rd Conference of the Caribbean Studies Association. Princess Hotel, Belize: 29–31 May 2003.

Rostow, Walter W. *The Stages of Economic Growth*. Cambridge: Cambridge University Press, 1960.

Rushton, J.P. *Race, Evolution, and Behavior*. New Brunswick, USA: Transaction Publishers, 1997.

Schansberg, D. Eric. Review of *Money for Nothing; Politicians, Rent Extraction, and Political Extortion*. *The Independent Review* 3, no. 1 (Summer 1998). http://www.independent.org/publications/tir/article.asp?issueID=29&articleID=363.

Schein, E.H. "Culture: The missing concept in organization studies." *Administrative Science Quarterly* 41, no. 2 (1996): 229–40.

———. *Organizational Culture and Leadership*. 2nd ed. San Francisco: Jossey-Bass, 1992.

———. "The Impact of Transnational Institutions on Cultural Values and Vice Versa." *Reflections: The SOL Journal* 3, no. 1 (2001): 41–48.

Schmidt, R.H. and C-P. Zeitinger. "Prospects, Problems and Potential of Credit-Granting NGOs." *Journal of International Development* 8, no. 2 (1996): 241–58.

Schrock, D. "Debt Causes...Hunger and The Borrower Is the Slave of the Lender." http://www.mcc.org/us/globalization/resources/hunger.html.

Schuftan, C. "What does the New UN Human Rights Approach Bring to the Struggle of the poor?" Afro-nets, 4 February 2001. http://www.afronets.org/archive/-200102/msg00015.php.

Schumpeter, Joseph A. *Capitalism, Socialism and Democracy*. New York: HarperCollins, 1976.

———. *The Theory of Economic Development*. 1934.Reprint, Cambridge, MA: Harvard University Press, 1959.

Seibel, H.D. and U. Parhusip, "Attaining Outreach with Sustainability. A Case Study of a Private Micro Finance Institution in Indonesia." *Institute of Development Studies (IDS) Bulletin* 29, no. 4 (1998): 81–90.

Sen, Amartya. *Development as Freedom*. New York: Knopf, 2000.

———. *Poverty and Famines: An Essay on Entitlements and Deprivation*. Oxford: Oxford University Press, 1981.

Shah, Meera Kaul. "A Step By Step Field Guide To Participatory Tools and Techniques." In *Embracing Participation in Development: Worldwide experience from CAREs Reproductive Health Programs with a Step-by-Step field guide to Participatory Tools and Techniques*. Eds. Meera Kaul Shah, Sarah Degnan Kambou and Barbara Monahan, 3.24–3.72. Lusaka, Zambia: CARE International, 1999.

Shah, Meera Kaul, with Rose Zambezi and Mary Simasiku. *Listening to Young Voices: Facilitating Participatory Appraisals on Reproductive Health with Adolescents*. Focus Tool Series 1. Lusaka, Zambia: CARE International, 1999.

Sheridan, Richard B. *Sugar and Slavery: An Economic History of the British West Indies 1623–1775*. Great Britain: A. Wheaton and Co. Ltd, 1974.

Shoman, Assad. *13 Chapters of a History of Belize*. Belize: Angelus Press, 1994.

———. *Party Politics in Belize, 1950–1986*. Belize: Cubola Productions, 1987.

Sibanda, V. "Corruption in the Private Sector: Its Causes, Extent and Effects." *Reports– Seminar on Corruption in the Private Sector*. 5 June 2001. http://www.kubatana.-net/tiz/html/reports/rep_fs.htm?corrpso10605.htm.

Sontag, Susan. *Illness as Metaphor and Aids and Its Metaphors*. New York: Picador, 2001.

Sperber, D., and L. Hirschfeld. "Culture, Cognition, and Evolution." In R. Wilson, and R. Keil, eds. *MIT Encyclopedia of the Cognitive Sciences* (cxi). Cambridge, MA: MIT Press, 1999.

Stoesz, David, C. Guzzetta, and M.W. Lusk. *International Development*. Allyn & Bacon, Inc., 1998.

Szasz, M.D., Thomas S. *The Myth Of Mental Illness: Foundations of A Theory of Personal Conduct, Revised Edition*. New York: Harper & Row, 1974.

Tang, Kwong-Leung. "The Marginalization of Social Welfare in Developing Countries: The Relevance of Theories of Social Policy Development." *Journal of Sociology and Social Welfare* 23, no. 2 (1996): 41–58.

Tilly, Charles. "War Making and State Making as Organized Crime." In *Bringing the State Back In*, ed. P.B. Evans, D. Reuschemeyer and T. Skocpol, 169–91. Cambridge: Cambridge University Press, 1985.

Tramo, M.J., W.C. Loftus, T.A. Stukel, R.L. Green, J.B. Weaver and M.S. Gazzaniga. "Brain size, head size, and intelligence quotient in monozygotic twins." *Neurology* 50, no. 5 (1998): 1246–52.

Turbayne, Colin M. *The Myth of Metaphor*. Columbia, SC: University of South Carolina Press, 1971.

Uphoff, Norman T. "Grassroots Organizations and NGOs in Rural Development: Opportunities with Diminishing States and Expanding Markets," *World Development* 21, no. 4 (1993): 607–22.

Wickramasekara, P. "Rural Employment Generation Schemes: Review of Asian Experience." *Indian Journal of Industrial Relations* 25, no. 4 (April 1990): 354.

Wilson, Peter J. *Crab Antics: The Social Anthropology of English-Speaking Negro Societies in the Caribbean*. Long Grove, IL: Waveland Press, 1995.

Woods, Louis A. and Joseph M. Perry. "Regional Integration, Foreign Trade and Economic Development: Caricom and Belize." *Fourth Annual Studies on Belize Conference*. SPEAReports 7, 25–47. Belize City: Society for the Promotion of Education and Research, 1991.

World Bank. *World Development Report: Attacking Poverty: Older Edition*. Oxford University Press, September 2000.

Yaron, J. *Successful Rural Finance Institutions*. World Bank Discussion Paper no. 150. Washington, DC: World Bank, 1992.

Index